ALSO BY JOHN NOBLE WILFORD

We Reach the Moon (1969)

Scientists at Work (1979)
(editor)

The Mapmakers (1981)

CO-AUTHOR:

Spaceliner (1981)
(with William Stockton)

The New York Times Guide to the Return of Halley's Comet (1985)
(with Richard Flaste, Holcomb Noble, and Walter Sullivan)

The Riddle of the Dinosaur

The Riddle of the Dinosaur

John Noble Wilford

DRAWINGS BY DOUGLAS HENDERSON

ALFRED A. KNOPF NEW YORK 1986

This is a Borzoi Book
published by Alfred A. Knopf, Inc.
 Published in the United States by
Alfred A. Knopf, Inc., New York, and simultaneously in
Canada by Random House of Canada Limited, Toronto.
Distributed by Random House, Inc., New York.

Grateful acknowledgment is made to *The New York Times*
for permission to reprint excerpts from "A New Look at
Dinosaurs" by John Noble Wilford, February 7, 1982,
magazine. Copyright © 1982 by the New York
Times Company. Reprinted by permission.

Library of Congress Cataloging in Publication Data
Wilford, John Noble.
The riddle of the dinosaur.
Bibliography: p.
Includes index.
1. Dinosaurs—Study and teaching—History. I. Title.
QE862.D5W55 1985 567.9'1 85-40015
ISBN 0-394-52763-1

Manufactured in the United States of America
Published January 14, 1986
Second Printing, March 1986

To

Beth and Fred

Contents

Color illustrations follow page 150.

The Riddle of the Dinosaur

Time in Utah

DRIVING SOUTH from Blanding, Utah, on the road to Mexican Hat, Jim Jensen spoke of the land thereabouts as it had been long ago in another age. He might have been speaking from personal memory or passing on recollections of a Mormon forebear; the images he evoked were that vivid. Some rock outcroppings had jogged his thoughts. Out of the Triassic and Jurassic shales and sandstones, especially the weathered pastels of the Morrison Formation crowning the mesas, he re-created with broad brushstrokes the American West as it had been tens of millions of years ago, when the few mammals around were too meek to inherit the earth, much less betray any latent tendencies toward evolving into humans who one day would drive down a road in Utah and contemplate time immemorial.

The bleached brown plateau country as far as one could see was high and dry now, but in the time that concerned Jensen, from about 225 million to 65 million years ago, this was a subtropical basin. The continents had begun drifting their separate ways with the disintegration of the most recent supercontinent, Pangaea, into two landmasses, Laurasia in the north and Gondwanaland in the south, and finally into the fragments that approximated the shapes of today's continents. North America was moving westward and northward. A widening gulf of water, the modest beginnings of the Atlantic Ocean, now separated America from the land to the east that it was leaving behind. The chunks that would be Europe and Asia headed to the east. Africa pulled away from South America, Antarctica away from Africa, and Australia away from Antarctica. But not all ties were severed. For a long time, creatures could migrate by land bridges between Europe and America, America and Asia. The world generally was warmer then. The poles were free of ice. Coral grew in the warm waters of Europe, then more of an archipelago than a continent. In this subtropical basin of North America, rivers flowed across broad floodplains. A warm, shallow sea encroached from the southeast, where the Gulf Coast states are now, and for millions of years the sea split the continent, mainly where the Great Plains are now. Along the shores of sea and stream, through the lush country, life flourished. But all was brown and green until some 100 million years ago, when flowering plants, the angiosperms, made their evolutionary debut. They introduced a springtime of color among the cycads and broadleaf conifers, dragonflies and flying reptiles, turtles and lizards and crocodiles, mousy little mammals cowering in the foliage, and the lords of all life then, the dinosaurs. These were the greatest animals in the time known as the Age of Reptiles.

THE APPROXIMATE POSITIONS OF THE CONTINENTS DURING THE MESOZOIC ERA.

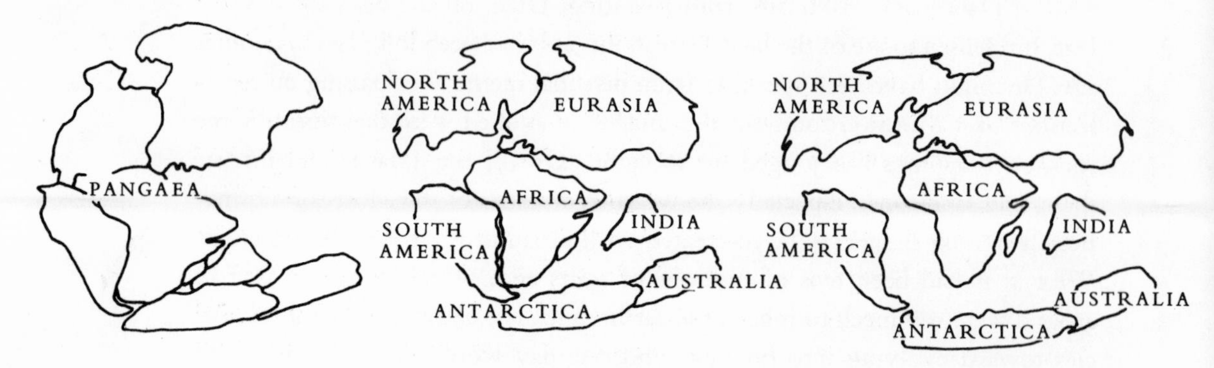

(Left to right) *Middle Triassic: Pangaea, the universal land mass, begins to break up. Late Jurassic: South America, with Africa still attached, has broken off from North America and Eurasia; Antarctica, while attached to Australia, has separated from Africa, while India drifts toward Eurasia. Late Cretaceous: North America is splitting off from Eurasia with the opening up of the Atlantic Ocean; Africa is almost into its present position; North and South America are still separate, but Australia has not yet separated from Antarctica.*

The dinosaurs emerged from primitive reptilian ancestors sometime in the Triassic period of geologic time, which extended from 248 million to 213 million years ago. They became dominant during the Jurassic, for the next 70 million years, and continued strong until the close of the Cretaceous, some 65 million years ago. Indeed, their extinction then, along with the demise of a staggering number of other creatures and plants, defined the end of the Cretaceous to the geologists who discovered the abrupt change in the fossil record signifying one of life's sharpest chronological boundaries. Each of these periods is characterized by distinctive layers of rock containing fossil accumulations unique to themselves, which is how geologists came to reckon relative time in earth history and how paleontologists learned to tell when species of dinosaurs, or other life, appeared and then disappeared. Triassic, Jurassic, and Cretaceous, these are subdivisions in the larger time-frame known as the Mesozoic, the era of "middle life" in the earth's history. The Mesozoic falls between the Paleozoic, beginning 590 million years ago with the appearance of fossils in abundance, and the Cenozoic, the era of the new animals, covering the last 65 million years.

Although dinosaurs populated all the large landmasses, with the possible exception of Antarctica, in the west of North America they seemed to have found the happiest of habitats. They were everywhere there in one form or another during the Mesozoic, from Texas and New Mexico up into Alberta. Not all of them, Jim Jensen noted, were the behemoths of popular lore. Some grew no bigger than rabbits or crows. Others in this subtropical basin and elsewhere reached twenty-five to thirty meters in length, with extravagant tails and necks accounting for a disproportionate share of the whole. Among these giants, *Diplodocus, Brontosaurus,* and *Brachiosaurus* were the largest terrestrial animals that ever lived. (The blue whale apparently is the largest animal ever.) Some dinosaurs stood on strong hind limbs, towering above all, and had horns, spikes, and armor plating as if prepared for mortal combat. The two-legged *Tyrannosaurus rex* had a large head, unusual for dinosaurs, and a menacing set of sharp teeth the size of bananas that made it a fearsome presence on the late Cretaceous landscape. Some others had bills resembling a duck's. Many had feet resembling a bird's. Some ran ostrichlike, while others seemed rooted in lethargy. Some were grazing herbivores, though there was nothing pastoral about a *Triceratops* charging like an angry rhinoceros. Others were carnivores that hunted in packs. Some 340 genera—groups of closely related species—of dinosaurs, large and small, fierce and docile, bipedal and quadrupedal, herbivorous and carnivorous, have been identified from their fossilized remains not only in North America but around the world. No genus survived through the entire Age of Reptiles, but dinosaurs of one kind or another flourished for 160 million years (humans may be 3 to 4 million years old, if the early hominids are counted), and then the last of them died off at the close of the Cretaceous. Their bodies sank into the sediments of these ancient shores and swamps. Their bones, those turning to fossil, became time capsules waiting to be discovered, exhumed, and puzzled over by the new lords of the land.

Nothing of the vanished world that Jensen described was known two centuries ago. If someone happened on a bed of dinosaur bones in earlier times, it did not occur to him that he was, in the words of Loren Eiseley, "intruding upon some gigantic stage not devised for him." Ancient bones were either ignored or, in the practice of the Chinese, ground up and purveyed as dragon-bone medicines and aphrodisiacs. Their meaning remained unsuspected, for time in all its vastness had not yet been discovered. The impermanence of life and of the land itself had not been recognized.

NOW THERE ARE EXPLORERS of time as well as of geographic space. Vanished worlds are their new worlds; extinct species, their aboriginal tribes. Much of science is an exploration of time. Science is not only a body of descriptive knowledge about concrete objects and observable forces, or a rational method of testing hypotheses, or an instrument for transforming society through technology. Science is all this, and more. Cosmology, geology, and evolution science are concerned with the temporal development of the natural world, at every level of the scale from the lifetime of an individual to that of the planet or the cosmos, and as such share many of the aims and attributes of history. Astrophysicists have been called the ultimate historians; they aspire to nothing less than a reconstruction of cosmic history. Looking out into space is equivalent to looking back in time, back toward the very beginning of the universe. Geologists plot the natural revolutions that have changed the face of the earth through time, much as historians chart the rise and fall of civilizations. Biologists and paleoanthropologists trace the evolution of life in general and of man in particular, a narrative with more fateful turning points than any traditional historian could ever find in the archives. Paleontologists are by definition explorers of time. The name "paleontology," coined by Charles Lyell in 1838, derives from three Greek words meaning "the science of ancient being." Paleontologists attempt to re-create the history of past life from fossils, and among the most marvelous and challenging material they deal with are the fossilized traces of dinosaurs.

There have been many dinosaur-bone hunters like James A. Jensen ever since dinosaur remains were first identified in the early nineteenth century. These explorers of time find the bones irresistible. They dig them because, like mountains to be climbed, they are there. They keep digging, like relentless detectives, because clues to the mystery of dinosaurian life and death may lie beneath the next stratum that will yield to their spades. The fact that the next scoop usually produces nothing, or else more new questions than answers, never seems to dispirit those who hunt dinosaurs. The past, a wondrous past, awaits them, they are sure, if they are but canny enough in choosing where to dig and inspired in deciphering the messages borne through time by the fossils they find.

Often as not, dinosaur hunters dig also because they never outgrew a childhood enchantment. Some of them freely admit this. Stephen Jay Gould, the Harvard University paleontologist who is a brilliant essayist on science, calls the paleontologist "one of those oddballs who parlayed his childhood fascination for dinosaurs into a career." He has never forgotten his own epiphany at the age of five. Seeing a tyrannosaur skeleton at a museum, a frightening sight at first, awakened in Gould the curiosity that would take him as an adult to the study of paleontology and the larger issues of evolution.

Others, more sensitive to the stifling notion that grownups should put away childish things, are somewhat apologetic about what they do and how they came to do it. But it does seem that, more than most other people, paleontologists, particularly those who hunt dinosaur bones, trace the origins of their careers back to childhood. Dale A. Russell, of the Canadian National Museum of Natural Sciences at Ottawa, explains the genesis of his interest this way: "As a child, I could imagine the world of dinosaurs. At times I was a dinosaur. And so rather than do something practical when I grew up, I just stayed with dinosaurs." John R. Horner, a paleontologist at Montana State University, says his father used to take him out on their ranch to pick up dinosaur bones. "I guess I never grew out of it," he says now.

Robert T. Bakker, an adjunct curator in paleontology at the University of Colorado Museum and formerly on the faculty at Johns Hopkins University, remembers seeing a mural of prehistoric life, including dinosaurs, reproduced on the cover of *Life.* He was eleven years old, and sitting on his grandfather's sun porch in New Jersey. "From that moment onward, I was a paleontologist," Bakker recalls. "My family and the doctor predicted it was just a hormonal stage that would pass. My parents still hope it will pass."

John H. Ostrom, of Yale University, is one exception. "I have absolutely no recollection of any interest in dinosaurs as a child," he says. "My father was a doctor, and I entered a premed program in college. I was taking a course in the theory of evolution and, as an assignment, was reading George Gaylord Simpson's book *The Meaning of Evolution.* I couldn't put it down. I was hooked. I decided to be a paleontologist so I could learn more about evolution." In this respect, his career is a reversal of the usual pattern; so many paleontologists approach the greater study of evolution by way of dinosaurs, but Ostrom, in pondering evolution, gravitated to investigations of the mysteries of dinosaurs.

Jensen, on the other hand, does fit the childhood-fascination pattern. When he was ten years old, he came upon some fossils in the mountains around the farm where he grew up in Utah. "I began collecting them and became curious as to what they were," Jensen says. "My father bought a used geology textbook, and in the back of it were pictures of dinosaurs. While some boys dreamed of a new bicycle, I dreamed of finding dinosaurs. I would always wake up before I could dig them up. I never did have a bicycle, but I've never stopped dreaming of dinosaurs."

As an adult, Jensen has lived his dream. Few hunters of dinosaur bones have been more indefatigable or successful in recent years than Dinosaur Jim, as Jensen enjoys being called. A self-taught paleontologist—his college career was brief—Jensen was, until his retirement in 1983, curator of the Vertebrate Paleontology Research Laboratory at Brigham Young University in Provo, Utah. But he was more in his element out in the field. In 1972, at Dry Mesa in western Colorado, near the town of Delta, he dug up bones of what was then the largest dinosaur ever found, an eighty-ton, twenty-five-meter creature that may have been an enlarged variation of *Brachiosaurus.* Jensen called it supersaurus, a name that has yet to be elevated to official scientific status. At the same site in 1979, he uncovered the shoulder blade and other bones of a dinosaur that must have been even larger, by several more tons and meters. If it stretched its long neck to full height, the creature probably could have peered into the sixth-floor window of a building. Dinosaur Jim named it ultrasaurus.

"I never dig until someone sees bone coming out of the ground," Jensen was saying on the drive down the road from Blanding. "Too many fossils out here and not enough time to be going out and digging at random."

Jensen is a big and hearty man who is never a stranger to anyone for more than a sentence or two. Over the years he developed a network of informants in the little towns of southern Utah and western Colorado. He would visit a rock shop in Moab, find out where a particular fossil came from, and file the answer in the back of his mind. He talked to herdsmen, farmers, and rockhounds, people who know the land, and they passed on tips. A sawmill operator in Delta, Eddie Jones, directed him to the Dry Mesa site. Jim Smith, in Henrieville, Utah, told him of a skeleton he had happened on thirty years before, and, when Jensen went to the place, he found the fossils still buried there, along with a note in a bottle, which read: "This critter belongs to Jim Smith. This is as far as I could lead him."

Some months before, a uranium prospector had told Jensen of bones he had seen along the bank of a dry wash south of Blanding. This was Dinosaur Jim's

James A. Jensen with dinosaur shoulder blade

immediate destination. Off to the left side of the road, he saw wheel tracks leading out through clumps of cheat grass. He swung the pickup off the paved road, stopped to adjust for four-wheel drive, and then followed the tracks left by uranium prospectors. Uranium and dinosaurs are often found together. The bones soak up and concentrate the uranium in the mineralization process that converts organic matter to fossil form.

One thing about a road fossil hunters travel—there is less and less of it the closer it gets to the bones. Two dusty ruts came to nothing over the crest of a ridge. There was a choice between the rocky low way or the eroded high way. Finally there was no choice but to get out and walk. Hiking the last couple of hundred meters, down a steep slope and into some gullies, Jensen came upon the junipers the prospector had said marked the place. There, underfoot, were some bone fragments. He stuck a sharp spade into the bank of gray clay, brown soil, and mudstone. After two or three scoops, penetrating ever deeper, he heard and felt something hard. He knew instantly that he had struck bone.

"It's the clunk noise, not as sharp a sound as when you hit rock," Jensen explained. "Somehow you just know you've hit a bone. Then you wonder if the bone is all there, or only a piece, and if it's something new, if it's big. You're always hoping for a big bone, not that little ones can't be just as important. Maybe you've come upon a whole skeleton, but not many of us are ever that fortunate."

Out of the dirt Jensen extracted and brushed clean several chunks of a spinal column, dorsal vertebrae from a dinosaur's rib section and several cervical, or neck, vertebrae. These were the remains of a herbivore, Jensen concluded. The interior structure of their bones lacked the distinctive layering found in the bones of a carnivore. Nor were these the bones of a giant, as dinosaurs went, but of a medium-size animal some ten meters long. Sitting in the gully and turning over a fossil in his hands, Jensen savored the moment. "Think about it," he said, presently. "This is the first sunlight to shine on that bone in 140 million years, the first human eyes ever to look upon that bone."

To share his reverie was to appreciate the appeal of exploring time and the reward of paleontology's fieldwork. Simpson, who was one of the leading paleontologists of the century, once described fossil hunting as "the most fascinating of all sports." In *Attending Marvels,* his account of an expedition to Patagonia, written in 1934, Simpson observed:

> [Bone digging] has some danger, enough to give it zest and probably about as much as in the average engineered big-game hunt, and the danger is wholly to the hunter. It has uncertainty and excitement and all the thrills of gambling with none of its vicious features. The hunter never knows what his bag may be, perhaps nothing, perhaps a creature never before seen by human eyes. Over the next hill may lie a great discovery! It requires knowledge, skill, and some degree of hardihood. And its results are so much more important, more worth while, and more enduring than those of any other sport! The fossil hunter does not kill; he resurrects. And the result of his sport is to add to the sum of human pleasure and to the treasures of human knowledge.

A century earlier, in much the same region, Charles Darwin experienced the thrill, too. "The pleasure of the first day's hunting," he wrote to his sister Catherine in 1833, "cannot be compared to finding a fine group of fossil bones, which tell their story of former times with almost a living tongue."

For Bob Bakker, the thrill begins before he reaches the field. He has written: "I know of no more exhilarating feeling than field fever—that special electricity generated when geological maps are spread out to mark spots for prospecting, the trucks are loaded with picks, awls, plaster and glue, and we count the days until we can set off for Como Bluff, or the Freezeout Hills, or any other spot in Wyoming where people are few, water is scarce, but fossil bones are abundant."

Jensen returned to the bank and dug some more, uncovering what appeared to be a petrified rope. "There's a neural canal, a mud cast of the spinal cord," he said. "Remember the poem about dinosaurs with a brain at both ends?" He launched into a recitation:

Behold the mighty dinosaur,
Famous in prehistoric lore.
Not only for his power and strength
But for his intellectual length.
You will observe by these remains
The creature had two sets of brains—
One in his head (the usual place),
The other in his spinal base.
Thus he could reason "A priori"
As well as "A posteriori."
No problem bothered him a bit
He made both head and tail of it. . . .
If something slipped his forward mind
'Twas rescued by the one behind.
And if in error he was caught
He had a saving afterthought.
As he thought twice before he spoke
He had no judgment to revoke.
Thus he could think without congestion
*Upon both sides of every question. . . .**

After a few hours of reconnaissance, Jensen reburied the bones with care and rolled boulders against the bank as some protection against further erosion.

*The verse was written in 1912 by Bert L. Taylor, a columnist for the Chicago *Tribune.* Its inspiration came from the discovery that *Stegosaurus* had a small brain, in the usual place, and a sacral plexus, about twenty times the size of its brain, at the point where the spinal cord passes through the pelvis. This was not a brain, however, but probably more of a junction box, where many nerves from the hindlegs and tail entered the spinal cord. Such an enlargement occurs in most reptiles, though it was more pronounced in some dinosaurs.

The bones were not as recent as he would have liked, from the Jurassic rather than the Cretaceous, but he hoped to come back some spring for serious excavations. "I've got dinosaurs standing in line waiting to be collected," Jensen said as he walked back up the slope to the pickup truck.

LATER IN THE DAY, Jensen headed west toward an excavation site where he had reason to believe Cretaceous dinosaurs would be standing in line. Storm clouds darkened the sky as he drove west, and what happened next, with fearful suddenness, brought home another aspect of time as revealing as the exhumed bones.

A cloudburst overcame the land all around. Within a minute, no more, a torrent of brown water only a little more fluid than moving concrete swept down off the slopes and across the road. It transported an avalanche of boulders, timbers, and tons of soil. Floods like these back in the Triassic buried fallen tree trunks with sand and silt to create the fossilizing conditions that produced the Petrified Forest of Arizona. These flash floods are still a scourge of this arid country. In a brief moment of time, punctuated by lightning bolts, a mountainside was shorn of its topmost soil and the valleys below were resurfaced. There was no telling how many creatures, mice and jackrabbits surely, deer and maybe even humans, contributed their bones in that instant to future fossilization deep in the valley sediments. The earth was undergoing one of its many alterations. Not only is life impermanent, as the bones in the gully by the junipers had made manifest, but so is the land. Bones and mud, fossils to be and new strata in the making, these are the stuff that made possible the exploration of time through paleontology.

Jensen drove out of the storm and by the next afternoon arrived at his excavation site not far from Bryce Canyon. After a bone-jarring ride across the trackless Pareah Wash, he found two of his students, Samuel Webb and William Little, digging into stony sediments laid down through the action of water sometime toward the end of the Cretaceous. A hummingbird guarded its nest in a nearby tree; it seemed incredible to think that this agitated little fairy of a creature might be, as some believe, a descendant of dinosaurs. Lying about the students were toe bones and skull bones, ribs and vertebrae, all part of one dinosaur. The animal probably had a body six meters long and a tail of four meters.

Back at the trailer in the base camp, Jensen compared a jawbone with drawings of known dinosaurs. "It was a carnivore," he said as he looked and thought. "Not *Allosaurus.* Not exactly *Tyrannosaurus,* either. It's something new, it must be something new."

Several weeks later, Jensen returned to the site, dug up more fragments of the mysterious animal, and showed them to Dale Russell, an authority on late Cretaceous dinosaurs. The two paleontologists surmised that they were looking at a new species of the tyrannosaurid family, the greatest predators of the Age of Reptiles. Jensen felt liberated. He had spent most of his career in the Jurassic, but finally knew where to look for fossils that would transport him some 70 million years forward to the end of the Cretaceous—and thus to the time of the mass extinction when the dinosaurs perished.

ONE MORE DINOSAUR had stepped out of the past and taken its place in the human mind, thereby making remote time somewhat less abstract and more comprehensible. This is the essential importance of dinosaurs in the exploration of time: they bring the past alive, a past of hitherto unsuspected dimension. Their bones and the rocks in which they lie are solemn reminders that, as Simpson said, the present is "only a random point in the long flow of time."

For several decades in the mid twentieth century, however, the field of dinosaur research seemed fossilized itself. Dinosaurs were considered so terminally extinct, and were so stigmatized by their irrevocable disappearance, that there seemed little to be learned about them or from them that was worth knowing. They made spectacular centerpieces at museums; little children might romanticize them; but serious paleontologists surely had more rewarding things to do.

Then, in the 1960s, paleontologists as well as biologists, geologists, and physicists began stepping over each other to introduce new findings and hypotheses about the life and death of the great beasts. Debates on these theories enlivened scholarly journals and scientific gatherings. New knowledge about dinosaurs, combined with advances in geology, biochemistry, paleomagnetism, paleobotany, and paleogeography, inspired new ideas about the evolution and extinction of life on earth.

Through the 1970s and into the 1980s, discovery after discovery revealed more of the wonder and variety of these creatures. Some fifty new kinds of dinosaurs were uncovered in the 1970s alone. As paleontologists pieced together the fossilized remains and pondered their meaning, a revised image of the dinosaurs began to take shape. No longer did it seem just to dismiss these animals with an epithet like "dim-witted" or to hold them up as symbols of overgrown obsolescence and monumental failure. Some dinosaurs may well have developed active, nonreptilian metabolisms; they could no longer be thought of simply as archaic lizards. Some of them may have been social beings and caring parents. Some dinosaurs may live on, in a sense, as today's birds. The dinosaurs' downfall, moreover, may have been not so much a result of their own physical or mental limitations as of hostile environmental forces, perhaps a global catastrophe.

In any event, they deserved considerable respect as a form of life. Their kind evolved, adapted, and survived over a period of 160 million years—an enviable record—and as long as they did so, mammals could not rise above their underprivileged status as inconspicuous, essentially nocturnal creatures subsisting mainly on a diet of insects. Dinosaurs, indeed, seemed to be worth knowing more about, as much now as when the explorers of time first began finding in the land and the bones entombed there a past of vast and astonishing dimension.

I

I

First Bones

THE WONDER OF DINOSAURS is not only that they lived so long ago, grew so large, and then became extinct under mysterious circumstances millions of years before humans came on the scene. The wonder also is that the human mind could resurrect the dinosaurs and through this resurrection begin to comprehend the fullness of time and the richness of life.

At first, there were only those intimations of bygone ages and bygone life. A few scraps of bone and some teeth, encrusted in ancient sediments, came to light in England in the first quarter of the nineteenth century. These were the bones of creatures long dead, relics of life in the distant past beyond human ken. No one knew then how long they had been dead, for no one knew then how long ago the long-ago could be. These were, judging by the evidence of those first bones and teeth, strange and monstrous creatures. But no one could know then—no one is quite sure yet—what they were really like. Whatever they were, these creatures that came to be known as dinosaurs, they seemed to be unlike anything now living.

This recognition in itself marked a critical departure from earlier thinking. It reflected a knowledge only recently gained, and somewhat reluctantly accepted, that many different forms of life existed in ages past and have since vanished. The fossils that were being found in increasing number and increasingly puzzling forms could not be interpreted any other way than as the remains of extinct life. This was the conclusion of Georges Cuvier, the foremost paleontologist of the early nineteenth century and the first scientist to present detailed and persuasive evidence for the reality of extinction as a general phenomenon in the history of life. Cuvier did not discover dinosaurs, but he did much to establish the intellectual conditions that made their discovery possible.

No one could have appreciated the fossils of what turned out to be dinosaurs unless there had been an awareness of extinctions. Now, of course, dinosaurs are a common metaphor for extinctions; nothing is "deader" than a dodo, unless it is a dinosaur. Moreover, attempts to solve the mystery of dinosaur extinction are central to what amounts to a rediscovery of the dinosaurs in recent years—another resurrection, and perhaps some new comprehension of earth's history. Here, too, one hears distant echoes of Cuvier. A variation on another of his themes, the idea that catastrophic geological upheavals contributed to many waves of extinctions, has emerged from the intellectual backrooms to influence not only the study of dinosaurs but the investigation of the causes and consequences of mass extinctions through time.

Georges Cuvier

In 1796, Cuvier made the first announcement about the extinction of species. He was only twenty-six years old, a short man with bright blue eyes and thick coppery red hair, but already prominent in French science. He was both brilliant and imaginative, qualities of a great scientist. Cuvier had been born in 1769 to a Huguenot family in Montbéliard, which then belonged to the duke of Württemberg and only later became a part of France. He was a precocious child who took an early interest in nature, collecting plants and bugs and sundry creatures, and with astonishing ease committed to memory long works on natural history. After his graduation from the duke's elite school in Stuttgart, he took a position as a tutor in Normandy, where he was captivated by the sea and the life teeming there. His dissections and descriptions of marine life as well as studies of fossils so impressed the established naturalists that they offered him a coveted research post in Paris.

In his first months there, Cuvier began examining the elephant bones that were being unearthed in Paris. Their discovery had caused a sensation. To think that elephants had once inhabited Paris! Parisians, astonished and fascinated, flocked to the excavation site as Cuvier tried to match the bones with the skeletons of living species. But they did not match. Thus, at a session of the National Institute of Sciences and Arts on January 21, 1796, he reported that the fossil elephants of Paris were distinct from either of the living forms, the Indian and African elephants, and that this species was now most certainly extinct.

More bones were brought to Cuvier from the gypsum quarries of Montmartre (the source of the original plaster of paris). These he found to be reptiles and other animals entirely different from any known creatures of the modern world. He realized that a whole fauna, not just elephants, had disappeared in the course of time. And the strangest and most enigmatic of these departed creatures were reptiles, whose fossils came to be prized by scientists. Cuvier was in the midst of digging up elephants and examining the Montmartre specimens when he was called upon to see what he could make of one particular fossil reptile.

The army of revolutionary France, fighting in the Netherlands in 1795, had shipped back to Paris a monstrous trophy of war. The French general had orders to find and seize it, and so he did in the small town of Maestricht. The priceless relic was kept there in a glass shrine in the residence of the local canon near the hill outside town where it had been unearthed to the astonishment of everyone. This was no bloodstained robe of a martyred saint or fragment of the True Cross, but a pair of fossil jaws more than one meter long. The jaws were the remains of some extraordinarily large antediluvian creature. Any bones of indeterminate origin and age were presumed to date back to the time preceding the Biblical Flood.

Workers in the Maestricht chalk quarries had discovered the jaws in 1770. They were accustomed to digging up fossil shells and an occasional bone, but nothing like the jaws. A retired German military surgeon and fossil collector, called to the scene, hauled the jaws off and had them examined by a couple of anatomists. It was an ancient whale, one decided. No, a gigantic marine lizard, the other declared. Was this possible? No lizards this large had ever been seen alive on land or in the sea. Still, as so many Europeans came to suspect, this did seem to be a prehistoric monster, something that might have lived before Noah, possibly before Adam, and passed out of existence. But this was, it seemed, something they were not sure they believed in.

Cuvier examined the jaws, comparing them with known animals, and concluded that they belonged to a lizard that could possibly be related to the monitors of the tropics. It was much larger, though, and must have led a marine, fish-eating life. Since it bore only a slight resemblance to living creatures, the animal must have lived in the very remote past. Some years later, the Rev. William D. Conybeare, in England, named it *Mosasaurus,* or "Meuse lizard," after the region in which it was found. The mosasaur was the first marine giant of the Mesozoic era to be dug up and identified. Cuvier's correct interpretation of those jaws established him as the foremost expert on large fossils. His influence on future fossil hunters was such that every time they dug up something large and old they had visions of ancient reptiles.

Additional evidence that not all species of life had survived to the present day came when an "unknown marine animal" that appeared to have wings was uncovered in Germany. From drawings—the discoverers would not let the fossil out of their hands—Cuvier identified the animal as a flying reptile, not marine but terrestrial, and named it *Pterodactyl,* from the Greek for "wing" and "finger." This was one of the pterosaurs, it has since been learned, which lived at the time of the dinosaurs and were the first true flying vertebrates. Some were as small as sparrows, while others had enormous wings spanning eight to ten meters. But they were now extinct, which was their important message to Cuvier.

In 1801, five years after his lecture on fossil elephants to the Institute, Cuvier elaborated on his thinking about extinctions as an apparent fact of nature. Nothing was more important, he said, than to "discover if the species which existed then have been entirely destroyed, or if they have merely been modified in their form, or if they have simply been transported from one climate to another." This reflected Cuvier's recognition of three alternative explanations to the distinct fossil forms he was seeing: extinction, evolution, or migration. He conceded that in some cases the latter explanation could apply, though it was highly unlikely that any of the larger ancient terrestrial animals had simply escaped the attention of explorers. In Cuvier's mind, this reduced the question to a choice between extinction and evolution. It was unfortunate for his reputation in history that Cuvier, otherwise so perceptive, locked himself into such either-or thinking. He rejected evolution, though, not out of any conscious desire to make his science conform to religion, but primarily as a defense of extinction. To Cuvier the fossil evidence seemed to favor extinction as the simplest and most obvious interpretation of what had happened to prehistoric life.

A few scientists had previously weighed the possibility of extinctions, yet could not bring themselves to accept the idea, fearing that it might be contrary to the Bible. They dared not ignore the words in Ecclesiastes 3:14: "I know that, whatsoever God doeth, it shall be forever: Nothing can be put to it, nor any thing taken from it. . . ." Perhaps, they thought, the creatures that seemed to be extinct had only disappeared from Europe and were alive and well in some remote, poorly explored part of the world. This was the migration explanation that Cuvier also raised. When Thomas Jefferson dispatched Meriwether Lewis and William Clark on their expedition into the American West, he felt sure that they would bring back reports of such survivors. In a few later instances, notably the discovery of a coelacanth in the waters off southern Africa and of an Australian marsupial named *Burramys parvus,* supposedly extinct animals did turn up alive. But when Cuvier, with his towering reputation and the evidence at hand, proclaimed the fact of species extinctions, nearly all doubt was erased.

Cuvier not only made scientists aware of extinctions, but he also developed methods of research that were widely emulated, and this, too, prepared scientists to deal with the first dinosaur bones.

What Cuvier did was to elevate comparative anatomy to a science of great value in the service of paleontology. One must draw on geology in searching for fossils and establishing their relative ages; but to identify the specimens and interpret their place in nature, one must know biology, particularly comparative anatomy. In this branch of science Cuvier excelled. He demonstrated that each major group of animals has its own peculiar body architecture. According to his principle of the "correlation of parts," the anatomical structure of every organ and bone is functionally related to all other parts of the body of an animal. (He mistakenly took this as evidence that species had not changed since their creation; each species, he believed, is too well coordinated, functionally and structurally, to have survived significant change through evolution.) Cuvier recognized that, by applying the correlation-of-parts principle, the species of an animal could often be identified from the shape of a single bone or, at most, a few pieces of bone. The toe bone is, after all, connected to the foot bone, the foot bone to the ankle bone, and so forth. Making these connections, as Cuvier did so well, instilled in paleontologists a confidence in their analytical powers that approached hubris. This confidence was reflected by Cuvier when he wrote: "The shape and structure of the teeth regulate the forms of the condyle [knuckle or other jointlike prominence], of the shoulder-blade, and of the claws, in the same manner as the equation of a curve regulates all its other properties. . . . Thus, commencing our investigation by a careful survey of any one bone by itself, a person who is sufficiently master of the laws of organic structure, may, as it were, reconstruct the whole animal to which that bone had belonged."

Hubris led paleontologists into some embarrassing mistakes. Jefferson, who counted paleontology among his many talents, once identified the claws of a giant sloth as belonging to a lion larger than the modern animal. Wrong though he was, Jefferson thereby gained another measure of immortality. The extinct sloth now bears the name *Megalonyx jeffersoni*—"Jefferson's giant nail." Henry Fairfield Osborn, the commanding presence in American paleontology during the early twentieth century, once announced, on the basis of a single tooth, that he had discovered the first human ancestor in the New World. The tooth turned out to be a pig's molar.

Cuvier also could be wrong, as one of the discoverers of dinosaurs would find out, but those occasions were the exception. He seemed to possess an almost magical facility for taking a few odd bones and reconstructing the whole skeletons of strange creatures, mammoths and mastodons as well as ancient forms of rhinoceros, hippopotamus, deer, and crocodile. Parisians saw this and were amazed. In Cuvier's hands paleontology seemed as much art as science. "Is Cuvier not the greatest poet of our century?" exclaimed Honoré de Balzac. "Our immortal naturalist has reconstructed worlds from blanched bones. He picks up a piece of gypsum and says to us 'See!' Suddenly stone turns into animals, the dead come to life, and another world unrolls before our eyes."

Not all of Cuvier's work was the poetry of laboratory reconstructions. He went into the field often with Alexandre Brongniart, a mining geologist, and there recognized that the deeper one dug, deep into the strata laid down in the more remote past, the less the fossils resembled animals now living. The strata revealed marked changes in the land and in life through time. Elephant bones appeared only in the uppermost layers. Below lay a succession of alternating deposits of sea and land fossils; at a certain depth, the large mammals disappeared altogether. Cuvier identified some 150 fossil species in the basin of the Seine, and 90 of them had no living counterparts. With these extinctions and the sharp boundaries between the strata in mind, Cuvier reasoned that a sequence of widespread upheavals had doomed earlier life and reshaped the surface of the earth. The basin of the Seine had been by turns dry and submerged. The strata from the times of these episodes seemed to tell the story of past life and catastrophic death.

So Cuvier presented his theory of earth's history in an 1812 treatise, *A Dis-*

course on the Revolutions of the Surface of the Globe. According to him, the sea or widespread floods had repeatedly inundated lands. Glacial ice advanced across continents that had been warm, which would explain some of the prehistoric animals that had recently been found frozen in Russia. Violent movements rent and overturned the earth's crust. These were catastrophes so sudden and complete, he said, that "the thread of Nature's operations was broken by them." The toll was great. "Living things without number were swept out of existence by the catastrophes," Cuvier wrote. "Those inhabiting the dry lands were engulfed by deluges. Others whose home was in the waters perished when the sea bottom suddenly became dry land; whole races were extinguished leaving mere traces of their existence, which are now difficult of recognition, even by the naturalist."

With his discovery of extinctions and a past generally unlike the present, with his skill at re-creating this past out of old bones, Georges Cuvier prepared nineteenth-century minds to think of earth history possibly extending back before Adam and to expect the land to yield more bones of creatures as fabulous as the mosasaur. "What a noble task it would be were we able to arrange the objects of the organic world in their chronological order," Cuvier wrote in 1812.

> The development of life, the successes of its forms, the precise determination of those organic types that first appeared, the simultaneous birth of certain species and their gradual extinction—the solution of these questions would perhaps enlighten us regarding the essence of the organism as much as all the experiments that we can try with living species. And man, to whom has been granted but a moment's sojourn on the earth, would gain the glory of tracing the history of the thousands of ages which preceded his existence and of the thousands of beings that have never been his contemporaries.

IT WAS AT THIS TIME that Gideon Algernon Mantell began hunting fossils and eventually came on the bones and teeth of what turned out to be the most celebrated victims of Cuvier's extinctions.

Fossil hunters like Mantell were legion in England then, amateurs and scientists alike, and the prizes they often sought were fossils of ancient reptiles. Such fossils were in vogue, in part because of Cuvier's mosasaur and in essence because they seemed to epitomize prehistoric life. Several recent discoveries had arrested the attention of scientists and the public. They were still talking about the incredible reptile Mary Anning had found in the cliffs at Lyme Regis, in southern England. If Dickens had written of paleontology,* he might have looked back to Mary Anning for inspiration. Without formal training in paleontology and scarcely literate, she supported herself and her widowed mother by selling natural "curiosities," mainly fossil shells. The tongue-twister "She sells seashells on the seashore" almost certainly refers to her. In 1810, when she was only eleven years old, Mary and her brother saw some bones protruding from a cliff and, after chipping away the rock with hammer and chisel, she traced the outline of a skeleton ten meters long. The creature, with its four flippers and a pair of long jaws full of sharp teeth, appeared both reptilian and piscine. As the word of her discovery spread, the savants of London, in effect, beat a path to Mary Anning's humble door. For she had found the first reasonably complete skeleton of the extinct marine reptile later to be known as *Ichthyosaurus,* from the Greek words for "fish" and "lizard." A few years later, she discovered the remains of another seagoing reptile, *Plesiosaurus.*

The savants did not so readily accept Mantell's discovery of the first recognized dinosaurs. Nor is it quite clear even now when and how he acquired the first dinosaur bones. The particulars of their discovery, like almost everything else about dinosaurs, are the subject of learned conjecture and dispute. The standard version of how the first dinosaur fossils were discovered, repeated time and again with mythic elaboration, can be summarized in the following way.

One spring day in 1822, Mantell, a surgeon, had driven by horse and carriage into the weald outside Lewes in Sussex, where the Ouse River flows south to the English Channel. There Mantell stopped at a house to attend a patient. While he was inside, the surgeon's wife, Mary Ann, strolled up and down the road. In her six years of marriage to Mantell, she had come to share his interest in fossils. They had just collaborated on a large volume, *The Fossils of the South Downs,* to be published that year, in which he described his collection, mostly ancient seashells, and she supplied the drawings. So nothing was more natural for Mary Ann Mantell, on her stroll, than to cast an appraising eye on a pile of rock dumped there for road repairs.

Her eye fell on one piece of sandstone in particular. Embedded in it was

*In the opening passages of *Bleak House,* Dickens did allude to contemporary thinking in geology and paleontology. "Implacable November weather," he wrote. "As much mud in the streets as if the waters had but newly retired from the face of the earth, and it would not have been wonderful to meet a Megalosaurus, forty feet long or so, waddling like an elephantine lizard up Holborn Hill."

Gideon Algernon Mantell

what looked like a large tooth. She showed this to her husband as soon as he emerged from the house. "You have found the remains of an animal new to science," Mantell supposedly told his wife. The tooth was, he said later, "wholly unlike any that had previously come under my observation."

Mantell returned to the wooded countryside many times that spring and summer, to the neglect of his medical practice. He was thirty-two years old and had been a surgeon for almost a decade, but his avocation, hunting fossils, had a way of taking precedence over his vocation. He visited the rock quarries and asked the quarrymen to alert him if they should find more teeth like the one his wife had picked up, or anything else beyond the usual shells. Some more teeth came to light, along with some strange bones, in a quarry in Tilgate Forest near Cuckfield in Sussex. These turned out to be the teeth and bones of the first recognized dinosaur.

This version is derived primarily from Mantell's report of the discovery in 1825 and his reminiscences late in life, in 1851. The story became legend through the biography of Mantell written in 1927 by Sidney Spokes and through countless retellings by scholars and popularizers of dinosaur lore. But Dennis R. Dean, a professor at the University of Wisconsin–Parkside, has now exposed serious flaws in the legend. In his research for a new, scholarly biography of Mantell, Dean examined the surgeon's journals and correspondence, including many previously unknown letters, and pieced together a revisionist version of the dinosaur discovery.

According to Dean's story, Mantell took an interest in the quarries at Cuckfield as early as 1818 and hired a quarryman named Leney to collect and send him unusual fossil specimens. Leney's shipments to Mantell in 1819 included many mystifying teeth and bones of what must have been some large reptiles.

A quarry in the Tilgate Forest, Sussex

In June 1820, Mantell received from Leney "a fine fragment of an enormous bone; several vertebrae, and some teeth of the Proteo-saurus."

This inspired Mantell to organize a collecting expedition. The purpose of all his visits to the Tilgate Forest, then as before and after, was invariably geological and paleontological, never apparently to see a patient. On August 15, 1820, Mantell's brother Thomas drove Mary Ann and another woman, probably her sister, to Cuckfield in his chaise. Mantell rode alongside on horseback. If Mary Ann Mantell did indeed pick up a tooth, as the surgeon would later claim, the incident must have occurred on this trip. But it seemed to have made no immediate impression on him. He reported in his journal that the party collected "nothing of consequence."

Other "good bones" were delivered to Mantell that year and in 1821, and he made at least two more collecting excursions, both in September 1821. On the first trip he found parts of an enormous bone. On the second, September 26, he came away from the Cuckfield quarries with "a fine lumbar vertebra of a crocodile and a tooth of the same kind of animal." Mantell, not being sure what he had, sought the opinions of established scientists. He showed one tooth, perhaps the one he had collected in September, to William Clift at the Hunterian Museum of the Royal College of Surgeons in London. Clift concluded that the tooth had belonged to a crocodile or a monitor lizard.

By November 1821, when he apparently wrote the section on the Tilgate fossils for *The Fossils of the South Downs,* Mantell had in his possession at least six teeth and many bone fragments of what would later be identified as a dinosaur. Writing months before Mary Ann's legendary springtime stroll, Mantell stated: "The teeth, vertebrae, bones, and other remains of an animal of the lizard tribe, of enormous magnitude, are perhaps the most interesting fossils that have been discovered in the county of Sussex." He noted that these animals somewhat resembled crocodiles, though they differed "in many important particulars from the recent species." Whatever they were, these animals had been gigantic. They exceeded in magnitude, Mantell remarked, "every animal of the lizard tribe hitherto discovered either in a recent or fossil state." The surgeon from Lewes had discovered dinosaurs without yet knowing it.

This version of the discovery story, as a journalist would say, does not read as well as the standard legend. It lacks the elements of science romance: no casual stroll down an English country road, no exotic fragment calling attention to itself in a pile of ordinary gravel, no moment of shared excitement as the wife shows the strange tooth to her husband the surgeon and amateur paleontologist. But, according to Dean's analysis, the legend perpetuates several errors of historical fact. He found no record of the surgeon and his wife taking a trip together into the Tilgate Forest in the spring or summer of 1822. Moreover, Dean's examination of *South Downs,* published in May of that year, showed that the surgeon had already gathered an extensive collection of dinosaur bones and teeth before 1822. Mantell drew particular attention to an "incisor tooth of a cuneiform shape," of which the crown only remained, and noted that several smaller specimens of the same type of tooth had been "discovered by Mrs. Mantell." One of these teeth, Dean concluded, is very likely the one Mantell later singled out as his original discovery of a dinosaur. On Mantell's known excursions to Cuckfield, as was pointed out, he was accompanied by his wife only on August 15, 1820. The first dinosaur tooth, therefore, may have been discovered by Mary Ann Mantell that day.

Even if the importance of her discovery went unrecognized at first, the more Mantell pondered the teeth, the more they excited his curiosity and puzzled him. The crown of one tooth, he noted, was worn down into a smooth oblique surface. This was clearly the tooth of a large plant-eating animal. It could not have masticated flesh. The tooth reminded Mantell of "the corresponding part of an incisor of a large pachyderm ground down by use." But he knew from Cuvier's discoveries of extinct elephants that remains of such prehistoric mammals were found only in the upper strata of relatively recent time, not in the more ancient strata from which he believed his fossils came. Mantell's thoughts, therefore, turned to ancient reptiles.

Since the apparent age of Mantell's fossil tooth seemed to rule out a mammalian connection, the surgeon of Lewes felt that it must be reptilian. But a characteristic of modern reptiles frustrated him in this line of thinking. "As no known existing reptiles are capable of masticating their food," Mantell said, "I could not venture to assign the tooth in question to a saurian."

Mantell took the tooth and other specimens to a meeting of the Geological Society of London. Some of the eminent scientists discouraged him by dismissing the fossils as rather uninteresting remains of a large fish related to the wolf-fish, *Anarhicas lupus,* or only some mammalian teeth. Perhaps Mantell had been mistaken in assuming the fossils' great antiquity. Only William Wollaston, the chemist, supported Mantell in his opinion that he had discovered teeth of "an unknown herbivorous reptile." Wollaston encouraged the surgeon to continue his investigation.

Mantell next turned to the great Cuvier himself. The surgeon heard that Charles Lyell, a young lawyer and geologist, would be visiting Paris and asked him to take the fossil tooth and show it to Cuvier. By then, 1823, Cuvier held three of France's highest scientific positions—professor of natural history at the Collège de France, professor of comparative anatomy at the Jardin des Plantes, and secretary of the Academy of Sciences. He had also grown fat and been made a baron, a title that matched his boundless vanity. He advised the government on education, lectured with eloquence, and turned out a steady flow of lucid research reports.

Lyell called on Cuvier at his studio near the natural history museum. These were the quarters of a tireless and methodical man, as Lyell would describe them several years later. Cuvier's "sanctum sanctorum," the English visitor recalled, was "a longish room . . . furnished with eleven desks to stand to, and two low tables, like a public office for so many clerks." On each desk lay "a complete establishment" of inkstand, pens, paper, books, and a manuscript in progress. All this, Lyell said, was "for the one man, who multiplies himself as author and, admitting no one into the room, moves as he finds necessary, or as fancy inclines him, from one occupation to another."

Cuvier examined the fossil and, without hesitation, pronounced it to be nothing more than an upper incisor of a rhinoceros. When Mantell, undaunted, sent Cuvier some of the bones, the verdict was likewise disappointing. The bones, Cuvier said, belonged to a species of hippopotamus.

Mantell persisted, the Geological Society and Cuvier notwithstanding. William Buckland, professor of geology at Oxford University, wrote to caution Mantell not to publish any claim that the fossils came from anywhere deeper than the superficial diluvian—that is, the uppermost sediments. There was no proof, Buckland said, that the fossils were old enough to be of an extinct reptilian giant. Still, Mantell persisted. He must have given the impression of a man obsessed, like an inventor of some antigravity device trying desperately to enlist backers.

Mantell eventually took the fossils to the Hunterian Museum in London. He spent hours poring over the museum's collection of reptilian teeth and bones, hoping to find something comparable to his specimens. His search proved fruitless. By chance, however, a young man named Samuel Stutchbury, who had been doing research on iguanas, was at the museum that day. When Mantell showed him the fossil teeth, Stutchbury remarked on their resemblance to the teeth of a Central American iguana. Mantell, as he examined Stutchbury's specimens, also saw the resemblance.

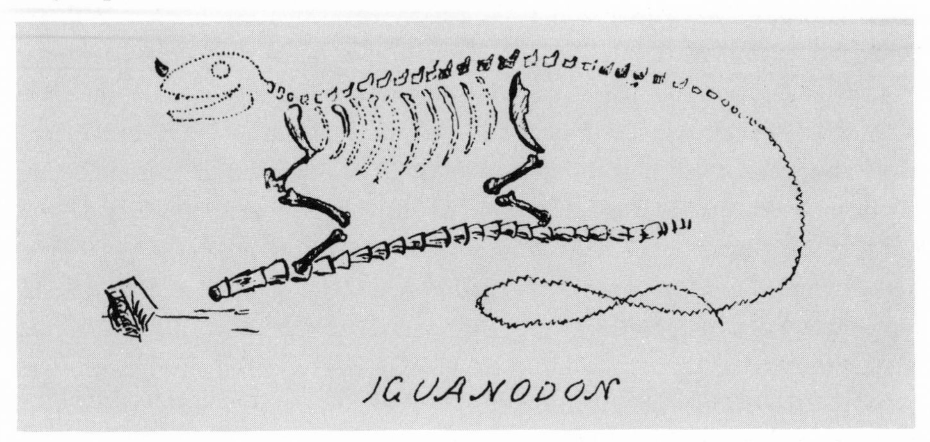

Iguanodon, *as restored by Mantell*

Mantell now felt confident that his teeth and bones were those of a huge plant-eating reptile. If an iguana had teeth this size, he speculated, the entire animal would be enormous, some eighteen meters long. At the suggestion of Conybeare, Mantell named the fossil reptile *Iguanodon,* meaning "iguana tooth." He then gave a full report of the discovery to the Royal Society in London in 1825.

Some of Mantell's assumptions about *Iguanodon* turned out to be erroneous. He thought the animal had walked on four legs in the manner of a scaled-up iguana. He mistook its spiky thumb bone for a horn and, in drawings, placed it on top of the snout, making the creature look like a rhinoceros. But Mantell made no mistake about the significance of his discovery. Long ago, before mammals flourished, he declared, reptiles more gigantic than any known today had lived on the earth.

When he learned of Mantell's findings, prior to publication, Cuvier graciously acknowledged his previous errors and proffered some thoughts of his own. Since all of the largest modern terrestrial animals were herbivores, it stood to reason that the largest of the ancient reptiles would also have been "nourished on vegetables." Accordingly, it should not be surprising that *Iguanodon,* being so large, had the teeth of a herbivore. As Cuvier anticipated and later discoveries revealed, many of the dinosaurs did turn out to have been plant-eating giants quite unlike today's reptiles.

WHILE MANTELL was agonizing over what to make of the *Iguanodon* fossils, between 1820 and 1825, a more eminent fossil hunter, William Buckland, examined an interesting collection of bones at the Oxford museum that had been found in a slate quarry. Most of the roofing slate for the shire came from the village of Stonesfield north of Oxford, and in recent years, as the quarry reached greater depths, workmen had encountered an increasing number of fossilized bones and delivered them to the museum. Some were relics of small mammals. Others appeared to be much older and larger. These bones included a lower jaw with large serrated teeth, some vertebrae, part of a pelvis, a piece of shoulder blade, and several fragments from a hind limb. Buckland decided that the bones were quite possibly reptilian. He, too, was influenced by Cuvier's mosasaur.

For some reason, probably the press of other research, Buckland took his time reporting on these fossils. But he called in friends and colleagues to have a look and give their opinions. One of them was so impressed by the huge, bladelike teeth that he published in 1822 the statement that the Stonesfield tooth belonged to a reptile of great length, which he called *Megalosaurus.* The author was James Parkinson, a physician who is best remembered for his description of the disease bearing his name. No one is sure, but the name *Megalosaurus* may also have been the inspiration of Conybeare, whose appellative faculty seems to have accounted for his most enduring contributions to paleontology.

Buckland waited two years to report the first full description of *Megalosaurus* in a scientific publication, the 1824 *Transactions of the Geological Society of London.* He thus beat Mantell into print by a year, though he had been preceded himself by Parkinson. This accounts for the confusion, persisting to this day, in assigning priority for the discovery of the first recognized dinosaurian fossils. Parkinson may have published the first account of a megalosaur fossil in 1822, but he failed to give a satisfactory scientific description. Buckland's was unquestionably the first formal scientific report on dinosaurian remains. Mantell's published paper on *Iguanodon* came a year later, in 1825, but the surgeon had discussed his findings before the Geological Society months prior to Buckland's publication and had described the teeth in his 1822 book on fossils. He might have published earlier had Buckland not counseled against "premature" announcement. If Mantell harbored any suspicion that Buckland acted out of selfish motives, the surgeon never betrayed his feelings in public. Mantell, writing of Buckland at the time, praised "the generous kindness which marked his character." Generous kindness would not always characterize relations between fossil hunters.

Although a case can be made for Mantell's priority of discovery—and his lonely struggle to win the establishment's support makes him a sentimental favorite, while his journal entries regarding saurian bones found in 1819 and 1820 support his priority—Buckland's announcement carried more weight. He was England's most respected geologist, professor of mineralogy and geology at Oxford and president of the Geological Society. He seemed to personify the recent emergence of geology as a full-fledged science and of fossil study, soon to be called paleontology, as its closely related discipline.

Buckland had been born at Axminster in 1784, the son of a clergyman, and after studies at Oxford, he also was ordained a priest in the Church of England. Several other of the country's leading geologists likewise combined careers in the church and science. Although he would become canon at Oxford and eventually dean of Westminster, geology and paleontology always commanded the better part of Buckland's energies. He was a bustling worker in the field, where he made an unforgettable impression scrambling about in his professorial robe and top hat. At a cave in Yorkshire, he identified the remains of scores of mammals that no longer inhabited Europe, including hyenas, lions, and elephants. His report on the discovery, which he inferred was a den of prehistoric hyenas, established him as a ranking paleontologist.

William Buckland

Buckland, however, had a restricted view of the possible. He was unshakable in his belief in the reality of Noah's Flood and that the animal bones in many such caves were from the unlucky victims of that catastrophe. He also believed that no humans could have inhabited Britain before the Flood. This led him, or required him, to misinterpret the bones in another cave, Paviland Cave in South Wales. There, deep in the sediments among bones of antediluvian animals, lay the skeleton of a human. It was stained red from the iron-rich earth and adorned with ivory beads. Buckland could not bring himself to believe that this was a human who lived at the time of the mammoths, which would have made it quite a sensational find—the oldest human remains ever to have been discovered by the 1820s. Instead, noting that the cave happened to be near an ancient Roman encampment, Buckland decided that this was a woman—no British man would wear beads—and that her profession had been less than respectable. "Whatever may have been her occupation," he wrote with a certain delicacy, "the vicinity of a camp would afford a motive for residence, as well as a means of subsistence." The skeleton, with its reputation thus stained the same color as its bones, became known as the "Red Lady of Paviland." Buckland's error was exposed much later. The Red Lady was a young man who died 18,000 years ago in the Ice Age.

No one could be indifferent to Buckland. His theatrical lectures captivated students. But Darwin, some years later, would find him "vulgar and coarse," with a "craving for notoriety." Visitors to the Buckland home found the place crawling with evidence that he was a cheerful eccentric. He delighted in discomfiting guests with platters of crocodile or ostrich meat and watching their reactions as guinea pigs nibbled at their toes and, according to John Ruskin, "polite little Carolina lizards kept off the flies." His bear, named Tiglath Pileser, after a king of ancient Babylon, would sometimes appear at garden parties dressed in an Oxonian cap and gown. But in his study of fossils, Buckland was absolutely serious about his effort to find evidence supporting Cuvier's catastrophist theory of geology. He was Cuvier's most tireless exponent in England. The bones in the Yorkshire cave, he was sure, were the remains of life in the final days before the last catastrophe, Noah's Flood.

Cuvier's influence was also evident in Buckland's work on *Megalosaurus.* It seems that Cuvier urged Buckland to go ahead and publish his paper, entitled "Notice on the *Megalosaurus* or Great Fossil Lizard of Stonesfield." Like Cuvier in his analysis of the mosasaur, Buckland confidently classified the fossils within the "order of Saurians or Lizards." Moreover, acknowledging a scholarly debt to Cuvier, he wrote: "From these dimensions as compared with the ordinary standard of the lizard family, a length exceeding 40 feet and a bulk equal to that of an elephant seven feet high have been assigned by Cuvier to the individual to which this bone [the thigh bone] belonged." Cuvier, it would appear, deserves a share of the credit for the discovery of *Megalosaurus*—and thus of dinosaurs. With his inspired work in comparative anatomy and species extinctions, Cuvier was at least the intellectual godfather of the discoveries of the 1820s.

In contrast to Mantell's plant-eating *Iguanodon,* the serrated teeth of Buckland's specimen were those of a flesh eater. But Buckland noticed something else about the teeth. They were set in sockets, as are the teeth of crocodiles; the teeth of lizards are attached directly to the jawbone. After Buckland cited anatomical reasons why this was not just an ancient crocodile, however, he failed to pursue the matter, never appreciating the importance of this feature. As Edwin H. Colbert, a modern authority on dinosaurs, has written, this was "unassailable proof" that *Megalosaurus* was not a gigantic lizard, as Buckland and Cuvier seemed to assume, but "something new, a reptile the like of which had never been imagined."

Earlier fossil collectors, as might be expected, had found megalosaur bones without knowing their significance. A "human thigh-bone" from Oxfordshire was described in 1676 by the Rev. Robert Plot, first keeper of the Ashmolean Museum at Oxford. It was actually the lower end of a dinosaur thigh, probably from a megalosaur. Alan Charig, of the British Museum (Natural History), recently discovered in the museum collection an *Iguanodon* bone that was picked up in Cuckfield in 1809, before the Mantells went fossil hunting there.

Buckland's interest in fossil giants waned with the years. He became more concerned with the big questions of geology and paleontology, as he saw them, which had to do with the reconciliation of geology and the Bible. He was a man of the church as well as of science.

Mantell, on the other hand, redoubled his search for fossils, driving his frail body and making life increasingly difficult for his family. He found the remains of another dinosaur in 1832, the year Cuvier died. Called *Hylaeosaurus,* it was a smaller creature with armor plating and large, hard, symmetrical spines running the length of its back. These and other bones filled his house to overflowing. The next year Mantell decided to leave Lewes and set up medical practice at Brighton, hoping for a more lucrative practice at the seaside resort in order to support his avocation. He published a popular book on geology and acquired the bones of another *Iguanodon,* found at Maidstone. But his medical practice suffered to the point that in 1838 he was forced to sell much of his fossil collection to the British Museum. The next year, after what must have been a domestic confrontation in which Mantell had to choose between his fossils and his family, his wife and their four children left him. By this time, Mantell had ceased giving Mary Ann credit for finding the original *Iguanodon* tooth.

Gideon Mantell spent his last years in London, a lonely and morose man, and died in 1852. William Buckland lived four more years, much honored but with his stature diminished because he had backed the wrong side in the century's war of geological philosophy. By the time of their deaths, nevertheless, Mantell and Buckland at least had the satisfaction of knowing that, with a few teeth and bones, they had fetched out of the dim past the first identifiable evidence of some of nature's most spectacular creations.

2 *Discovery of Time*

NEARLY ALL of earth's history remained unknown and largely inconceivable at the beginning of the nineteenth century. Science had long since discredited the pre-Copernican idea of a small, earth-centered universe, thereby freeing people to think of the heavens in virtually limitless dimensions. Chemistry, physics, and physiology were being pursued with fewer restraints imposed by dogma. The way things were seemed fit for rigorous, objective inquiry, but not the way things had come to be—not earth's history. Its study had yet to be liberated from the inhibiting influence of traditional belief. Its study, with a few as yet unappreciated exceptions, was constrained by a concept of time woefully deficient in time.

No one then could glimpse the history we know now with a fair degree of certainty. No one knew the age of the planet earth, 4.6 billion years, or could imagine the progression of life that apparently had its beginning sometime before the end of earth's first billion years, perhaps as early as 4.2 billion years ago. In the beginning, the planet was sterile. The land took form, pocked with meteorite craters, lit by the fires of countless volcanoes, and drenched by rain that fed the young oceans of liquid water. The air was of nitrogen, carbon dioxide, and other gases, but no oxygen yet. Vast stores of compounds containing carbon and hydrogen and a few other chemicals had accumulated on the land and in the waters. Life arose from nonlife in this primordial chemical soup, the compounds coming together with the help of lightning discharges and the sun's ultraviolet radiation. (An alternate theory emphasizes the role of ordinary clay as the site for storing the energy and information for processing inorganic raw material into the more complex molecules from which the first life arose.) Molecules eventually combined into more complex molecules leading to self-replicating, single-celled organisms, something like blue-green algae—life. The simplest definition of a living entity is something that can reproduce itself. Then, after a seeming eternity when nothing much appeared to change, some cells with a latent sense of community clumped together to form multicellular organisms with more elaborate chemical machinery. Early life, the proliferating algae and bacteria, learned to use light as the source of energy for growth. The photosynthetic organisms that followed broke down water to capture the hydrogen and release oxygen into the environment. The air became polluted with oxygen, which must have destroyed many ancient species. Extinction was as much a part of the process of life on earth then as it would be later. Out of this early global catastrophe arose new forms of life that thrived on oxygen. An atmosphere enriched with oxygen was conducive to the more complex chemistry that created the earliest forms of animal life. Jellyfish, worms, and other soft-bodied creatures appeared some 1 billion years ago. Animals with external skeletons—the trilobites, coral, and sea scorpions—began to flourish 590 million years ago. Within a few million years, in an unprecedented explosion of new life, nearly all major groups of invertebrates with hard parts made their first appearance on earth. The horseshoe crab that washes up on the beach is like a message in a bottle from that time, for it has survived more or less intact over some 500 million years. Then came fish, the first animals with backbones. Life was still confined to water. But as the land rose and plant life washed ashore, some fish with lungs crawled out of the water on their stumpy fins and established a beachhead about 400 million years ago. Their kind evolved into amphibians, ancestors of frogs, toads, and salamanders. Life's conquest of the land became complete with the emergence 300 million years ago of reptiles, the first vertebrates to be independent of water. From these early reptiles descended nearly every animal with a backbone that lives on earth today, humans included, and many other animals that have vanished, most notably the dinosaurs.

But at the turn of the nineteenth century most scientists as well as laymen could not envisage time and life on such a vast scale. They might accept Cuvier's extinctions, a first step toward comprehension. They might view with fascination the many fossil discoveries, suggesting a readiness to contemplate prehistory. But they could not yet conceive of dinosaurs and their whole world because, in a sense, they had yet to discover time.

Cuvier, for example, could do no more than suggest an age of "some thousands of centuries" for the fossil-bearing strata around Paris. And he was a scientist in the tradition of the Enlightenment, open to new ideas derived from scientific inquiry. Many other scientists, particularly in Britain, clung to assumptions that militated against an understanding of life's vast time-scale. They assumed that God had created the earth a relatively short time before; thus, there was not enough time for nature to have had a past all that different from its present. They assumed the fixity of the species; life in the past could not have been all that different from life now. They also assumed that the world was made for man's benefit; hence the difficulty they had in conceiving of a world without man, a world dominated by nonhuman species.

Such intellectual baggage is hardly recommended for travels back to the time of dinosaurs. But carry it scientists did, willingly for the most part, though sometimes uncomfortably, as they crossed the threshold of the century that would revolutionize the study of natural history.

Although evidence to the contrary lay everywhere underfoot and was beginning to attract notice, much of Christian Europe still tended to believe the earth could be no more than 6,000 years old. This time barrier, erected in the name of religion, seemed insurmountable. The Englishmen who eventually made the first dinosaur discoveries, and even the great Darwin, grew up with the firm belief that God had created the earth and man and all the other species in the year 4004 B.C.

ANY DATE that specific suggests a basis in fact, and factual it was to James Ussher, the Protestant prelate who worked out the date in the seventeenth century. Ussher, the archbishop of Armagh in the Church of Ireland, was a devoted scholar of the Bible, the one book he knew and valued above all others. He harbored no doubt whatsoever of the Bible's historical accuracy. Accordingly, he pored through the genealogies of the Old Testament, the lists of who begat whom, and made calculations of the length of each generation of the many patriarchs, priests, judges, and kings. In so working his way back through time, Ussher determined to his satisfaction that the Creation must have occurred in 4004 B.C. and the Flood in 2349 B.C. This he published in 1650.

Ussher was exploring time the best way he knew how, a way with a long and honored tradition. Indeed, as Martin J. S. Rudwick, a Cambridge University historian of science, noted in his 1972 book *The Meaning of Fossils,* the idea that the earth had a history first entered "scientific" debate not from the realm of science but from that of theology, particularly from chronologists like Ussher. In the fourth century, a historian of the early Christian church, Eusebius, developed a chronology not unlike Ussher's. Later church scholars tended to avoid such literal interpretations of Biblical accounts and even suggested that the Genesis story of the Creation might better be thought of as allegory. Then Martin Luther came along and reestablished the Biblical age of earth more firmly than ever. Luther and the other Protestant reformers looked to the Scriptures as the ultimate authority rather than accept the pronouncements of the Roman Catholic Church, which they considered too corrupt to be trusted. Luther's date for the Creation was a rounded-out 4000 B.C.

But, alas for Ussher's reputation in history, it is his name that is associated with the belief that the earth and life were less than 6,000 years old. Ussher's date made a lasting impression because, after all, it came to be printed right there in the margins of the King James Bible as plain as the words "In the beginning . . ." Those who wished to be more exact about such an important event heeded John Lightfoot's refinement of Ussher's date. In checking Ussher's calculations a few years later, Lightfoot, a Hebrew scholar and vice-chancellor of Cambridge, concluded that, to be more precise, God had created the earth at nine o'clock on the morning of Sunday the twenty-third of October in the year 4004 B.C.

Like it or not, scientists had to squeeze their observations of nature into a scale of time based on a 6,000-year-old world. Those who entertained doubts usually recoiled from the heretical implications of their doubts. When Carolus Linnaeus, the eighteenth-century Swedish botanist, said that he "should like to believe" the earth was older, he dutifully dismissed the notion, saying that "the Scriptures do not allow this." Others, however, were less cautious. Georges Louis Leclerc, comte de Buffon, the French naturalist, wrote in the mid eighteenth century, "Nature's great workman is time," and to him six millenia were hardly sufficient to account for the fossils and sediments running to such depths over the planet. By his reckoning, including an estimate based on how long a molten sphere the size of earth should take to cool and solidify, Buffon declared the earth's age to be at least 75,000 years, perhaps as much as half a million years. In the same century, Immanuel Kant, writing his *Cosmogony,* assumed a world many millions of years old. The house of Ussher's chronology showed signs of falling.

By the time of Mantell and Buckland, the evidence of ancient, extinct life and of "catastrophes" reshaping the landscape through time cried out for new interpretations of the earth's age. Cuvier's description of extinctions associated with periodic catastrophes appealed to many scientists like Buckland because it afforded a means of reconciling geology with Genesis. The catastrophist theory added countless years to the earth's age. After each catastrophe, according to Cuvier's inspired disciples in Britain, God had started over again with a new creation. The Book of Genesis dealt only with the last of these creations.

God, it seems, had neglected to reveal the previous ones to Moses because they did not concern man. Noah's Flood was presumably the last of the catastrophes and not one of the classics of annihilation, for the Bible says that many creatures, two by two, managed to ride out the deluge.

William Buckland, writing in 1836, seemed prepared to accept the growing evidence that the earth might be older than Ussher's date. As a man of science, he bowed to the findings of the new geology. Still, as a man of the cloth and of the early nineteenth century, he had lost none of his faith in the popular belief that the hand of God was everywhere revealed in nature. The first dinosaur bones were pondered in this light.

The coal fueling the Industrial Revolution and the British Empire, Buckland wrote, had been "laid up in store" by God ages ago "in a manner so admirably adapted to the benefit of the Human Race." This was the essence of the idea that nature was so ordered for man's benefit, an unspoken premise of human activities to this day. It flowed logically from the scientific-theological doctrine known variously as the *Scala Naturae,* Great Chain of Being, or Ladder of Perfection. All things were created at the same time and occupied fixed places on the ladder, from minerals upward through the lower forms of life to man on the highest rung. Man stood at the apex of nature.

A corollary to the *Scala Naturae* was a body of thought known as natural theology, which was widely believed at the time. The "bible" of natural theology was a tome by the Rev. William Paley of Cambridge, published in 1802 and reprinted almost annually over several decades for an eager audience. The book's title serves as a synopsis: *Natural Theology: or, Evidences of the Existence and Attributes of the Deity collected from the Appearances of Nature.*

The book opens with the analogy of a watch. If someone came upon a watch on the heath, Paley wrote, he would have no trouble seeing "that its several parts are framed and put together for a purpose" and thus inferring that "the watch must have had a maker." Likewise, according to Paley, the varied and intricate works of nature, all the plants and animals, including man himself, cannot be the product of mere chance; they, too, have been designed. Paley concluded: "There cannot be design without a designer; contrivance without a contriver; order without choice; arrangement, without any thing capable of arranging; subserviency and relation to a purpose, without that which could intend a purpose; means suitable to an end, without the end ever having been contemplated, or the means accommodated to it."

Paley, anticipating objections, conceded that some of God's designs, as for vision, could have been simpler. Yet if things were too simple, he argued, people might not perceive the skill and superior intelligence that had gone into God's creation of nature. And how could anyone dispute one of Paley's more winning illustrations of God's handiwork? Characterizing the divine skill in designing the human anatomy, the author of *Natural Theology* observed: "It is the most difficult thing that can be to get a wig made even; yet how seldom is the face awry!" Voltaire, the relentless anticlerical writer, had scoffed at such thinking years before Paley. In *Candide,* Voltaire has Dr. Pangloss assert: "Everything was made for a purpose; everything is necessary for the fulfillment of that purpose. Observe that noses have been made for spectacles; therefore we have spectacles."

Implicit in natural theology were the beliefs in the divine origins of earth and life (probably not too long ago), the immutability of species (nothing could be more haphazard, or without design, than Darwin's higgledy-piggledy natural selection), and the utilitarian view, popular then, that everything in nature was designed as the means to some end, usually for the greater good of man. Thus, it seemed unlikely that people would be dredging up a past in which the Designer was presumably so profligate, whimsical, or just plain careless that He would put hordes of large animals on earth, long before they could be of any use to man, and then wipe them off the face of the earth, as if they had been a mistake He wished to forget.

Although few scientists accepted natural theology in its entirety, they believed enough of it not to challenge it, or else lacked the inclination or information to do so. Darwin recalled that, as an undergraduate at Cambridge in the 1820s, he did not question Paley's premises and, indeed, was "charmed and convinced by the long line of argumentation." Later, Darwin would reverse himself. After marshaling the evidence for evolution by natural selection, he wrote: "There seems to be no more design in the variability of organic beings, and in the action of natural selection, than in the course which the wind blows."

But when Darwin sailed on the *Beagle* in 1831, like most Englishmen he did not in the least question the literal truth of the Bible. The captain, Robert FitzRoy, also an educated gentleman, was convinced the voyage would give Darwin an opportunity to find evidences for the first appearances of all created things on earth, in accordance with Genesis. Darwin and FitzRoy embodied the times. One would go forward and become the Copernicus of natural history.

On the voyage, Darwin began to cast the old intellectual baggage over the side. He read a new book on geology, by Lyell, that was a parting gift from his Cambridge mentor, John Stevens Henslow. From it Darwin got a glimmering of insight into the possible age and history of earth. There might still be a God, but not the designer Paley imagined. There might have been a divine creation, but long before Ussher estimated it to have occurred. Geology afforded this new perspective on time through a theory, promoted by Lyell, on the long, slow, cyclical nature of earth history, in contrast to the catastrophism of Cuvier and Buckland, and through the emerging ability to reconstruct the past through those relics of bygone life, fossils. The discovery of time was thus made through a careful reading of the land and the fossils therein.

JAMES HUTTON read the mountains, riverbeds, and coastal outcrops of his native Scotland and discovered that the earth was incredibly old, virtually ageless. He broke the time barrier in the last decades of the eighteenth century, although his accomplishment remained largely unappreciated until the 1830s, in time to have an important bearing on the discovery of dinosaurs and on Darwinian evolution.

James Hutton

One of the paradoxes of history is that in the society of Ussher and Paley and Buckland, with its staunch belief in supernatural causes, there could also flourish the Age of Reason, with its equally strong belief in man's ability to comprehend causes and in the probability that the causes might have little or nothing to do with the supernatural. Hutton inclined very much to the latter tradition. Born in Edinburgh in 1726, he was by turns a lawyer's apprentice, physician, chemical manufacturer, scientific farmer, and, finally, in the remaining three decades of his life, a full-time gentleman of leisure and intellectual inquiry. In those years Hutton developed a new theory of the earth.

The dominant theory then was Neptunism, championed by Abraham Gottlob Werner, a professor of mineralogy in Saxony who was deemed infallible in matters of geology. Werner believed, and therefore nearly everyone believed, that all the rock in the earth's crust had precipitated out of a primeval sea that had covered the entire planet. All features of the present landscape, the plains and valleys and mountains, owed their shape to the same universal waters. Where the waters went Werner never bothered to explain, nor did anyone press him to explain. Who dared question a theory that had the virtue of being compatible with the Biblical Flood?

Hutton saw no evidence of the universal flood. He believed instead that every rock formation, no matter how old, appeared to be derived from older rock. All features of the present landscape, to Hutton, were products of gradual change. "From the top of the mountains to the shore of the sea," he declared, "everything is in a state of change."

In an address to the Royal Society of Edinburgh in 1785 and in the book *Theory of the Earth,* published in 1795, Hutton described the earth as a dynamic, self-regulating "world machine" run by natural laws. There was no need to invoke singular events of creation and revolution to explain the face of the earth. Given enough time—this was the crux of Hutton's theory—geologic activity at its present rates could have produced all the rocks and accounted for the shape of the landscape.

According to Hutton, the earth's surface is at once deteriorating and being renewed through the four-stage cycle of erosion, deposition, consolidation, and uplift. Hutton the farmer had watched streams carry soil to the sea. The land is worn away by wind, rain, frost, and surf, the first stage in the cycle. The materials of erosion are eventually deposited as sediment in the depths of the ocean, the second stage. There the sediments are compacted and consolidated into layers of rock, the third stage. This much had been recognized by some of Hutton's predecessors.

There has to be a fourth step in the cycle, Hutton realized, or else the old continents would all be smoothed down and the oceans filled up. There must be a restorative force, and volcanoes suggested to him the mechanism for this fourth step. Werner and the Neptunists dismissed volcanism as the superficial effect of spontaneous combustion of buried seams of coal. Hutton perceived volcanism as the manifestation of "the liquefying power and expansive force of subterranean fire." Erupting volcanoes issued new rock, basalt and granite, from the earth's depths. Werner thought granite was the most ancient of all rocks, having been created as sediments on the floor of the universal ocean. Hutton thought otherwise, having seen in the Scottish highlands many veins of granite cutting up through older layers of sedimentary rock, the sandstones and shales. Interior heat was not only supplying new rock, Hutton further postulated, but it was responsible for lifting rock out of the sea and folding it up as new mountains and continents. He saw evidence of this in the angular unconformities exposed in the sides of the Scottish hills. The tilted and tortured strata implied a process of crustal uplift "which has for principle subterranean heat." Marine fossils betrayed the origins of the strata. Seeing one of these revealing unconformities on a field trip with Hutton, John Playfair, Hutton's Boswell, wrote: "What clearer evidence could we have had of the different formations of these rocks, and for the long interval which separated their formation, had we actually seen them emerging from the bosom of the deep? . . . The mind seemed to grow giddy by looking so far into the abyss of time."

It was unimaginable that wind, rain, surf, and imperceptible crustal movements could have shaped the earth's surface in only 6,000 years. After outlining the "chain of facts" supporting his cyclical notion of the earth's history, Hutton asked, "What more can we require?" His answer: "Nothing but time." In his view of geologic change through existing processes, the earth was surely the product of almost limitless time. Hutton concluded the treatise with his famous phrase that to earth history "we find no vestige of a beginning,—no prospect of an end."

Predictably, critics accused Hutton of atheism. He never questioned a divine creation, only the progression of events that ensued once the Creator had rested on the seventh day. Even so, critics subjected Hutton to ridicule, as in William Cowper's poem *The Task:*

> *. . . some drill and bore*
> *The solid earth, and from the strata there*
> *Extract a register, by which we learn*
> *That he who made it, and reveal'd its date*
> *To Moses, was mistaken in its age.*

Hutton did not live to see his triumph. Geological orthodoxy shifted away from Neptunism, but not to Hutton's theory. It moved to Cuvier's catastrophism, which did not require an indefinite amount of time and, moreover, invoked primeval oceans that bore a reassuring resemblance to Noah's Flood. It was left to Charles Lyell, born in 1797, the year Hutton died, to establish

Hutton's theory as the new orthodoxy. This he did in the three-volume *Principles of Geology,* the first volume of which Darwin took with him on the *Beagle.* Lyell's concept of gradual change and unlimited time, which became known as uniformitarianism, set the stage for modern geology and paleontology. It influenced Darwin to think of time on a scale sufficient for the slow processes of evolution and afforded paleontologists a freedom to imagine vanished worlds inhabited by creatures that lived and became extinct long before the patriarchs of the Bible.

Although uniformitarianism survives to this day, new evidence has shown that Hutton's world machine does not always function in smooth cycles. Cataclysms have rearranged the face of the earth many times over. The dynamics of sea-floor spreading and continental drift, the so-called plate tectonics rather than Cuvier's catastrophic floods, are continuing processes whose cumulative effect on climate and life can be revolutionary, a circumstance that in a sense represents a convergence of uniformitarianism and catastrophism.

Sufficient for the nineteenth century, however, was the new knowledge that the earth was old enough to have a history of unsuspected length and variety—time enough for dinosaurs. It remained for William Smith, reading the fossils in the land, to learn how to tell geologic time and enable others to establish the temporal framework of natural history.

3 *Measuring Time*

ON THE EVENING of January 5, 1796, the twenty-six-year-old William Smith set to paper a thought that had been germinating for several years. It was a totally new insight into the significance of fossils. Smith might have seemed an unlikely source of a transforming concept in geology and paleontology, for in that day science was largely the pursuit of gentlemen of means, men like Hutton and Cuvier, and Smith's origins and occupation were humble. He made his living as a surveyor of mines and canals and was, as a contemporary said, "a plain and moderately lettered man." His father, a mechanic in the Cotswolds, had died when Smith was not yet eight, and the boy went to live with an uncle who showed little sympathy for his desire to learn something more than farming. But Smith was industrious and observant. He taught himself surveying and, while holding the rod and dragging the chain, became curious about fossils and even more curious about the way certain layers of rock containing fossils always lay in a definite order. It occurred to Smith that the strata could be identified by the distinctive fossils within them.

Smith became convinced of this as he tramped along measuring the route of the new Somerset Coal Canal. Excavations had proceeded through Triassic marls and over beds of limestone and clay, reaching the village of Dunkerton in Somerset by early 1796. There, after a long day's work, in the same month that Cuvier in Paris delivered his pronouncement on extinct elephants, Smith returned to his room at the Swan Inn, on the Bath Turnpike, and wrote the following memorandum:

> Fossils have long been studdied as great Curiosities collected with great pains treasured up with great Care and at great Expense and shown and admired with as much pleasure as a Childe rattle or his Hobbyhorse is shown and admired by himself and his playfellows—because it is pretty. And this has been done by Thousands who have never paid the least regard

> to that wonderful order & regularity with which Nature has disposed of singular productions and assigned to each Class its peculiar Stratum.

Smith had recognized the second of two fundamental principles of stratigraphy. It had already been established to the satisfaction of Hutton and the more practical geologists, if not to some theorists and theologians, that strata of the earth occur in regular order and that under ordinary, undisturbed circumstances the lower strata are the more ancient of the layers. This served Smith as a guiding principle in his pioneering geologic mapping of England. His new discovery was that the organic remains buried within the strata also occur in the same regular order. This second principle, which every geologist and paleontologist now takes for granted, may seem too simple for comment, but no one had plucked it out of the ground until William Smith, the "moderately lettered" surveyor. He became known thereafter as "Strata" Smith.

William Smith

After writing the memorandum, Smith spent years preparing a log of fossils and the strata to which they belonged. If the fossils had scientific names, Smith did not always know them, or need to. He simply recognized them by their shapes and usually called them by their common names: the tiny mollusc shells known as pundibs, the thick sea urchins called poundstones, the familiar horn-shaped fossils that were ammonites. More important than names to Smith was the realization that the most distinctive aspect of a particular layer of the earth was not its thickness, color, or mineral composition—these varied from place to place in the same stratum, depending on the origin of the sediments—but the fossils embedded therein. Certain fossils he found in one stratum and nowhere else. They were the remains of creatures that lived at the time a particular sediment was being laid down, and at no other time. These are now known as "index fossils." By heeding the "wonderful order & regularity" of these index fossils, Smith said, it is possible to correlate strata in outcrops many miles apart, even continents away. The humblest fossils are the most useful in this regard; dinosaurs, mosasaurs, and saber-toothed cats are too large and rare to serve as guides to geologists trying to identify a stratum.

Since strata, no matter how different they may appear, are of the same age when they contain the same index fossils, William Smith had discovered a means of measuring time. Not absolute time in thousands and millions of years; such measurements were still more than a century away. But relative time; each layer of rock, according to Smith, represented an interval of time identifiable by its distinct assembly of fossils, and the sequence of layers represented the progression of time and geologic events. Thus, life itself, past life preserved in fossil form, was the key to telling geologic time.

FOR SO LONG, up to the century of Smith, people had not been sure what they should make of these curiosities they sometimes called figured stones. Prehistoric people must have found them fascinating. They left drawings of fossils on cave walls and fashioned them into necklaces and amulets. They considered fossils special enough, talismans perhaps, to be worthy adornments for the dead when they were laid to rest. But no one seems to have suspected their true nature before the ancient Greeks.

In the sixth century B.C., Pythagoras is said to have recognized fossils as the remains of living creatures. Because some fossils found in the mountains looked like small marine creatures, he surmised that the sea had once reached such elevations. A century later, Herodotus examined tiny fossils preserved in the stone of the Egyptian pyramids and, being a historian, decided that they were most likely petrified lentils, leftovers from the food supply of the pyramid builders. Elsewhere, Herodotus saw "shells upon the hills" and reasoned more correctly that they were from the sea and that the sea must have once covered the Libyan desert.

A Chinese scholar of the twelfth century A.D., Chu Hsi, was even more observant, anticipating both Hutton and Smith. "I have seen on high mountains conchs and oyster shells, often embedded in the rocks," the scholar wrote. "These rocks in ancient times were earth or mud, and the conch and oysters lived in water. Subsequently, everything that was at the bottom came to be at the top, and what was originally soft became solid and hard. One should meditate deeply on such matters, for these facts can be verified."

Those in the Middle Ages of Europe who meditated on such things, however, preferred to think of fossils as simply "sports of nature." They were minerals that just happened to look like bones or shells. As late as the eighteenth century, a German professor announced his certainty that fossils were nothing other than a divine hoax to test man's faith.

In this matter, as in so many others, Leonardo da Vinci proved himself ahead of his time. In the early sixteenth century, he came upon many fossils in the Apennines and correctly perceived that they were remains of marine organisms that had become embedded in rocks forming on some ancient sea bed. The rocks containing the fossils were then somehow elevated to their present dry-land position. Leonardo's interpretation was not made known to his contemporaries. It remained buried in his notebooks, to be dug up later and marveled at as the fossil of a brilliant but ignored insight. A generation later, Gabriele Fallopio, the skillful anatomist who is remembered, if at all, for his functional description of the Fallopian tubes, puzzled over the elephant bones, sharks' teeth, and many smaller marine fossils that were being uncovered in Italy. He could not imagine that the waters of the Biblical Flood had reached Italy's highlands (marine fossils found on land were by then usually attributed to the Flood). So Falloppio, reverting to medieval thinking, pronounced them to be nothing more than mineral concretions. There was safety in such an interpretation. In 1589, a Huguenot named Bernard Palissy was burned at the stake as a heretic for daring to write that fossils were the remains of living creatures.

A name for them, whatever they were, came into being about this time. The word "fossil" was apparently introduced by Georgius Agricola, a sixteenth-century German physician. He derived the word from the Latin *fossilis,* meaning "something dug up." For a while, the word defined almost anything dug out of the earth—coal, minerals, and metals as well as these mysterious sports of nature. The more narrow definition, which is that fossils are the relics of past life, came to be generally accepted by the early nineteenth century.

Fossils are not always the remains of living things themselves, but sometimes only traces of their existence. For example, an animal may be buried and eventually decay, though it retains a solid form long enough to leave a cavity in the rock, a mold of its former self and nothing more. Several victims of the Mount Vesuvius eruption that covered Pompeii left molds of themselves in the volcanic ash. (But this is a matter for archeologists, who study artifacts, the works of man, not fossils. Anything younger than 10,000 years, and thus not prehistoric, is not considered a true fossil in the eyes of paleontologists, whose interests run to earlier times.) In other cases, the mold may fill up with sand, clay, or other substances to make a cast. Other traces classified as fossils include the imprints of leaves in sandstone and shale, preserved burrows and borings of animals, and footprints left in mud that later solidified. Tracks in the Old Red Sandstone formation of the Orkney Islands record the passage of a primitive fish in the earliest-known invasion of the land by vertebrates. Two king crabs that lived 300 million years ago were indiscreet enough to leave trails in Cornwall made while they were engaged in sexual intercourse. No less revealing of past life are coprolites, fossilized feces that can betray the diets of extinct species. More sublime, though rare, are the insects preserved in amber, a fossilized pine resin found most often along the shores of the Baltic Sea. And whole bodies of mammoths, with dried blood still in the veins, have been found under the ice of Siberia and Alaska.

But the most common forms of preservation have been by carbonization and petrification. Oil and coal are known as fossil fuels because that is what they are, the residue of wood and other vegetable matter transformed through carbonization, which is a process of incomplete decay in the absence of air but the presence of extreme pressures. Of most interest to paleontologists, though, are the more identifiable fossils produced through petrification.

So much depends on chance and circumstance in preservation after death, as in life and death itself. Only exceedingly few plants and animals pass from life to such a timeless state by petrification, and this is just as well in view of the world's finite carrying capacity. The weight of all organisms that have lived on earth in the last half-billion years, it is estimated, would equal the total mass of the earth. However, almost all organic material disappears after death; it is, in today's ecological idiom, biodegradable. The flesh is consumed by scavengers, from microbes to vultures. The bones crumble, dust to dust. Nothing recognizable remains. As Loren Eiseley has written: "Nature has no interest in the preservation of the dead; her purpose is to start their elements upon the eternal road to life once more."

An organism's chances of becoming a fossil are greater, though still not good, if it has a solid and resistant skeleton or a mineralized shell. The "fossilization potential" of soft-bodied creatures like worms is quite low, though exquisite imprints of ancient jellyfish are occasionally found. The circumstance of a quick and thorough burial further enhances an organism's chances of petrification. Burial protects the organism from oxygen and oxygen-breathing agents of decay. This allows time for mineralization to take place. Water containing dissolved minerals soaks into the pores of bone or shell, slowly destroying much of the original material and replacing it molecule by molecule with the minerals. The result is a stony fossil, a petrified replica of the original form that contains little or none of the original organic material. The most favorable conditions for such fossilization exist in the sediments of the sea, bogs, swamps, and small, stagnant bodies of water. Animals that die on dry land are less likely to get the burial suitable for fossilization, a fact that tends to skew the fossil record.

Scientists, consequently, will never know how many dinosaur species lived in the shadow of Mantell's *Iguanodon* or Buckland's *Megalosaurus* and became extinct without leaving fossils to memorialize their existence. Every age leaves an incomplete fossil record. Of the 3 million species of living things in the world today, only a small fraction stands much chance of leaving identifiable fossils. The largest order of animals on earth embraces the 300,000 beetle species, a fact that led the geneticist J. B. S. Haldane, when asked what traits of the Creator were evidenced by life on earth, to remark: "He must have had an inordinate fondness for beetles." But few if any of the beetles will survive as fossils. Most of the other species today are plants, also poor fossil candidates. There are 8,600 birds and 4,000 mammals, whose prospects are somewhat better. Still, only a few of these species—and most of them, a reading of nature's actuarial tables indicates, should be extinct 10 million years from now—will leave fossils to suggest what life was like back in the time when one particular species began to fathom the meaning and importance of fossils.

THIS UNDERSTANDING of fossils began, somewhat tentatively, with two scientists in the seventeenth century who published the first comprehensive analyses of the phenomenon. They were Robert Hooke and Niels Stensen, usually known by his latinized name Nicolaus Stenonis, or simply Steno. Their prescient observations won few adherents until much later, and William Smith probably knew little or nothing of their ideas.

Hooke, an English mathematician with wide intellectual interests in the time of Isaac Newton and Edmond Halley, offered proof that fossils were either the remains of organisms turned to stone or the impressions left by them. His reasoning took him beyond conventional wisdom. Since so many fossils had marine origins, he said, they indicated that the surface of the earth had undergone a marked transformation since the Creation, sea giving way to land, land to sea, and so on—as Cuvier, with more evidence, would later establish. As for the significance of fossils, Hooke wrote:

> I do humbly conceive (tho' some possibly may think there is too much notice taken of such a trivial thing as a rotten shell, yet) that men do generally too much slight and pass over without regard these records of antiquity which Nature have left as monuments and hieroglyphick characters of preceding transactions in the like duration or transactions of the body of the Earth, which are infinitely more evident and certain tokens than anything of antiquity that can be fetched out of coins or medals, or any other way yet known, since the best of those ways may be counterfeited or made by art and design. . . . [Fossil shells] are not to be counterfeited by all the craft in the world, nor can they be doubted to be, what they appear, by any one that will impartially examine the true appearances of them: And tho' it must be granted that it is very difficult to read them, and to raise a chronology out of them, and to state the intervalls of the times, wherein such or such catastrophes and mutations have happened; yet 'tis not impossible. . . .

Modern geologists might describe the importance of fossils differently, but not any better. These "monuments and hieroglyphick characters of preceding transactions," if deciphered, could lead to the discovery of earth's chronology. Hooke was circling the insight that Smith homed in on. Hooke's reference to coins and medals, of course, betrays his belief that the fossils would correspond to the period of human life.

Steno was a Danish physician who, while serving a Florentine duke, took time to investigate the marine fossils of Tuscany. He recognized their internal structure from his knowledge of anatomy, and demonstrated that they could only be the relics of living creatures. But being a man of his time—he would eventually convert to Catholicism and become a bishop—Steno did not allow himself to imagine that the fossils were any older than Noah's Flood. Nor could he believe the elephant bones, then being discovered, to be prehistoric. They were, he declared, the remains of the African elephants brought into Italy by Hannibal.

Steno, nonetheless, cast a more perceptive eye on the layered conformation of the land than anyone else in the seventeenth century. He concluded that the strata of the earth had been laid down in the form of watery sediments that then hardened into rock, and that in any normal sequence the upper strata were younger than the lower strata. This principle of superposition is now an axiom of stratigraphy. It was the principle Cuvier applied when he recognized the fact of species extinctions back through time and postulated that it was the consequence of a series of widespread catastrophes.

As Hooke had glimpsed the significance of fossils for telling geologic time, though falling short of Smith's more precise observations, Steno recognized that the strata of the earth's crust also contained a chronological record of major events in the earth's past, each stratum being like a chapter in earth history. They approached the discovery of earth's unsuspected age, but did not go far enough.

There the matter stood for several generations until William Smith. German geologists, applying Steno's principle of superposition, had established with greater certainty the fact that different layers of rock represent discrete episodes of geologic time—the first principle of stratigraphy. Other scientists had identified and classified many fossils and reached a consensus that they indeed were remains of past life. But no one quite realized the revealing relationship between strata and fossils, not until Smith put the two together and showed how to read geologic time.

OVER THE NEXT few decades, as the sequence of crustal layers and fossils became more familiar, scientists devised the geologic time-scale in use today. This became the standard calendar of geochronology. The calendar's "seasons," "months," and "weeks" entered the language of geology and paleontology to express the great divisions of time as they are measured in the rocks.

The seasons are the eras: Precambrian, Paleozoic, Mesozoic, and Cenozoic. The divisions, except for Precambrian, were proposed in the 1840s by John Phillips, a nephew and apprentice of William Smith. They reflect clear transitions, punctuated by mass extinctions, from one system of predominant life to another—the primitive life of the Paleozoic, the large reptiles of the Mesozoic, and the mammals of the Cenozoic. Earlier, in the Precambrian, which embraces time from the formation of the earth to the appearance of abundant multicellular life, the strata bear few fossils.

The months of geologic time are the divisions known as periods. They are, in chronological order, the Cambrian, Ordovician, Silurian, Devonian, Carboniferous, and Permian, all divisions of the Paleozoic era; in the United States, the Carboniferous formations are classified instead as the Mississippian and Pennsylvanian periods. The periods mostly bear names from the areas where their strata were first studied in detail. The Ordovician and Silurian periods, for example, carry names of ancient Welsh tribes; Cambrian is derived from the Roman name for Wales; Permian is from the province of Perm in Russia; Devonian, from Devonshire. The Carboniferous is descriptive, meaning "coal-bearing."

For dinosaur hunters the three most important months, or periods, are those of the Mesozoic: Triassic, Jurassic, and Cretaceous. They took their names from strata in southern Germany with distinctively tripartite rock structure, from the Jura Mountains, and from the Latin word meaning "chalk," after the chalk beds in the strata near Paris where the period was categorized. Nearly everywhere else that geologists encounter Cretaceous layers, with the notable exception of the Dover White Cliffs, they consist of sandstone and shale and would probably escape recognition if it were not for Smith's index fossils.

The Cenozoic is divided into two major periods: Tertiary and Quaternary. But with the abundance of fossil discoveries, these two periods came to be subdivided into epochs known as the Paleocene, Eocene, Oligocene, Miocene, Pliocene, Pleistocene (the time of the most recent ice age), and Holocene, which includes the last 10,000 years to the present.

STANDARD CHRONO-STRATIGRAPHICAL SUCCESSION

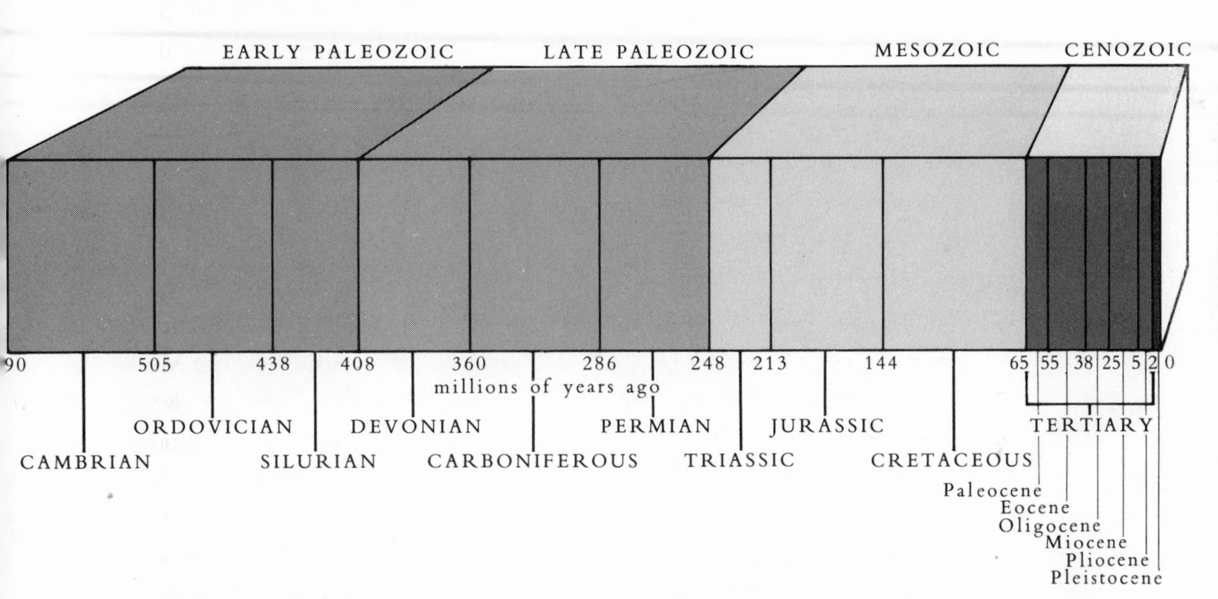

This was a calendar without dates, however. Since geologists could not assign absolute ages to the strata, paleontologists who made the major dinosaur discoveries in the nineteenth century and well into the twentieth knew only that these creatures lived in one or another of the Mesozoic periods. They could tell, for example, that the small coelurosaurs came from rocks indicating that they lived in the Triassic. They could likewise assign allosaurs and brontosaurs and stegosaurs to the Jurassic. Iguanodonts and tyrannosaurs were definitely creatures of the Cretaceous. Paleontologists thus knew where various dinosaurs fit in the progression of time, but they were at a loss to fix the absolute ages of these periods of dinosaur predominance. It was as if a historian, knowing only relative ages, could do no more than place the discovery of America in some dateless period between the Crusades and the Industrial Revolution.

Scientists who sought to calculate the earth's absolute age came up with many different answers, none of them satisfying. William Thomson, the famous Lord Kelvin, based his calculations on assumptions of how long it had taken the planet to cool down to its present crustal temperatures. But his answer, 20 to 40 million years, was disputed vigorously by geologists who needed more time than that to account for the progression of change recorded in the strata. Estimates based on the thickness of sediments ran to 100 million years. However, most geologists quite properly doubted that sedimentation rates had been uniform through time. Another estimate, derived from calculations of the amount of salt washed into the sea, yielded ages of 80 to 90 million years. These estimates were not even close, but no one could be sure of that until scientists happened on the fact that the rocks themselves contained atomic "clocks" that had been ticking away since their formation. In 1905, Bertram Boltwood, a Yale University chemist, noted a mother-daughter relationship between uranium and lead. Atoms of the same element with differing atomic weights, owing to variations in the number of neutrons, are called isotopes. Radioactive decay is a spontaneous process in which an isotope of an element (the parent) loses particles from its nucleus to form an isotope of a new element (the daughter). Some isotopes that decay slowly are used as atomic clocks. The radioactive breakdown of uranium, which was a newly discovered phenomenon, produces lead. The amount of lead mixed in with uranium would provide a measure of the time that had elapsed since the mineral had been formed. Samples of rock from older formations, as determined by fossil dating, were found to contain a lower proportion of uranium to lead than those from the younger formations. Formations of the same fossil age had the same uranium-lead ratio. Other atomic clocks useful to geology today rely on the parent-daughter ratios of isotopes of thorium and lead, rubidium and strontium, and potassium and argon.

When Ernest Rutherford, a New Zealand–born physicist, then calculated the rate of change from uranium to lead, scientists proceeded to make their first attempts to obtain radiometric ages of rock and of the earth itself. Boltwood's ages ranged up to 2 billion years.

Further refinements in the method, along with more sophisticated analytical instruments, produced progressively greater age estimates for the earth. A geology book published shortly after World War II would have reported an age of 3 billion years. A text of the 1950s would have said 4.5 billion. Now, with a certainty never before possible, the age is fixed at 4.6 billion years, a time-scale much closer to Hutton's than to Ussher's. The "atomic clocks" in the rocks, moreover, enabled scientists to assign absolute dates to the calendar of geologic time: 590 million years ago for the beginning of the Paleozoic; 248 million years for the beginning of the Mesozoic; and 65 million for the end of the Cretaceous and of the dinosaurs.

Such a stretch of time has little meaning to creatures whose lives span some three score and ten years, our own very real time barrier. One way of approaching comprehension, though, is to compress the entire 4.6 billion years into a single year, as Don L. Eicher does in his book *Geologic Time.*

On that scale, Eicher writes, the oldest known rocks date from about mid-March. Living things first appeared in the sea in May—or, according to new discoveries, a little earlier. Land plants and animals emerged in late November. Dinosaurs became dominant in mid-December, then disappeared on the 25th. Humanlike creatures appeared sometime during the evening of December 31st. Rome ruled the Western world for five seconds from 11:59:45 to 11:59:50. Columbus discovered America three seconds before midnight. James Hutton discovered the magnitude of geologic time and William Smith learned to read strata and fossils slightly more than one second before the end of the year, which was also the time when a few scientists were just beginning to suspect that not all the species that ever existed managed to survive to modern times and when the bones of the most spectacular of these extinct species were coming to light.

4

A Name for a Phenomenon

ONLY THOSE with nimble tongues could pronounce their way through the discoveries that followed Buckland's *Megalosaurus* and Mantell's *Iguanodon* and *Hylaeosaurus.* Joining the ranks of archaic reptiles by 1841 were *Macrodontophion, Thecodontosaurus, Palaeosaurus, Plateosaurus, Cladeidon,* and *Cetiosaurus,* and their fossil remains were trying to tell scientists something about Mesozoic life. These newly discovered creatures seemed to have been sufficiently different from modern reptiles or from the marine giants like Cuvier's *Mosasaurus* and Mary Anning's *Ichthyosaurus* to warrant a family name all their own. They thus became known collectively by the more pronounceable name of Dinosauria—dinosaurs.

This name was the inspiration of Richard Owen, a brilliant anatomist and paleontologist who was hailed in his day as the English Cuvier. His ascent to such exalted professional heights had been swift. Born at Lancaster in 1804, he became a surgeon's apprentice and, while still a teenager, learned anatomy by performing countless autopsies on prisoners. The experience set the course of his career. Soon, as the Hunterian Professor at the Royal College of Surgeons, his renown was such that his opinions were sought on all matters of comparative anatomy and fossil reptiles. He gave names to the two newest fossil discoveries: *Cladeidon,* from the Triassic, and *Cetiosaurus,* from the Jurassic.

Owen commanded respect but hardly affection. He was pompous. He disliked being called the English Cuvier because he believed himself superior to the Frenchman. He held himself to be infallible, and delivered opinions accordingly, as pronouncements freighted with obscure polysyllables. Over the years, colleagues had reason to distrust him because, they said, he would not hesitate to take credit for someone else's achievement. "It is deeply to be deplored," wrote Mantell, "that this highly eminent and gifted man can never act with candour and liberality." Owen's appearance reenforced his reputation as a cold, remote man. He was tall and ungainly, with a massive head and lofty forehead. He had a large, tight mouth and a projecting chin. His bulging fish eyes could be terrifying.

Richard Owen

This was the forbidding figure that stood before the annual meeting of the British Association for the Advancement of Science, convened at Plymouth on August 2, 1841. Owen had given much thought to fossil reptiles, particularly *Iguanodon, Megalosaurus,* and *Hylaeosaurus.* These were undoubtedly gigantic creatures, he knew, but were they gigantic lizards? Although Mantell had surmised that they were somehow different from all other archaic reptiles, most scientists thought of them as no more than overgrown lizards, having been misled, Owen suspected, by Cuvier's correct identification of the mosasaur as an extinct type of lizard. In his scrutiny of the fossils, Owen observed many characteristics that, as he told the audience at Plymouth, he "deemed sufficient grounds for establishing a distinct tribe or sub-order of Saurian Reptiles, for which I propose the name Dinosauria."

Owen coined the name from the Greek *deinos,* meaning "terrible" or "fearfully great," and *sauros,* meaning "lizard"—Dinosauria, terrible lizard. It is odd that he chose a word meaning lizard when he had in mind setting these creatures apart from lizards, but then he probably thought of *sauros* in the more general sense of "reptile."

For two and a half hours Owen droned on, elaborating on his reasons for the new classification of extinct animal life. The most obvious reason was that, unlike the other giant saurians, these were terrestrial rather than marine creatures. Another difference was that, in contrast to other reptiles, they shared the characteristic of having five vertebrae fused to the pelvic girdle. Their huge skeletons—small dinosaurs had not yet been discovered—also suggested that they had more massive bodies than the streamlined lizards and mosasaurs. They reminded Owen of pachydermal mammals. "From the size and form of the ribs," he said, "it is evident that the trunk was broader and deeper in proportion than in modern Saurians, and it was doubtless raised from the ground upon extremities proportionally larger and especially longer, so that the general aspect of the living Megalosaur must have proportionally resembled that of the large terrestrial quadrupeds of the Mammalian class which now tread the earth, and the place of which seems to have been supplied in the oolitic ages [the ancient time when certain rocks, like limestone, were laid down] by the great reptiles of the extinct Dinosauria order."

In this description Owen was, in effect, drafting the first sketch for the murals and dioramas of Mesozoic life that would come to enchant mankind. He had no doubt that these had been imposing creatures, terrible lizards of elephantine stature. But Owen felt that some of their size estimates, which were extrapolations based on lizards as a standard, were ridiculous. By a comparison of the teeth and clavicle of *Iguanodon* with those of the iguana, for example, paleontologists had arrived at dimensions of thirty-five meters in length for the extinct reptile. Owen proposed instead that the calculations be based on the size and number of the vertebrae, a method still employed today. This produced a more reasonable length for *Iguanodon* of eight meters and for *Megalosaurus* of nine.

Owen's interest in dinosaurs went beyond their size and shape. As he continued his "Report on British Fossil Reptiles," he revealed his true colors. He was essentially an antievolutionist, at least an anti-Lamarckian. Though he believed that species had changed over time, Owen was convinced that all the animals within each major group were variations on a single theme, the "ideal archetype," and that the "Divine mind which planned the Archetype also foreknew all its modifications." His preplanned evolution was antithetical to the heretical ideas of Jean Baptiste Lamarck, a contemporary of Cuvier. Cuvier had believed in the extinction of the species, but not in evolution. Lamarck believed in evolution, but not in extinction; species did not so much disappear as gradually change into something different and, in his mind, better.

Although Darwin had yet to publish his theory, evolution was already a divisive issue in science. Those who continued to believe that God had created the species in their present, unchanging forms—or, as Owen believed, "foreknew" all the modifications—led the attack on Lamarck's scheme of things. In 1809, Lamarck had postulated that there was an intrinsic tendency of organisms to strive toward perfection; they evolved progressively from simpler to more complex forms. This was, he said, the "observed" trend in nature. But this was not the way the trend looked to Owen as he contemplated the fossils of what he called dinosaurs.

If there was some kind of Lamarckian ascent from simplicity to complexity, Owen argued, the principal reptiles populating the world today would not be such comparatively lowly creatures. Dinosaurs, not lizards and crocodiles, stood at the apex of reptilian development. *Iguanodon* and *Megalosaurus* fossils, he asserted, revealed dinosaurs to be "the crowns of reptilian creation" and "the nearest approach to mammals." And yet where were the dinosaurs? Long dead, and every one of their reptilian replacements was a simpler creature by far. If this was evolution, it was retrograde evolution. Owen had, indeed, exposed a weakness in Lamarck's concept of evolution. With relish, for he knew it bolstered his argument, Owen emphasized the superiority of dinosaurs over other reptiles. Adrian J. Desmond, in *The Hot-Blooded Dinosaurs,* writes: "Owen literally populated his Mesozoic earth with dinosaurs as a ploy against the evolutionists."

Owen went on, in his authoritative manner, to declare that dinosaurs had not evolved from some lower reptilian stock but had been created by God. Moreover, God had placed them on earth at the particular time of the Mesozoic because they were peculiarly suited to conditions then. From the abundance of large reptiles then and the absence of any significant mammals Owen inferred that the Mesozoic atmosphere had been deficient in oxygen. Reptiles, being cold-blooded and less energetic, required less oxygen than warm-blooded mammals, according to his reasoning. Eventually, an "invigoration" of the atmosphere with more oxygen made the world unhabitable for the dinosaurs. This seems to have been the first theory advanced to account for dinosaurian extinction, though most certainly it would not be the last.

Toward the end of his report, Owen also introduced some provocative ideas about dinosaurian metabolism. "A more cautious observer would, perhaps, have shrunk from such speculations," Owen acknowledged, but speculate he did. Dinosaurs, he said, may have led more vigorous lives than that associated with reptiles. Their "thoracic structure" indicated that they could have had a four-chambered heart more like those of mammals and birds, instead of the three-chambered reptilian heart. "Their superior adaptations to terrestrial life," Owen said, were further evidence that they must have "enjoyed the function of such a highly-organized centre of circulation in a degree more nearly approaching that which now characterises the warm-blooded Vertebrata." This was the first inference that dinosaurs may have risen above typical reptilian cold-bloodedness, though most certainly it would not be the last.

Richard Owen had presented the first comprehensive report on dinosaurs. Perhaps only a man of his arrogance would have dared make so much out of so few bones representing the partial remains of no more than nine genera of archaic reptiles. Yet, whatever his motives, however flimsy some of his evidence, Owen "created" dinosaurs that day in 1841.

Owen properly isolated dinosaurs from the usual run of reptiles, modern and archaic. He gave them a name, though Dinosauria is not, strictly speaking, a recognized scientific grouping of animals. Almost nothing learned about them suggests that they form a single natural group. Indeed, since the late nineteenth century, most scientists have come to believe that the so-called dinosaurs consisted of two separate groups that were rather distantly related. These are Saurischia, or "lizard hips," and Ornithischia, "bird hips." As the names suggest, saurischians and ornithischians have quite different anatomies that mark them as being perhaps no more related to each other than they are to other members of the reptilian family tree, such as crocodiles and pterosaurs.

Together, the saurischians and ornithischians, the crocodilians and pterosaurians, are members of that larger assemblage known as archosaurs, or "ruling reptiles." These four orders evolved from the most primitive archosaurs, the thecodonts. (Of the archosaurs, only some crocodilians—alligators and gavials as well as true crocodiles—survive to this day.) Archosauria is variously described as a superorder or subclass of the class Reptilia. Thus, the place in nature of one of the most familiar dinosaurs is as follows:

Class Reptilia
- Subclass Archosauria
  - Order Saurischia
    - Suborder Theropoda
      - Infraorder Carnosauria
        - Family Tyrannosauridae
          - Genus Tyrannosaurus
            - Species rex

Tyrannosaurus rex was a lizard-hipped (Saurischia) biped (Theropoda) that was a heavily built meat-eater (Carnosauria). There is no official reference to it as being a dinosaur. Those who found and named *Tyrannosaurus rex* in Montana in the early 1900s are classified as follows:

Class Mammalia
Subclass Eutheria
Order Primates
Suborder Anthropoidea
Superfamily Hominoidea
Family Hominidae
Genus Homo
Species sapiens

Homo sapiens, the self-styled "wise humans," are vertebrates that feed their young with milk from mammary glands (Mammalia), nourish their young *in utero* (Eutheria), have five-digit hands and feet usually equipped with nails instead of claws (Primates), have forward-directed vision and large brains (Anthropoidea), have forelimbs specialized for manipulation (Hominoidea), and are bipedal so that they can hunt with weapons held in their forelimbs.

But only the purists among *Homo sapiens* insist on expunging Owen's dinosaurs from the scientific language, and there are few such purists. Besides, dinosaurs, both saurischians and ornithischians, did share one feature that is lacking in every other reptile. All stood in a "fully erect" position with their limbs supporting the body from beneath. In this they were more like mammals than reptiles. Most other reptiles are sprawlers, with their limbs projecting sideways from the body. Modern crocodiles pull themselves up into a semi-erect posture only when they want to move off at a trot, which is not often. The limb structure supporting the dinosaurs in their erect posture also enabled many of them to evolve true bipedality—to stand on their hind legs. In this, too, they were unlike other reptiles. Alan Charig, the British paleontologist, finds this "some justification" for the use of the popular term "dinosaur" to cover both the saurischians and the ornithischians.

With or without justification, Owen's dinosaurs survive as an ineradicable part of the language. Nearly all scientists, even in their most august gatherings, refer without apology to their fascinating subjects as dinosaurs. As the Supreme Court is alleged to do, the scientists read the election returns and realize that their arcane nomenclature keeps losing to the ever-popular dinosaurs, by acclamation.

THE POPULAR APPEAL of dinosaurs, by whatever name, became evident when they had a debut of sorts at the Crystal Palace in London in 1854. Owen had a hand in this, too, but mostly it was the work of an artist whose imagination compensated for the scarcity of knowledge about the creatures.

After the first world's fair, the Great Exhibition of the Works of Industry of All Nations in 1851, closed at Hyde Park, the central building, an enormous iron-framed glass structure known as the Crystal Palace, was dismantled and reerected on the outskirts of London, in a park at Sydenham. It was decided that the grounds should be decorated with replicas of the recently discovered prehistoric beasts. A sculptor, Benjamin Waterhouse Hawkins, was given the task, as he said, of "revivifying the ancient world." Working closely with Owen, Hawkins shaped out of cement, stone, bricks, and iron life-size restorations of extinct amphibians, crocodiles, and plesiosaurs, as well as the three dinosaurs that had received the most attention—*Iguanodon, Megalosaurus,* and *Hylaeosaurus.* Hawkins created the illusion that modern man knew more about these creatures than in fact he did. Some of the replicas looked suspiciously

Waterhouse Hawkins's model of Iguanodon

like overgrown frogs and turtles. The *Iguanodon* resembled a reptilian rhinoceros, for Hawkins perpetuated Mantell's mistake by fashioning a horn for the creature's nose. The *Iguanodon* and *Megalosaurus* were also made to stand on four legs, for scientists had not yet divined their bipedality.

Nonetheless, it was with great pride that Hawkins celebrated his restorations by holding one of the most incredible dinner parties in the history of science. Invitations were inscribed on simulated wing bones of a *Pterodactyl.* Twenty-one guests, all prominent scientists, arrived at the park on the eve of the new year, December 31, 1853, and were seated at a festive table laid out in the interior of the partially completed *Iguanodon.* Owen sat at the head of the table, which was in the head—where else?—of the animal. The revelers saw in the new year of 1854, drinking toasts and hailing Hawkins as the modern Pygmalion, and the *Quarterly Review* reported the occasion in effusive style: "Saurians and Pterodactyles all! dream ye ever, in your ancient festivities, of a race to come, dwelling above your tombs . . . dining on your ghosts, called from the deep by their sorcerers?" *Punch,* in an article entitled "Fun in a Fossil," ignored the iguanodont's herbivorous nature in declaring: "We congratulate the company on the era in which they live, for if it had been an early geological period they might perhaps have occupied the Iguanodon's inside without having any dinner there."

The exhibit was opened to the public later that year, and the Victorians came in droves, according to one account, "to witness the monsters that inhabited the earth before Noah." People have stood in wonder before restorations of dinosaurs ever since. Their fascination, as Hawkins remarked, is "almost romantic in its influence upon the imagination."

In 1868, Hawkins accepted an invitation from New York City to build a similar set of models for its new Central Park. Noting the "almost romantic interest" in extinct creatures, the park commissioners outlined a plan to celebrate the "Huge fishes, enormous birds, monstrous reptiles, and ponderous uncouth mammals" that inhabited the world before man established "a record of his pre-eminence." The prehistoric creatures were to occupy an island in the center of the Paleozoic Museum, which was to be erected on the west side of the park opposite Sixty-third Street. Hawkins set up a workshop in the park and was busy making the molds and casts for the restorations when the whole project ran afoul of some unsavory city politics. The Tammany Hall machine of William Marcy ("Boss") Tweed had nothing but contempt for the project. Who did this Englishman Hawkins think he was, wanting to fill

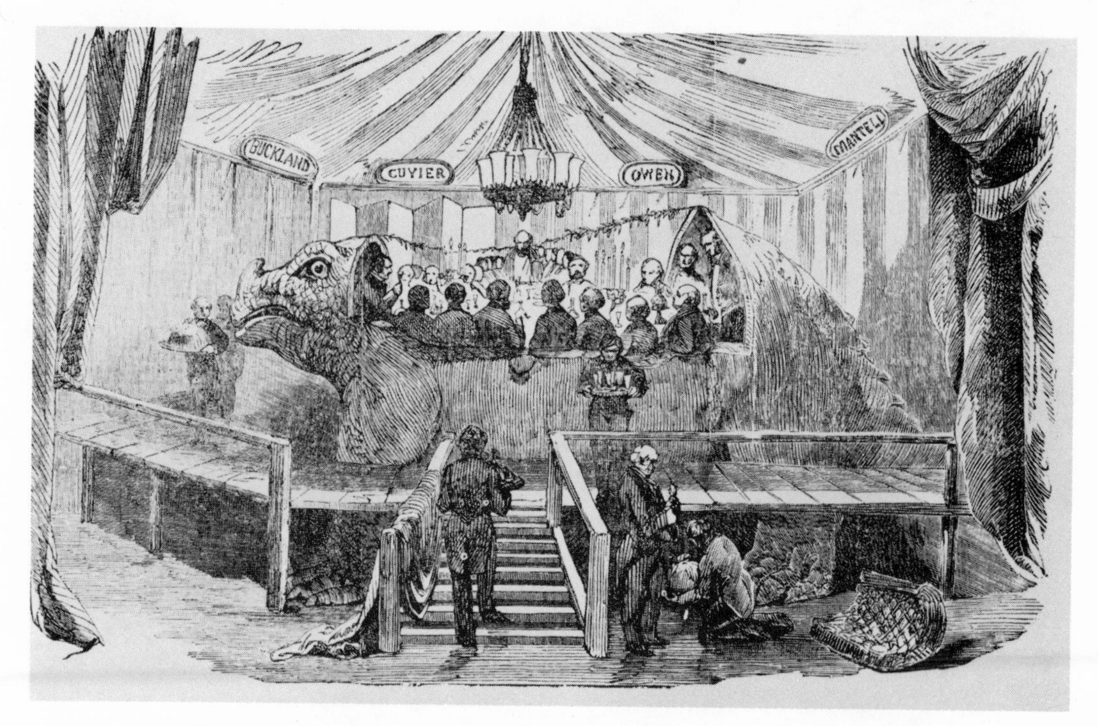

Illustration of dinner held in Waterhouse Hawkins's restoration of Iguanodon

a museum with dinosaurs and such? Tweed replaced the park commisssioners with his own men, who were skeptical of the antiquity of dinosaurs, referring to them sarcastically as "specimens of animals alleged to be of the pre-Adamite period." Moreover, it was foolish, the Tweed commissioners said, to build a museum "devoted wholly to paleontology—a science which, however interesting, is yet so imperfectly known as not to justify so great a public expense for illustrating it." The museum was expected to cost $300,000; in eighteen months, the Tweed machine had spent $8 million of public money on patronage jobs for 4,000 park workers, which Tweed presumably thought was a fair price for their votes. Seeing no profit in the museum, Tweed had the foundations demolished in 1870. Hawkins continued work on the models, hoping that some other museum would buy them. But in the spring of 1871, on orders from Tweed functionaries, park laborers broke into Hawkins's workshop, smashed the dinosaurs with sledgehammers, and hauled away and buried the pieces in the park. Only a few weeks after this act of vandalism, Tweed himself was broken. He was convicted of fraud and sentenced to prison. Most of the fragments of dinosaurs and other prehistoric creatures were dug up four years later and found to be utterly worthless. But a few "dinosaur bones" may still lie buried in Central Park, artifacts of an extinct political machine.

Hawkins, heartbroken, abandoned prehistoric sculpture and spent most of his remaining years at Princeton painting murals of Mesozoic creatures. His London models, if not the ones intended for New York, still stand as relics of the earliest perceptions of those animals Owen christened dinosaurs.

WHY DO DINOSAURS so fascinate mankind? Why do dinosaurs, of all the extinct creatures, evoke such vivid images of past life? What their special quality is may be as impossible to identify as the source of dragon lore.

A staple of mythology is the hero, Beowulf, Siegfried, or St. George, battling the dragon. It is the struggle with mysterious forces. When the hero triumphs by slaying the dragon, fear is vanquished. Almost invariably this symbol of fear is large and basically reptilian. People who came upon giant bones, probably the remains of mammoths and mastodons, could be excused for believing that these must be evidence of those dragons of yore. By the nineteenth century, however, science had disabused most people of the reality of dragons. In their place, filling some psychoecological niche, as it were, appeared the dinosaurs.

Dinosaurs so resembled the mythical dragons that some scholars proposed that they had actually inspired the dragon legend. It was, they suspected, a case of "racial memory." Encounters between protohumans and dinosaurs in the remote past must have left indelible scars on the human psyche. But no one takes this seriously any more. Caveman movies and comic strips like "Alley Oop" and "B.C." notwithstanding, no dinosaurs shared the earth with any remote human ancestors. Moreover, as Daniel Cohen points out in *A Modern Look at Monsters,* the whole concept of "racial memory" is suspect because, though people hunted the mammoth and some elephantlike creatures in Europe 10,000 years ago, European folklore contains nothing about elephants or similar creatures; the discovery of living elephants in Africa and Asia came as a complete surprise to Europeans.

Some of the earliest depictions of the great reptiles fostered a belief in the similarities between dinosaurs and dragons. In 1840, a year before Owen's report, a British geologist named Thomas Hawkins published *The Book of Great Sea Dragons,* which was based loosely on the discoveries of Cuvier, Anning, Buckland, and Mantell. Illustrations in the book showed monstrous reptiles of land, sea, and air battling in gloomily gothic landscapes. They reminded one modern writer, L. Sprague de Camp, so much of medieval dragon lore that "one half-expects an armored knight to clatter into the scene on his destrier." The dragon book enjoyed wide popularity, and has not lacked for imitators.

Paleontologists, even behavioral scientists, seem to be at a loss to account for the hold dinosaurs have on the psyche. It must be elemental, for children are the ones most likely to become enamored of dinosaurs, and at an early age. Many children go through a dinosaur phase. Dinosaurs were big and scary, the stuff of fantasies; size and ferocity must be a factor in their popularity, because small dinosaurs are seldom mentioned by children. The larger something or someone is, the more impressive it is to a child's mind. And these creatures were real, which apparently makes them more awesome and exciting than the Creature from the Black Lagoon or Superman. "Superman is not real," one child said, putting down a friend's fascination with that figure, "but my Mom said that dinosaurs are." So dinosaurs were real, but safe. They are safe because they are completely gone; those who know nothing else about dinosaurs remember seeing them trudging across the barren landscape of Walt Disney's *Fantasia* and crashing down to die to Stravinsky's music. People seem to enjoy being scared a little, but at a safe distance.

John E. Schowalter, professor of pediatrics and psychiatry at the Yale University Child Study Center, was surprised a few years ago to find that little effort had been made to explain why children love and identify with dinosaurs. He conducted a poll of nursery-school teachers and collected observations from parents and his own psychotherapy practice. He found the fascination with dinosaurs not only common but generally healthy. Those children most interested tended to be the brighter, more imaginative ones.

The dinosaur, Schowalter concluded, assumes an important role in the fantasy play of growing up. The child learns in fantasy how to cope in a world of giants, grownups. To children, for example, the ferocious *Tyrannosaurus rex* frequently represents the father, while the large but docile *Brontosaurus* represents the mother. In one classroom mural, he noted, children drew a skirt on the *Brontosaurus.* It may even be a source of reassurance for children to know that the giant dinosaurs are now extinct; the old order changeth, Schowalter observed, and the future belongs to the smaller members of the rising generation.

Dinosaur fantasies also involve wish fulfillment. At times, Schowalter said, a child identifies with the most aggressive dinosaur and terrorizes the others.

Another theme is that in which the child saves the parent figures from hostile dinosaurs, thereby protecting and rising above them simultaneously. One child tried repeatedly to overthrow a ruling dinosaur, but always failed. According to Schowalter, only when he became more assertive in real life at home, and did not suffer retaliation, did he dare sometimes to vary the fantasy to end in his own favor.

Dinosaurs afford children an early opportunity to triumph over their peers and adults. Children learn to pronounce the difficult names of dinosaurs, a facility beyond many adults, and to recite all their vital statistics. So armed, they are eager to pounce on those with an inferior command of such knowledge. For this the child is often praised and taken seriously. This may be the first time the child experiences a sense of grownup intellectual accomplishment.

In childhood and beyond, dinosaurs inspire wonder, the wonder that stirs imagination. Arthur C. Clarke, the science-fiction writer, remembers as a boy riding with his father in a pony cart. "As he opened a pack of cigarettes, he handed me the card inside; it was one of a series illustrating prehistoric animals," Clarke writes. "From that moment, I became hooked on dinosaurs, collected all the cards on the subject I could and used them in class to illustrate little adventure stories I told the other children in the village school. These must have been my first ventures into fiction. . . . To this day I retain my fascination with dinosaurs and eagerly look forward to the time when the genetic engineers will recreate the tyrannosaur."

Dinosaurs evidently satisfy a human need for mystery and adventure. Their appeal may be as simple—or complex—as that. They lived in a time so long ago that it can be imagined only through some of the most remarkable adventures of the mind. They were mostly big and bizarre, nothing quite like anything before or since. And then they died off and were no more, their fate an enduring mystery. As science seeks so diligently to explain and quantify, it is heartening to have something left to the imagination.

But dinosaurs also entered the human consciousness at a propitious moment, when people were beginning to contemplate time and life on a scale far exceeding traditional belief. Dinosaurs not only lent spectacular substance to scientific theory but, more than trilobites, ammonites, and giant sloths, made mental travel back into remote time exciting and popular. They came to epitomize prehuman life. And man, for all his day-to-day preoccupation, has as abiding a curiosity about the past as about his present surroundings on earth and beyond. He is forever seeking to know his place in nature and the cosmos, even at the risk of being humbled sometimes by what he learns.

In her 1969 book *Hunting for Dinosaurs,* Zofia Kielan-Jaworowska, an eminent Polish paleontologist, wrote:

> No scientist familiar with the intellectual adventure of studying animals from times long past will have any hesitation in affirming that to travel millions of years back into the past, which is what paleontological study amounts to, is much more fascinating than the most exotic geographical travel we are able to undertake today. The study of animals that lived on earth millions of years ago is not merely a study of their anatomy, but first and foremost a study of the course of evolution on earth and of the laws that govern it.
>
> All the philosophical systems ever developed by man are essentially anthropocentric, with the tragic consequences for humanity which we know from history and which we are experiencing today. Studying the evolution of animals that inhabited earth for millions of years and comparing this with the history of mankind—so short on the geological scale—puts man's position in the living world in its proper perspective and helps counteract anthropocentric ideas.

Of all the prehuman animals, the creatures Owen called dinosaurs and Hawkins revivified in stone became irresistible to the public and to an increasing number of scientists. They became the big game of fossil hunters in the last half of the nineteenth century and well into the twentieth, paleontology's own Mesozoic era—when giants roamed the world in search of bones and sometimes their territorial and intellectual clashes resounded through the land.

II

5 *Early Bird*

IN NOVEMBER 1859, twenty-three years after the return of the *Beagle,* Charles Darwin delivered himself of the theory that would immortalize him and revolutionize biology and all sciences related to biology, including paleontology. He did so reluctantly. He had become convinced as early as 1837 that the species were mutable, not fixed, and that changes occurred through a process of gradual transformations in organisms that led in time to distinctive new organisms. New forms of life descended from older forms, some reptiles becoming feathered birds and some apes evolving to humans. But foreseeing the controversy his ideas were sure to provoke, and eschewing intellectual combat, Darwin put off publication of his theory of evolution through assorted procrastinations in geology and a definitive study of barnacles. He would have held back even longer if he had not learned in 1858 that another English naturalist, Alfred Russel Wallace, had independently reached much the same conclusions and was prepared to publicize them. No scientist, not even the retiring Darwin, could sit back and let another get full credit for an idea for which he could claim priority. And so Darwin rushed to publish in late 1859 his book of books, *On the Origin of Species by Means of Natural Selection, or the Preservation of Favored Races in the Struggle for Life.*

Although a few others had bucked tradition and dogma to make a case for evolution, no one before Darwin, and then Wallace, had conceived of a plausible explanation of how it came about. Not even Lamarck, the foremost evolutionist of the early nineteenth century. Lamarck's concept of spontaneous generation of simple forms, from which higher forms evolved progressively, left too much unexplained. His notion of a mechanism by which evolutionary change occurred—the inheritance of acquired characteristics—might be valid as an explanation for the passing on of cultural and behavioral traits, but not organic features. That is, a giraffe did not stretch its neck to reach the leaves high in a tree and then pass on to succeeding generations a longer neck. The mechanism by which evolution worked, as Darwin came to believe, was something else. It was natural selection, which was Darwin's most profound and original insight.

Natural selection, as opposed to the artificial selection already widely practiced by animal and plant breeders, was a matter of the "survival of the fittest," a phrase Darwin did not use in the book's first edition but which would come to characterize his theory and be perverted in political usage. From his experience as the naturalist on the *Beagle* and from his reading of Thomas Malthus's views of population, Darwin made two simple but significant observations: that individual organisms within the same species have varying characteristics, and that most organisms produce far more offspring than will actually survive. Those organisms that vary in ways most suitable to their environment will survive and reproduce, Darwin concluded, and those that do not will die. Those individuals with attributes giving them a competitive edge over others—a stronger wing, perhaps, or a sharper tooth—should live longer and produce more offspring, which will tend to inherit those advantageous attributes. Whereas Lamarck believed that environment-induced changes in plants and animals would be inherited by the next generation, Darwin held that in any given population random variants are present and the environment "selects" which of the variants will be hereditarily favored. Among the giraffes with longer and shorter necks, natural selection "picked" the ones with long necks because they were the ones capable of reaching more food and surviving, and so all giraffes today have long necks. Darwin's random variants, such as an individual giraffe's longer neck, were already coded in the organism's genes, and only changes in genetic makeup can be inherited. Through time and cumulative inheritances a species is thus modified to a point where it becomes something else, another distinct species. In Darwin's botanical metaphor, the tree of life grows and changes with the appearances of "fresh buds and these, if vigorous, branch out and overtop on all sides many a feeble branch." This is the evolution of species by natural selection, according to Darwin.

Life is infinitely creative, in this view, but where among the fossils were the transitional forms between ancestral and descendant groups of organisms? Darwin, in *Origin of Species,* recognized this weakness in his case for natural selection, calling the absence of fossil intermediate forms "probably the gravest and most obvious of the many objections which may be urged against my views." He devoted an entire chapter, "On the Imperfections of the Geological

Record," to attempting to explain this absence. Much of the evidence, he conceded, was irretrievably lost. Gaps in the fossil record were inevitable because fossils were formed only in exceptional circumstances. Many organisms undoubtedly came and went without leaving a fossil trace, and the traces of others might have long since been obliterated by geological upheavals. But Darwin felt sure, or wanted to believe, that some of the crucial transitional forms were buried in the ground and, with time and greater effort, should be uncovered. Paleontology, after all, was a young science.

Critics, like wolves sensing the weakest member in a herd of caribou, pounced on this admitted vulnerability and sought to devour the entire theory. *Family Herald,* an anti-Darwinian publication in England, attacked with ridicule: "We defy any one, from Mr. Darwin downwards, to show us the link between the fish and the man. Let them catch a mermaid, and they will find the missing link."

"Missing link" was another phrase, like survival of the fittest, that caught the public fancy. The link had to be found, or else the theory might never gain acceptance among many scientists as well as the public. Bones of the Neanderthal man, the first extinct form of man ever studied, had been found near Düsseldorf in 1856, but scholars were not yet sure what to make of them. Some scientists suspected that they were the remains of a diseased idiot or perhaps a Cossack from the Napoleonic wars. Even Darwin's supporters felt that the Neanderthal man, though prehistoric, was too humanlike to establish a link to the apes.

One missing link would not be missing much longer. Less than two years after Darwin's publication, stonecutters in Bavaria made one of the most fascinating and famous paleontological discoveries of all time. They found the fossil remains of what looked like a reptile, possibly a small dinosaur, that in some respects bore a resemblance to a bird, for it had feathers. Darwin had hypothesized that birds must have developed from reptiles, and there was the evidence, so it seemed, in the reptile-bird known as *Archaeopteryx.* Evolutionists could scarcely believe their good fortune.

The discovery was made in the pastoral Altmühl Valley near the town of Solnhofen, which is northwest of Munich and south of Nürnberg. Since the time of the Roman Empire, the valley had been known for its yellow-gray limestone of marblelike beauty and durability. Solnhofen slabs were used in paving roads and for decorating Roman baths in Bavaria. Today, most of the older buildings in towns along the Altmühl River are roofed and floored with

Solnhofen limestone. Renewed demand for the stone came after 1793, when Aloys Senefelder found it to be the perfect material for lithography, the new process he was developing for printing from stone plates.

With the growing popularity of lithography in mass printing, the Altmühl stonecutters redoubled their efforts and, in so doing, began turning up strange fossils. The pterodactyl Cuvier described came from one of these quarries. Other flying saurians were preserved in stone, as well as exquisite specimens of insects, shrimp, crabs, fish, crocodiles, and marine tortoises. The quarries were a veritable mine of fossils, a paleontologist's Comstock or Kimberley.

The Solnhofen limestone had formed out of sediments that accumulated 150 to 160 million years ago along the northern shore of a Jurassic sea. The uplifting and consolidation of Europe as a continent lay millions of years in the future. Overhead in this place and time in the Jurassic glided pterosaurs, which somewhat resembled brown pelicans in appearance and perhaps also in the way they plunged into the water to catch fish. Giant dragonflies swarmed over the marshes. Along the shores of fern, cycad, gingko, and yew shrub, dinosaurs no bigger than chickens, *Compsognathus,* ran about chasing after tiny mammals and reptiles. And there were these birdlike creatures, *Archaeopteryx,* which were no bigger than crows.

This scene has been reconstructed from the fossilized bones that were buried in lime mud. F. Werner Barthel, a modern geologist who grew up in the Solnhofen region, believes that the mud was washed by storms into shallow bays and lagoons and settled there behind barrier reefs. The same storms would have blown many flying creatures into the lagoons, where they would have been trapped in the mire that in time would become the thick beds of uniformly fine-grained limestone.

In quarrying these limestone beds, workers handled each slab as if it were precious stone and so enhanced their chances of finding rare fossils. The stone, if it is thoroughly weathered, splits along the planes of sedimentation so that a block can be opened into thin segments like leaves in a book. Each slab was scrutinized by as many as a dozen workers, checking for soundness, looking for flaws, hand cutting it to desired dimensions, hand carrying it to sheds, and ever looking for fossils. John Ostrom, the Yale paleontologist who has visited nearly all of these quarries, said that these unusual handling methods are still practiced; most quarries elsewhere are now highly mechanized, but not those around Solnhofen. "Every quarry worker has eyes peeled for a fossil trophy which he can perhaps hide from the quarry owner and sell to a collector, thereby supplementing his meager paycheck," Ostrom said. "This is why we now have these fascinating and incredible specimens of *Archaeopteryx.*"

It was in this way that workers in late 1860 or early 1861 saw the faint impression of a feather in one of the Solnhofen slabs. The discovery was surprising in two respects. It is rare that soft tissues, such as feathers, are preserved. And no one had at that time ever found any trace of birds having lived as early as the Mesozoic; the air then belonged to the pterosaurs and not until their demise, it was assumed, did birds come into their own. But there in the Solnhofen limestone of the Jurassic time was the imprint of a solitary feather about sixty millimeters long. Only birds, no other creatures, were known to have feathers. This must have been the early bird.

The fossil feather was brought to the attention of Hermann von Meyer in Frankfurt. He was one of Germany's most industrious and respected paleontologists, despite the handicap of clubfeet that kept him out of the field and a preoccupation with politics that limited the time he spent on science. Von Meyer was the author of the five-volume *Fauna of the Ancient World,* which included his descriptions of many new genera and species of pterosaurs discovered in the Solnhofen quarries. He was also the author of a cautionary addendum to Cuvier's law of the correlation of parts. "I found," von Meyer wrote, "that in one or several parts a creature could have correspondences bordering on similarity with another creature, without being related to it." Ichthyosaurs, therefore, may resemble dolphins in some respects and pterosaurs may resemble birds or bats, but this is merely a convergence, not a real kinship. An awareness of the phenomenon of convergence has surely spared many a paleontologist much embarrassment. It was something to bear in mind when examining the fossil feather.

Von Meyer approached the object with some skepticism, but finally decided that it was not a hoax. In his report published in a German scientific journal in August 1861, he declared the feather to be genuine, very old, and perhaps avian. He cautioned that it "need not necessarily be derived from a bird" and could be a "feathered animal, differing essentially from our birds."

One month later, before the scientific world had time to react to the first report, von Meyer announced a more startling discovery. A headless skeleton had been found in the limestone, and with it also was the distinct impression of feathers. The fossil, indeed, looked like one of Darwin's missing links. Von Meyer gave it the taxonomically neutral name of *Archaeopteryx lithographica*—"ancient feather from the lithographic limestone."

THE FOSSIL'S VALUE was appraised at first not in scientific but in monetary terms. Its owner believed that museums would pay a substantial sum for what appeared to be the oldest bird in the world—*Urvögel,* "first bird," as the Germans came to call it. The owner held out for his price.

The skeleton was found in a quarry owned by a man named Ottmann. But somehow it came into the hands of Karl Häberlein, the district medical officer in the nearby village of Pappenheim. Perhaps it was turned over in payment for medical treatment. Häberlein realized that fossils from these quarries often aroused great scientific interest, and certainly this should be true for a fossil looking like a cross between a reptile and a bird. He let it be known that the fossil was available for a then forbidding price equivalent to £700. He wanted the money, it is said, to provide a dowry for his daughter.

Scientists and museum representatives paid calls on Häberlein and his bird. They could look, to assure themselves that this was no fake,* but they could not make drawings. Some drawings were accomplished on the sly, however, and found their way to Andreas Wagner at the University of Munich. This "mongrel creature," he noted, had the feathers of a bird but the tail of a reptile. And this worried him. Wagner, an anti-Darwinist, was quick to recognize what the evolutionists might make of this discovery and, therefore, decided to strike first with an identification and name that might discourage Darwinian missing-link interpretations. In a report based on the drawing and hearsay, Wagner called the specimen a reptile, perhaps a kind of pterosaur, and gave it the name *Griphosaurus problematicus,* "the problematical griffin lizard," which was a statement more than a taxonomic description. In Greek mythology, a griffin was a fabulous creature, half bird, half lion.

Writing to "ward off Darwinian misinterpretation of our new Saurian," Wagner asserted: "At first glance of the *Griphosaurus* we might certainly form the notion that we had before us an intermediate creature, engaged in the transition from the Saurian to the bird. Darwin and his adherents will probably employ the new discovery as an exceedingly welcome occurrence for the justification of their strange views upon the transformation of animals. But in this

*Much later, in 1985, skeptics charged that Häberlein may have engaged in fossil making. Lee Spetner, an American-Israeli physicist, led the attack, producing enlarged photographs of the 1861 specimen which, he claimed, indicated that the feathered sections were added to a genuine reptilian fossil by applying a layer of cement to the original rock and making impressions of feathers in it. "Codswallop," asserted Alan Charig, speaking for other paleontologists who strongly rejected the charge of fossil forgery.

they will be wrong." Darwinians, he continued, must establish the evidence of such an intermediate step by which the transition of some living or extinct animal form or class is made to another form. "If they cannot do this (as they certainly cannot), their views," Wagner concluded, "must be at once rejected as fantastic dreams, with which the exact investigation of nature has nothing to do."

Still, interest in buying the specimen was keen. Wagner had unwittingly accentuated its potentially sensational import. Richard Owen, who was now superintendent of the British Museum, read Wagner's report and in 1862 sent George Waterhouse to Pappenheim with authorization to pay £500 for the fossil. Häberlein held firm. Owen finally persuaded the museum trustees to meet Häberlein's price, just as German museum officials were beginning their own belated negotiations. The Germans learned to their dismay that, as the author Herbert Wendt would put it much later, the bird had flown to London.

After the specimen (still embedded in limestone) arrived in London in October 1862, Owen examined it in every detail. He was no friend of Darwinism. Owen believed in "continuous creation," which mimicked evolution, but

Archaeopteryx *at British Museum*

could not accept Darwin's natural selection with its absence of predetermined design. Still, Owen was an expert anatomist. At a glance, he could see that the creature possessed, as Wagner had said, "a combination of characters that nothing more surprising and odd could be imagined." Except for the missing head, the skeleton was unusually complete and well-preserved. It had several reptilian features: a long bony tail; three clawed fingers at the end of its forelimb or wing; saurian ribs and vertebrae. But, plainly, it also had some birdlike feathers, which were arranged on wings in the manner of modern birds. To Owen the feathers tipped the balance. This, he reported to the Royal Society in November, was "unequivocally" an ancient bird and should not be construed as evidence of a Darwinian missing link. He did not discuss the matter further.

Evolutionists, however, hailed the creature's "extreme importance" in documenting Darwin's theory. This was surely a missing link between reptiles and birds. Eventually, Thomas Henry Huxley joined the battle and made certain the world knew the importance of *Archaeopteryx*.

HUXLEY was known as Darwin's "bulldog," a pugnacious role he took upon himself with relish and carried off with eloquence and devastating effect. But he was a brilliant scientist in his own right, the first of a long line of Huxleys to distinguish themselves in science and the arts. Thomas Henry Huxley was born in 1825, the son of a schoolmaster of modest means. Though trained in medicine, Huxley took an early interest in physiology and natural history rather than in the practice of medicine. His study of jellyfish, conducted while serving as assistant surgeon on a British navy vessel in the waters of Australasia, won him election to the Royal Society at the age of twenty-seven. He then accepted a post as lecturer in paleontology and natural history at the School of Mines in London, where he came to the study of fossils and to prominence in the Darwinian wars.

While Darwin's book was still in press, Huxley foresaw the coming battles and wrote his friend: "As to the curs which bark and yelp, you must recollect that some of your friends, at any rate, are endowed with a combativeness which (though you have often and justly rebuked it) may stand you in good stead. I am sharpening up my claws and beak in readiness."

Despite reservations about some aspects of Darwin's theory, Huxley published a favorable review of the book and journeyed to Oxford in June 1860 for the first pitched battle. His prey was none other than the bishop of Oxford,

Thomas Henry Huxley, from a caricature that appeared in Vanity Fair

Samuel Wilberforce, whose unctuous manner earned him the sobriquet "Soapy Sam." Wilberforce was to lead the anti-Darwinian attack at the final session of the British Association for the Advancement of Science. Darwin avoided the meeting, saying he was too ill, but Huxley was there, sitting on the platform not far from Wilberforce. Many in the audience of 700 were sympathetic to Wilberforce, but not a few Oxford undergraduates were there lusting for episcopal blood.

Wilberforce spoke, as Huxley recalled, "for full half an hour with inimitable spirit, emptiness and unfairness." He had presumably been coached by Owen, but contemporary accounts differ as to what line of reasoning he developed in an effort to refute Darwin's theory of evolution. All agreed, however, that in the speech the bishop made a slanderous allusion to Huxley's simian ancestry, which prompted Huxley to whisper to a neighbor: "The Lord hath delivered him into mine hands."

When he took the floor, Huxley disarmed the bishop and won the respect, if not the complete conversion, of the audience. In a letter to a friend, he gave this account of his speech:

> . . . I spoke pretty much to the effect—that I had listened with great attention to the Lord Bishops speech but had been unable to discover either a new fact or a new argument in it—except indeed the question raised as to my personal predilections in the manner of ancestry—That it would not have occurred to me to bring forward such a topic as that for discussion myself, but that I was quite ready to meet the Right Revd. prelate even on that ground—If then, said I, the question is put to me would I rather have a miserable ape for a grandfather or a man highly endowed by nature and possessed of great means of influence & yet who employs those faculties & that influence for the mere purpose of introducing ridicule into a grave scientific discussion—I unhesitatingly affirm my preference for the ape.

This riposte, according to Huxley, set off "inextinguishable laughter" and applause, after which the audience "listened to the rest of my arguments with the greatest attention." Darwin, hearing of this, was appalled but pleased: "How durst you attack a live bishop in that fashion? I am quite ashamed of you! Have you no respect for fine lawn sleeves? By Jove, you seem to have done it well!"

Belatedly, Huxley enlisted *Archaeopteryx* in his attacks on Wilberforce, Owen, and others who could not bring themselves to share Darwin's view of the course of life. Huxley was struck by the specimen's many reptilian features; but for the feather imprint, it would probably have been misidentified as a reptile, as did happen with other *Archaeopteryx* fossils. A few years later, in 1867, Huxley published a classic report establishing the evolutionary relationship of birds and reptiles. He cited fourteen anatomical features that occur in birds and reptiles alike, but not in mammals, to support his case for classifying the two together in a new taxonomic category, which he called Sauropsida. (The proposed category was rejected by scientists, even though they came to agree with the reptile-bird relationship and much later would revive the issue of regrouping some reptiles—dinosaurs—with birds.) Moreover, Huxley argued that the creatures most nearly intermediate between birds and reptiles, the connecting link that had been missing, were some types of dinosaurs.

No longer, Huxley felt, did evolutionists have to be on the defensive about gaps in the fossil record, not with *Archaeopteryx* in hand. He elaborated on his thinking in a popular lecture in February 1868. The speech was vintage Huxley, of whom Darwin once said: "He never says and never writes anything flat." The speech also was a reflection of how times and thinking were changing.

Those who hold the doctrine of evolution, Huxley the evolutionist said in beginning his speech, "conceived that there are grounds for believing that the world, with all that is in it and on it, did not come into existence in the condition in which we now see it, nor in anything approaching that condition." He followed this with a succinct summation of Hutton, Lyell, and Darwin all rolled into one. Evolutionists, he said, "hold that the present conformation and composition of the earth's crust, the distribution of land and water, and the infinitely diversified forms of animals and plants which constitute its present population, are merely the final terms in an immense series of changes which have been brought about, in the course of immeasureable time, by the operation of causes more or less similar to those which are at work at the present day."

But how is it, Huxley then asked, if all animals "have proceeded by gradual modification from a common stock," that great gaps exist between, say, fish and mammals, reptiles and birds? "We, who believe in Evolution, reply that those gaps were once non-existent; that the connecting forms existed in previous epochs of the world's history, but that they have died out."

Huxley, once again anticipating the next question, led his audience on. "Naturally enough, then, we are asked to produce these extinct forms of life," he said, conceding that most of them were lost and probably beyond recovery, but not all of them. Naturally enough, Huxley cited *Archaeopteryx* as his primary piece of evidence. He agreed with Owen that this was a bird, but of a transitional kind. There were the feathers and wishbone of a bird, but there was the long bony tail of a reptile as well as other reptilian features throughout its skeleton.

Another fossil animal from the same Solnhofen limestone, thus a contemporary of *Archaeopteryx,* was next introduced by Huxley to strengthen his case not only for the reptile-bird link but, more specifically, for the dinosaur-bird link. This was the small dinosaur that Andreas Wagner in 1861 had described and named *Compsognathus.* Huxley had fixed his mind on *Compsognathus* as a missing link before he joined other evolutionists in support of *Archaeopteryx* in such a role. If *Archaeopteryx* was a bird that looked something like a dinosaur, *Compsognathus* was a dinosaur that looked something like a bird. It was less than two-thirds of a meter long, the smallest dinosaur ever identified and not much bigger than *Archaeopteryx.* Of even more interest to Huxley was this animal's long, delicate hind limbs. The dinosaur seemed clearly to have

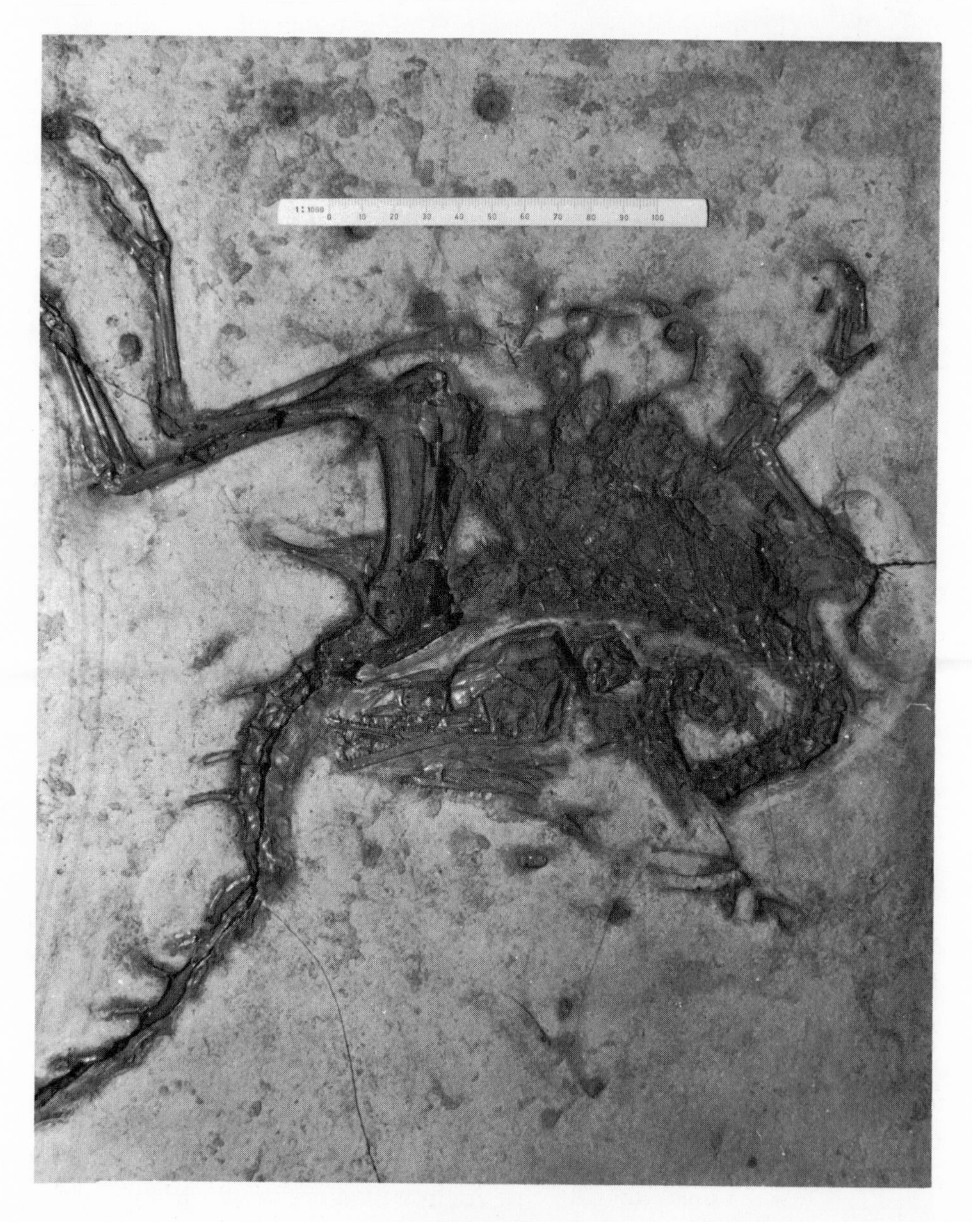

Fossil of Compsognathus

been bipedal. Its foot and ankle joint were remarkably birdlike. "It is impossible to look at the conformation of this strange reptile," Huxley told his audience, "and to doubt that it hopped or walked, in an erect or semi-erect position, after the manner of a bird, to which its long neck, slight head, and small anterior limbs must have given it an extraordinary resemblance."

Huxley recognized that as a contemporaneous species *Archaeopteryx* could not be descended from *Compsognathus.* But finding a reptilelike bird and a birdlike reptile living at approximately the same time in the Jurassic closed the evolutionary gap between the reptilian and avian classes, which Huxley offered as further support for his Sauropsida classification and for Darwin's theory of evolution.

Out of Huxley's emphasis on the reptile-bird relationship in his defense of Darwin emerged a new appreciation of dinosaurs. Early discoveries were reinterpreted. It was the first of paleontology's many "rediscoveries" of dinosaurs. Recent findings, particularly those in North America, took on new meaning.

The first North American fossils identified as dinosaurian were dug up in the 1850s in Montana and New Jersey. A United States Army mapping expedition, working in the Judith River badlands of present-day Montana, came upon assorted teeth in Cretaceous clays. These fossils were examined in 1858 by Joseph Leidy, professor of anatomy at the University of Pennsylvania and director of the Academy of Natural Sciences in Philadelphia. Leidy pronounced them to be the first evidence that dinosaurs had also lived in America during the Mesozoic. One specimen was a herbivore that he named *Trachodon,* meaning "rough tooth." It is now known to be one of the duck-billed dinosaurs and also goes by the name of *Anatosaurus,* or "duck lizard." Some fangs from another Judith River creature inspired Leidy to name the carnivore *Deinodon horridus,* "most horrible of the terror teeth."

In the summer of the same year, William Parker Foulke, a fellow of the Academy of Natural Sciences, learned of some bones in a marl quarry at Haddonfield, in New Jersey near Philadelphia. He investigated and found a mass of large bones, an almost complete skeleton of a creature some six to eight meters long. After careful examination, Leidy concluded that Foulke had found a dinosaur and gave it the name of *Hadrosaurus foulkii,* for the town and the discoverer. This was one of the duck-billed dinosaurs that later discoveries would show to have been most abundant in Cretaceous North America. Leidy also noted from the teeth that this hadrosaur appeared to be related to the *Trachodon* of Montana and the *Iguanodon* of England.

It was something to think about: dinosaurs might well have ranged the world.

What surprised Leidy most of all was the disproportionate size of the animal's front and hind limbs. The thigh bone was almost twice as long as the humerus of the upper arm. If they had not been found together, he might have assumed that they were from different animals. Reporting to the academy,

Leidy said: "The great disproportion of size between the fore and back parts of the skeleton of *Hadrosaurus,* leads me to suspect that this great extinct herbivorous lizard may have been in the habit of browsing, sustaining itself, kangaroo-like, in an erect position on its back extremities and tail."

Huxley saw the significance of Leidy's finding. Not all dinosaurs walked and ran on all fours; Owen's rhinocerine dinosaurs misrepresented reality. Some were bipedal, another general similarity between dinosaurs and birds. Huxley then reexamined Mantell's *Iguanodon* and noted that its hindquarters and three-toed foot "wonderfully approached" those of birds. The *Iguanodon,* contrary to the quadrupedal image of it in the Crystal Palace exhibit, must have been capable of erect posture and of hopping or running on its hind legs, an observation that eventually would be confirmed.

This reminded Huxley of certain "bird" tracks in the Connecticut River Valley of New England. They had mystified farmers and scientists alike since their discovery in the early years of the century. One day in 1802, a college student named Pliny Moody, while plowing his father's field in South Hadley, Massachusetts, turned up a sandstone slab bearing the imprint of a large three-toed foot. It looked like the footprint of a giant turkey or raven. Those who saw this wonder decided, in a moment of pious fancy, that the print must have been made by the raven that Noah had released from the ark to search for dry land. Other tracks of Noah's raven were found over the years, always in the Triassic sandstone that would become the source of the "brownstone" favored in the construction of Manhattan townhouses. A collection of these fossil tracks, some of which were half a meter long, came into the hands of Edward Hitchcock in 1835. He was a geologist and president of Amherst College. Since there were no skeletons associated with the tracks, Hitchcock could only imagine what these animals had been. He concluded that the Connecticut valley had once been populated by some extraordinary three-toed wading birds several times the size of ostriches. "They must have been the giant rulers of that valley," Hitchcock said. No one knew then that dinosaur tracks had been discovered, but misidentified, several years before the first bones were identified in England.

If some dinosaurs were bipedal and had birdlike feet—and *Hadrosaurus, Iguanodon,* and *Compsognathus* seemed to remove any doubt—Huxley reasoned that Hitchcock's "stony bird tracks" could be those of dinosaurs living in the early Mesozoic. Perhaps some of the smaller tracks were left by birds, he conceded, having no way of knowing then that birds had yet to evolve in the early Mesozoic. But most of the tracks, certainly the big ones, were made by bipedal dinosaurs. "The important truth which these tracks reveal," Huxley asserted, "is, that at the commencement of the Mesozoic epoch, bipedal animals existed which had the feet of birds, and walked in the same erect or semi-erect fashion."

It was something else to think about: dinosaurs were even more ancient than had been imagined, and possessed some birdlike features well before the time of *Archaeopteryx.*

Time would prove Huxley right about the tracks. With the subsequent discoveries of bones, nearly all of the New England tracks are now attributed to a variety of Triassic dinosaurs. At Dinosaur State Park, in Rocky Hill, Connecticut, some 2,000 well-preserved tracks are believed to be those of such creatures as *Stegomosuchus, Dilophosaurus,* and *Coelophysis,* the latter of which is thought by some scientists to occupy a place in the mainline ancestry of birds.

It was sufficient for Huxley's immediate purpose to have demonstrated in this way the confusing similarity between the tracks of birds and dinosaurs. Birds evolved from dinosaurs or other archaic reptiles, Huxley declared with more certainty than ever, and one of the creatures of the transition, one of the connecting links, was the reptilelike bird from the Solnohofen limestone, *Archaeopteryx.*

THE ARCHAEOPTERYX in the museum in London had no head, and some anti-Darwinists made the most of this. If the *Archaeopteryx* had had a toothless beak, as they wanted to believe, then it was surely a bird, however ancient, without any obvious evolutionary message. Even Huxley doubted that the early bird had teeth, though others who had examined the fossil believed they could see the remains of an upper jaw with four teeth. If it had had a reptilian mouth with teeth, then Huxley and his allies would be reinforced in their hypothesis of its evolutionary link between reptiles and birds. The bird in hand would be worth more if they could only find another in the quarry, one with a head.

The next discovery came in 1877, also in the Solnhofen region, and this specimen was more complete and more splendid than the first. Alan Feduccia, an American zoologist writing in 1980, said that this *Archaeopteryx* fossil "may well be the most important natural history specimen in existence, perhaps comparable in value to the Rosetta stone." Its head was intact, a Huxley head. The skull was birdlike with a mouth evolving toward a beak shape, but set in the jaws were pointed reptilian teeth. In contrast to the London specimen, the skeleton of this one was articulated in a natural pose with the wings extended. The dinosaurlike arms and hands were adorned with a great span of feathers nearly identical in detail to those of modern birds, and more feathers were preserved on either side of the long reptilian tail. *Archaeopteryx* now looked even more like the missing link.

The second specimen also found its way to the Häberlein family. The doctor had died, but his son Ernst was equally enterprising, offering the fossil for sale at three times the price the first specimen had fetched. After much bargaining, Werner Siemens, the industrialist, bought the fossil to insure that it remained in Germany and resold it to Berlin University. In tribute, the fossil was classified as a special genus, *Archaeornis siemensi.* Later studies, however, established that the second specimen probably belonged to the same genus, if not the same species, as the first *Archaeopteryx.* Among paleontologists the second *Archaeopteryx,* now owned by the Humboldt University Museum in East Berlin, is commonly referred to as the Berlin specimen.

Since then, three other *Archaeopteryx* skeletons have been identified. The next discovery was a long time coming. In 1956, a German geology student happened on a badly decomposed specimen lying almost forgotten in a quarryman's shed a few hundred meters from where the London specimen had been dug up. For some years the fossil was displayed at a small museum in Maxberg, and so it is called the Maxberg specimen.

Another skeleton was identified in 1970. As it turned out, this one had been around since 1855, six years before the discovery of the solitary feather and the London specimen. John Ostrom, while in Europe in the course of studying the London, Berlin, and Maxberg specimens, was visiting the Teyler Museum at Haarlem in the Netherlands. There he came upon a specimen identified as a pterosaur that to him did not look like a pterosaur. The legs and feet, he noted, were disproportionately large for a pterosaur of that age. The three fingers on the claws were of different lengths, not the same length, as is characteristic of pterosaurs. Could this be a misidentified *Archaeopteryx*? It came from the same quarries. So Ostrom, his curiosity piqued, got permission to remove the fossil from its display case for a closer inspection. Tilting the limestone slab up to the light, he saw the faint impressions of feathers, something no one had previously detected because they had no reason to suspect they would find anything so strange. Pterosaurs were flying or gliding reptiles with wings of leathery membrane, not feathers.

Ostrom asked the Teyler curator if he could borrow the fossil and take it home to Yale for more study. He explained his suspicion that the pterosaur

Berlin Archaeopteryx

might, in fact, be an *Archaeopteryx,* which any museum curator would be happy to hear. Ostrom left the museum clutching a shoebox whose contents were insured for $1 million.

Ironically, the same Hermann von Meyer who had applied the name *Archaeopteryx* to the solitary feather and had reported the London specimen was the one who first described—and misidentified—the Teyler specimen. He did this in 1857, before any fossil birds had been recognized in the Solnhofen limestone. Von Meyer did observe that the "wing membrane" had a strange appearance unlike other pterosaurs he had seen. Still, he reported it as a new species of pterosaur. Ostrom, back at Yale in the fall of 1970, confirmed his first impression and announced the rediscovery, so to speak, of another *Archaeopteryx*. Although the Teyler specimen "is very fragmentary and far less spectacular" than the London and Berlin specimens, Ostrom said, it possessed well-preserved claws providing "important new evidence that is not preserved in any of the other specimens." A horny sheath, something like a human fingernail, surrounded the claws.

Speaking of his "lucky" discovery several years later, Ostrom drew a moral: "My find is a classic example of why a paleontologist or museum should not throw things away that can't be absolutely classified as worthless." It also underscored an increasingly strong trend in which major discoveries are as often made in the laboratory or museum as in the field. "Ever since I've had to give up field work," Ostrom added, "I've said the best discoveries are made in museum storerooms."*

The fifth and most recent *Archaeopteryx* specimen to come to light was reported in 1973. It, too, had been dug up earlier, in 1951, and was thought to be something else, the small dinosaur *Compsognathus*. The confusion would have pleased Huxley. It was understandable, though, because this specimen lacked any distinct feather impressions. If it had not come from one of the Jurassic limestone quarries, near Eichstätt, the possibility that it was an *Archaeopteryx* might not have occurred to anyone. A professor in Eichstätt, Franz X. Mayr, acquired the specimen and in time recognized it as yet another *Archaeopteryx*.

So there are now five specimens of this rare early bird known to exist: the London, Berlin, Maxberg, Teyler, and Eichstätt specimens, as well as the solitary feather, which is in a Munich museum. Rumors of others circulate from time to time. In 1983, German paleontologists thought they had two likely candidates. But one turned out to be a fish. The other, not so strangely, was found to be the remains of a pterosaur; mistaken identities cut two ways. No birds any older have thus far appeared in the fossil record. In 1978, Jim Jensen, digging in Colorado, announced what he called a possible rival for *Archaeop-*

*Ostrom was repeating an opinion he first heard expressed by Donald Baird of Princeton. Not that Ostrom does not miss fieldwork, which he abandoned for reasons of health.

teryx, but the fossils are so few and fragmented that no other scientists are prepared to agree with Jensen.

But it took only one, the first of the 150-million-year-old birds from the Solnhofen limestone, the first reptilian-avian *Archaeopteryx,* to bolster Huxley's effective defense of Darwinian evolution through natural selection. There was no longer any serious question that birds had evolved from archaic reptiles. Othniel Charles Marsh declared in 1877 that Huxley had virtually bridged the gap between reptiles and birds. *Compsognathus* and *Archaeopteryx,* he said, served as "the stepping stones by which the evolutionist of to-day leads the doubting brother across the shallow remnant of the gulf, once thought impassable." For some years Huxley's hypothesis that birds were direct descendants of early dinosaurs enjoyed wide support, only to fall out of favor by the time of his death in 1895. The hypothesis has since been revived and, with new evidence, has drawn a new generation of staunch supporters. *Archaeopteryx* is still the best example known of the kind of creatures Darwin's theory predicts: a species that represents an intermediate step between two great classes of organisms.

The discovery of *Archaeopteryx,* coming shortly after the publication of Darwin's *Origin of Species,* elevated the study of dinosaurs to a higher and broader plane. They came to be seen as more than monstrous curiosities. Dinosaurs quite possibly were key figures in some of the more transcending developments in the course of life on earth. Sensing this, sensing that the discovery of dinosaurs had only begun, scientists increasingly committed their careers and lives to the exploration of time as revealed through the bones of these creatures.

6 *Cope and Marsh: The Bone Wars*

FROM OUT of the American West in 1877 there came three messages about discoveries of unusual bones that would become objects of contention in the bitterest rivalry in the history of paleontology. They set in motion explorations that uncovered some of the richest dinosaur graveyards in the world and led to the discovery of such popular bygone creatures as *Brontosaurus* and *Diplodocus, Stegosaurus* and *Triceratops.* The new findings revealed beyond all doubt that dinosaurs had lived in great number in the Mesozoic and had come in an unsuspected variety of shapes and sizes.

The first message was from Arthur Lakes, an Englishman teaching school in Golden, Colorado, a town west of Denver. Lakes had studied geology at Oxford and was a part-time fossil collector. In the early spring, he and H. C. Beckwith, a navy captain from Connecticut, were hiking in the mountains near the neighboring town of Morrison. They were looking for fossil leaves and examining the strata along the banks of Bear Creek. When they reached a sandstone ridge, Lakes found some huge bones embedded in the rock. These were, as he wrote in April in a letter to Yale University, "apparently a vertebra and a humerus bone of some gigantic saurian."

Lakes addressed the letter, along with two small sketches of the bones, to Othniel Charles Marsh, professor of paleontology at Yale, who was widely known as a wealthy man prepared to pay for new specimens. Marsh was slow to respond. Meanwhile, Lakes dug up other "colossal" bones of "no less than six different animals if not different species." Eventually, he sent ten boxes of the bones to New Haven for identification and, not being sure that Marsh was interested, followed this up with a shipment of similar specimens to a paleontologist in Philadelphia. This was Edward Drinker Cope, another man of wealth who was an independent scientist of prehistoric life. The two cargoes were certain to provoke a reaction. Cope and Marsh hated each other.

The reaction was swift and predictable. When Marsh received his shipment, he sent $100 to Lakes and asked him to keep the discovery site a secret. On July 1, he published a description of the Lakes discoveries in the *American Journal of Science.* To the animal with the large bones he assigned the name *Titanosaurus,* later changed to *Atlantosaurus.* But when he learned of the correspondence between Lakes and Cope, Marsh wired Benjamin Mudge, his chief field collector, to proceed immediately from Kansas to Morrison, Colorado, to secure Lakes's services and loyalty and to take charge of the excavations. Before Cope could publish his own interpretation of the bones, Lakes wrote him that the specimens should be shipped on to Marsh. Cope did so, though he must have seethed at this latest triumph of his rival.

By this time, however, a second message of discovery had arrived from the West, and this one was addressed to Cope. In the same spring, O. W. Lucas, an amateur naturalist who also was a teacher, was collecting plants near Cañon City, Colorado, and came upon an assortment of large fossil bones. Lucas shipped several of the specimens to Cope, who encouraged him to dig for more. By late summer, Cope had seen enough samples to conclude that the Cañon City dinosaurs had been herbivores, about twenty to twenty-five meters long, exceeding "in proportions any other land animal hitherto described, including the one found near Golden City by Professor Lakes." This was *Camarasaurus.* In no time Marsh, hearing of the Cañon City finds, instructed Mudge to leave the Morrison excavations and prospect the area where Lucas was working for Cope. Mudge reported to Marsh that, indeed, Lucas was finding bones for Cope much larger than anything Lakes had dug up. With Marsh's approval, Mudge brought in Samuel Wendell Williston from Kansas to set up a rival quarry near Cañon City. It had been several years since Marsh had done any fieldwork himself. He relied mainly on men like Mudge and Williston, experienced fossil collectors who worked for themselves and took on paid assignments from the professional paleontologists back east. They were a new breed in dinosaur hunting, the full-time hired collectors. Mudge was a professor at Kansas State Agricultural College (now Kansas State University), in Manhattan, and Williston had been one of his students. Williston would go on to become an accomplished paleontologist in his own right, but at Cañon City in 1877 he had little luck for Marsh. He reported that Lucas was getting all the best bones for Cope and had rejected entreaties that he should quit Cope and work for Marsh. Neither man, Cope or Marsh, was above suborning the other's collectors.

Marsh had no time to nurse the disappointment at Cañon City, for he had reason to believe that he was within reach of an even greater prize. In late July of 1877, the third message of discovery in the West reached him at New Haven. The letter was sent from Laramie and signed "Harlow and Edwards." It read:

> I write to announce to you the discovery not far from this place, of a large number of fossils, supposed to be those of the Megatherium, although there is no one here sufficient of a geologist to state for a certainty. We have excavated one (1) partly, and know where there is several others that we have not, as yet, done any work upon. The formation in which they are found is that of the Tertiary Period.
>
> We are desirous of disposing of what fossils we have, and also, the secret of the others. We are working men and are not able to present them as a gift, and if we can sell the secret of the fossil bed, and procure work in excavating others we would like to do so.
>
> We have said nothing to any-one as yet.
>
> We measured one shoulder blade and found it to measure four feet eight inches 4 ft. 8 in. in length.
>
> One joint of the vertebrae measures two feet and one half 2 1/2 in circumference and ten inches (10) in length.
>
> As a proof of our sincerity and truth, we will send you a few fossils, at what they cost us in time and money in unearthing.
>
> We would be pleased to hear from you, as you are well known as an enthusiastic geologist, and a man of means, both of which we are desirous of finding—more especially the latter.
>
> Hoping to hear from you very soon, before the snows of winter set in. . . .

The boxes of bones from Harlow and Edwards finally reached Marsh in October, along with a letter referring to even more discoveries. The bones were definitely dinosaurian, and gigantic. The two men had been mistaken in placing them in the Tertiary and so this side of the age of the great reptiles. Marsh immediately sent them a letter with instructions for future collection and shipment, questions about the geology of the discovery site, and a check for $75 payable to Harlow and Edwards. (This may not seem like much compensation, but in Wyoming Territory then a man's monthly wage was often considerably less.) In their next communication, the two men seemed ready to work for Marsh but warned that "there are plenty of men looking for such things" in the vicinity. This was all Marsh had to hear. Cope's agents, he feared, might be closing in on *his* bones.

So Marsh dispatched Williston to the scene, which had by then been revealed to be Como Station, on the Union Pacific Railroad west of Laramie near Medicine Bow, the rough-and-tumble place Owen Wister would ensconce in western lore in *The Virginian.* Williston stepped off the train late one night in November to find that the station consisted of little more than two rude shacks set out on a windswept plain. He asked the station agent about a hotel and was pointed in the direction of the section-house. He asked where he might find Harlow and Edwards and was told that they lived on a ranch far off in the country. "A freshly opened box of cigars, however, helped clear up things," Williston recalled. The agent grinned and allowed that he and the section foreman were Harlow and Edwards. Williston showed the agent a telegram from Marsh to establish his identity, and the next morning he was taken out to survey the wealth of bones along the ridge south of the station, the ridge known as Como Bluff.

As Williston wrote in a letter to Marsh shortly after arriving at Como, Harlow and Edwards were, in fact, William E. Carlin, the agent, and William H. Reed, the foreman. They had used false names to conceal their connection with the fossils, possibly because they had been collecting them on railroad time. The subterfuge had cost them. They had not been able to cash Marsh's check. But there was nothing false about their reports of fossils. The bones, Williston wrote, "extend for seven miles and are by the ton." Several tons of bones had already been gathered and packed, awaiting shipment to New Haven.

Two days later, on November 16, Williston wrote Marsh with even more enthusiasm. "Cañon City and Morrison are simply nowhere in comparison with this locality both as regards perfection, accessibility and quantity," Williston declared. He recommended that Marsh employ Carlin and Reed at $75 a month each. He also cautioned: "There will be great danger next summer of competition."

Marsh must have shared Williston's sense of urgency. He drew up a contract with Carlin and Reed for $90 each, not $75, and stipulated that they were "to take all reasonable precautions to keep all other collectors not authorized by Prof. Marsh out of the region and to use their best efforts in every way to promote Prof. Marsh's interests." Williston was instructed to remain at Como to supervise excavations.

The stage was thus set for one of the most intense and productive periods of dinosaur discovery, in Colorado and Wyoming and then to the north. Practical-minded settlers looked upon the early fossil hunters and naturalists as a curious lot. "For anyone to go chasing about over the West hunting for petrified bones, or even bugs, was conclusive evidence of his lack of good horse sense," recalled James H. Cook, a game hunter and rancher who knew both Cope and Marsh and came to realize on his own the "real thrills" of finding fossils in western Nebraska. Fossils were showing up everywhere, and this was a time in which the scope and character of dinosaur hunting changed forever. Amateurs who made chance discoveries were eclipsed by professional paleontologists and their hired collectors, who brought to the hunt an acquisitive fervor that mirrored the expansionary times. The Indians were being battled into submission, the buffalo slaughtered, and the land fenced off for range and the plow. The new transcontinental railroad brought in settlers and fortune seekers by the droves. The dinosaur hunters, in the spirit of the time and place, staked out their own claims and guarded them jealously, sometimes belligerently, and grubbed for a measure of fame and fortune. At places like Como Bluff, they fought the elements and each other. They pioneered the methods of wide-ranging, systematic paleontological exploration. They developed new techniques of protecting delicate fossils for the long journeys back to the museums and laboratories in the East. And these shipments ran into the carloads, tons and tons of dinosaur bones bound mainly for Philadelphia and New Haven and the eager, grasping hands of Cope and Marsh.

COMPETITION IN SCIENCE, as in any human endeavor, is normal and can be healthy; it can bring out the best in bright, ambitious people. It brought out the worst in Cope and Marsh. They were bright and ambitious, but also arrogant and vindictive and greedy for fame. Theirs was a contest for scientific supremacy, marked by jealousy and mistrust, in which the one did not simply want to succeed, but wished the other to fail.

Cope was the more brilliant of the two, an impetuous genius with a volatile temperament. His quickness of mind gained him early recognition by the science establishment. His interests ranged through the whole of nature, but centered on herpetology and vertebrate paleontology, and wherever his mind lighted he published his observations readily—hastily, some said—and never shied from speculation. In 1867, at the age of twenty-seven, he published *Origin of Genera,* a treatise in which he accepted evolution but rejected natural selection. This book marked him as a leading exponent of the American school of evolution, or Neo-Lamarckism. Essentially, though, Cope was not a leader but a loner. He was one of the last of the scholars who worked independent of an academic institution. He could never be collegial. His impatience and

Edward Drinker Cope *Othniel Charles Marsh*

fiery temper alienated other scientists; he could never conceal his feelings when it might have been diplomatic to do so, any more than he could forgive or forget a critic or rival.

The faces of the two men bear more than a hint of their characters. Cope's elegant chestnut mustaches bespeak the comfort and respectability to which he was born. The intense eyes and jutting jaw betray his pugnacious side. The Cope jaw has been called an affront to the peace. Marsh, bearded and bald, presents a more stolid, sternly complacent image. His face expresses little emotion, something that his seclusive nature could not bring him to share with others. This is the image of a self-centered man used to having his way through power rather than persuasion.

Marsh was a slow but sure thinker who had a genius for recognizing and concentrating on the more compelling issues and quests of science. He became a staunch defender of Darwin in the United States. He went for the biggest, most impressive fossils in the West. But Marsh, too, was a loner. Although he had many allies in the high places of government and science and enjoyed the camaraderie of fashionable clubs, he apparently was incapable of close friendship. He had an aloof bearing and a suspicious nature. A colleague noted in Marsh "an absence of the complete exchange of confidence which normally exists between intimate friends." He remained a bachelor all his life, which led a classmate to remark that Marsh handled many bones but somehow never acquired a rib.

OTHNIEL CHARLES MARSH, who preferred to be called "Oh See," after his initials, was nine years older than Cope. He had been born in Lockport in western New York in 1831, the son of a farmer, and he might have become a farmer also if his mother had not been the sister of George Peabody, the wealthy financier. Marsh had a rather lonely childhood. His mother died when he was only three years old, and he grew up mostly with aunts and uncles. He showed no particular ambition or aptitude, except for collecting fossils exposed in the widening of the Erie Canal near his home. When he was twenty, however, fortune plucked Marsh from the farm. Receiving a legacy from his mother's estate, which had been provided by Peabody, Marsh entered Phillips Academy at Andover, Massachusetts, where he spent five years and found himself as a student and a young man with a growing sense of purpose. He wrote Uncle George in London that "in so far as it may be in my power to prevent it, you shall never have the occasion to regret the kindness which you have shown me for my dear mother's sake." Marsh wanted money to go to Yale, which he got. At the age of twenty-five, he enrolled as a college freshman and spent six years as an undergraduate and then as a student at Yale's new Sheffield Scientific School, always living well in a four-room apartment overflowing with his collection of minerals and fossils. After Yale, Uncle George's generosity took Marsh to Europe, beginning in 1862 and lasting through most of the Civil War; it is not clear whether he was avoiding military service, as some wealthy people did, or if, according to various accounts, his eyesight disqualified him. In any event, he used the time abroad to study at universities in Germany, visit museums, and go salmon fishing in Scotland with Uncle George. Marsh seems to have caught what he was after. When he returned to New Haven in 1866, he brought with him a gift of $150,000 from George Peabody to endow a museum of natural history, which was only one of the many Peabody philanthropies to American education. Marsh was rewarded with a professor's chair at Yale. This, and the additional money he received at Peabody's death in 1869, set O. C. Marsh up for life.

It is a wonder that Marsh did not discover the dinosaur beds at Como Bluff in 1868. On his first trip west, he took the newly completed Union Pacific Railroad to Como to look for, among other things, a tiger salamander in the lake there. When the train stopped briefly to take on water at Antelope Station, in western Nebraska, Marsh examined a scattering of fossils in the dirt around a new well. He identified the bones of several extinct animals, including a miniature horse. When the conductor called "all aboard," Marsh left reluctantly, but only after he had persuaded the station master to collect more bones and have them waiting when he passed through again on the return trip east. At Como, Marsh found the salamander he sought, although he somehow failed to notice the dinosaur bones lying everywhere like logs. They would have to await discovery by Carlin and Reed. Perhaps Marsh's mind was still back at Antelope Station. On his return there, Marsh received "a hatfull of bones" from the station master. "As we shook hands," Marsh wrote, "I left in his palm glittering coin of the realm."

This was Marsh's way, dispensing his wealth in the acquisition of fossils, but in this case the fossils were worth every coin. The fossil horse at Antelope Station was an important discovery. It was one of the most famous pieces of paleontological evidence for the validity of Darwin's theory. His recognition of this missing link brought Marsh to the attention of world scientists. He was more sure than ever that paleontology would be his life's work.

Marsh returned west as the leader of four expeditions of Yale students, from 1870 through 1873, working mostly in western Kansas and Wyoming. Influential Yale alumni in Washington arranged for him to obtain provisions from military garrisons and cavalry escorts for his movements through hostile Indian country. The soldiers were not always appreciative participants. As Charles Betts, one of the students, related: "After fourteen hours in the saddle, one of the soldiers, exhausted with heat and thirst, finally exclaimed, 'What did God Almighty make such a country as this for?' 'Why,' replied another more devout trooper, 'God Almighty made the country good enough, but it's this deuced geology the professor talks about that spoiled it all!' "

Even the stolid Marsh seems to have given in to the romantic urge to exaggerate his experiences in the West. He was not the first or last Easterner to do so after a western experience. And it was not unlike him. Several of his hired fossil hunters complained that Marsh often appropriated credit for explorations conducted while he was safely back in New Haven. Samuel Williston, writing in 1897, said:

> In his publications Professor Marsh has stated, or left it to be inferred, that his personal explorations in this as in other fields were extensive and that the larger part of the fossils described by him were the results of these explorations. The actual fact is that since 1875, when my personal relations with Professor Marsh began, he himself did no field work, his knowledge of the formations being derived from a few transient and hasty visits to the

> different fields where his collectors were at work. His reference to the personal dangers encountered by hostile Indians is amusing in the extreme to all those who know the facts. I think I can say without fear of dispute . . . that Professor Marsh never ran any greater danger from Indians than when he entertained Red Cloud at his home in New Haven.

Red Cloud was the great war chief of the Sioux, whom Marsh had befriended in 1874. In order to get permission to hunt fossils in the Sioux country of Nebraska and the Dakotas, which would be Marsh's last expedition, he agreed to deliver to Washington Red Cloud's complaints against the corrupt government Indian agents who were distributing rotten food and defective supplies to the starving Sioux. Marsh did so. In addition, he brought the fraud to the attention of newspapers. The ensuing investigation exposed one of the many scandals of the Grant Administration and led to the ouster of the head of the Bureau of Indian Affairs.

The whole affair brought Marsh his first taste of national celebrity, which he basked in and came to seek and expect. This coincided with his election to the National Academy of Sciences. After a slow, uncertain start, his place in science seemed secure. He had influence in Washington, professional honors, and crates of fascinating specimens, including toothed birds and pterodactyls with six-meter wingspans, to fill the museum his Uncle George had bestowed on Yale. Marsh, moreover, had finally achieved a stature in paleontology comparable to that of his younger rival, Edward Drinker Cope.

COPE HAD BEEN BORN in 1840 into the family of a prosperous Philadelphia shipowner and merchant. Despite the death of his mother when he was three, the same age at which Marsh lost his mother, Cope grew up in a close family atmosphere and enjoyed the loving encouragement of his father and stepmother. The boy showed an early interest in nature, exploring the woods outside Philadelphia and making notes and sketches of the fossils he saw at the Academy of Natural Sciences. On a trip by sea to Boston with his father, he filled his journal with excellent drawings of jellyfish and grampuses. There seemed little doubt that he would pursue a life of science. After school, Cope in 1860 studied anatomy under Joseph Leidy at the University of Pennsylvania, but he had no further formal college training. Instead, he trained himself, spending two years recataloguing the herpetological collection at the Academy of Natural Sciences and then, like Marsh, traveling to Europe to visit museums and scientists. His European sojourn occurred in 1863–64, during the Civil War. Cope was a devout Quaker and thus a pacifist. His father apparently also wanted to separate his son from a woman he was in love with. On his return, Cope took over the management of a farm his father had bought him, taught zoology for a while at Haverford College, and married a distant cousin, Annie Pim.

The traits that would make Cope such a difficult, unhappy man were already manifest. He was restless, impatient, and quarrelsome. He suffered from his own brilliance and made others suffer, as well. He quit farming, in which he had no interest, and resigned from the Haverford faculty because of differences with the administration. As a young man, Cope wrote to his father: "I am not constructed for getting along comfortably with the general run of people." Or, for that matter, the special run of people, his friends and scientific peers. Once, in the halls of the august American Philosophical Society, Cope came to eye-blackening blows with a close friend over some difference of scientific opinion. Many others were victims of his sharp tongue. Leidy said of Cope: "He does things in an unnecessarily offensive manner."

In 1867, Cope moved with his wife and baby daughter to Haddonfield, New Jersey, where he could be close to the fossil beds in which the first hadrosaur had been discovered in the previous decade and where, with an independent income, he could devote himself full-time to the study of modern reptiles and fossil vertebrates. Though still in his twenties, Cope had already published numerous scientific reports and, as always, felt pressure to put more of his thoughts and observations on the record. In his career he wrote more than 1,400 articles and several books.

Cope's introduction to the West came in 1871 when he traveled to western Kansas. He had read of Marsh's explorations in the Smoky Hill River region and wanted to sample the remains of Cretaceous life in the chalk beds there. On this trip he teamed up with Charles H. Sternberg, a young freelance fossil hunter, and their efforts resulted in a rich haul of fossil turtles, sea serpents, mosasaurs, and sharks from the land that had once been an ancient sea floor. Sternberg was an unusual man in that he got along well with Cope and expressed nothing but admiration for his intelligence, stamina, and indomitable spirit in the field.

On another expedition, in 1876, Sternberg accompanied Cope on a search for fossils in the Judith River badlands of Montana, traveling by train and stagecoach as far as Helena. There they heard the news of the Sioux massacre of Custer's troops at Little Big Horn. Cope was advised against proceeding to the badlands, which was the neutral ground between the Sioux and their hereditary enemies, the Crow. The fossil hunters might be killed by either tribe, which would lay the blame on the other. But, as Sternberg recalled, Cope reasoned that now was the perfect time to enter the region. Every Sioux warrior would be with Sitting Bull and would not be able to reach the Judith River country for another month or two. So Cope and Sternberg moved on to Fort Benton, a frontier town where, Sternberg noted, the streets were "paved with playing-cards." They bought a wagon and team of mules, engaged the services of a cook and some mule skinners, and set forth. Cope's instinct had been right; they never encountered any threatening Indians. Some visiting Crow chiefs were enchanted by Cope's taking out his false teeth and putting them back in. For days on the trip Cope and Sternberg never saw another human. From sunup to sundown Cope trudged the ravines and hillsides, looking for fossils and picking up the pieces of such dinosaurs as *Trachodon, Monoclonius,* and several varieties of horned and duck-billed dinosaurs. The water they drank was "like a dense solution of Epsom salts," Sternberg said, and had predictable consequences. At night, after one of the cook's usual indigestible meals, Cope would read aloud from the Bible and then try to rest between bouts of insomnia and tumultuous nightmares. "Every animal of which he had found traces during the day played with him at night, tossing him into the air, kicking him, trampling upon him," Sternberg wrote. "When I waked him, he would thank me cordially and lie down to another attack."

Cope, nonetheless, would be ready at dawn for another arduous day. No one could ever say of Cope that he did not pay his full dues as a field paleontologist. Henry Fairfield Osborn, his biographer, noted that "as a field explorer in geology and vertebrate paleontology, Cope far surpassed either of his fellow co-founders of the latter science: Joseph Leidy and Othniel Charles Marsh."

THE WARFARE between Cope and Marsh had broken out several years before the 1877 discoveries. The two were once friends of sorts. In 1867, Cope named a fossil species for Marsh, and Marsh returned the compliment a couple of years later. In the spring of 1868, Marsh visited Cope at Haddonfield and toured the fossil beds in the vicinity. They were wary of each other, as was their mutual nature, but all seemed amicable.

Their exchanges of letters were at first cordial. Cope referred to himself as "thy friend." But soon the letters became filled with carping remarks about each other's mistakes. Marsh never let Cope forget his error in reconstructing a fossil skeleton with the head at the tail. Then any pretense of cordiality ended in 1872, the summer Cope invaded what Marsh considered to be his private fossil-hunting turf in the Bridger Basin of southwestern Wyoming and adjacent parts of Utah.

The most coveted fossils in the basin were primarily mammals of the Eocene, and, strictly speaking, Marsh could not claim priority in their discovery. For several years a doctor at Fort Bridger had been collecting fossils and sending them to Leidy for description. Marsh explored the area on his 1871 expedition and was there again in 1872. It was in July of that year that Cope, exploring under the auspices of Ferdinand V. Hayden's mapping survey, arrived at Fort Bridger. He bought supplies and secured the services of one of Marsh's men, who guided him to some of Marsh's digging sites.

After weeks in the field, Cope returned to the fort delirious with fever but with the will to call up enough strength to dash off several articles on the uinatheres, mammals that became extinct in the Eocene. Marsh was outraged. Bridger Basin was his territory, and the uinatheres were his animals; indeed, in later years the more methodical Marsh would publish a definitive study of these animals. "I have of late been subjected to a very unscrupulous rivalry," Marsh wrote to some of his fellow scientists, "and have thus lost more than half of the discoveries for which I have risked my life during my western explorations."

This was all so typical of each man. The impetuous Cope rushed in to grab some bones, as if spoiling for a fight, and rushed out to publish what he had learned, as if he alone could interpret the messages of the fossils and as if time to do it were running out. Marsh's reaction, on the other hand, reflected his need to possess whatever he touched and his fear that someone was always trying to rob him of his possessions. Charles E. Beecher, a Yale colleague, wrote of him: "He not only had the means and the inclination, but entered every field of acquisition with the dominating ambition to obtain everything there was in it, and leave not a single scrap behind."

The West, though big enough for the most expansive dreams, seemed not to be big enough for both Cope and Marsh in their consuming reach for scientific greatness. And there was certainly no room anymore for a third paleontologist, the retiring Joseph Leidy. In a letter to a foreign scientist, Leidy wrote: "Formerly, every fossil one found in the States came to me, for nobody else cared to study such things, but Professors Marsh and Cope, with long purses, offer money for what used to come to me for nothing, and in that respect I cannot compete with them."

Cope and Marsh, said Nathan Reingold in his book *Science in Nineteenth-Century America,* "were robber barons trying to corner the old-bones market."

AT COMO BLUFF, beginning in 1877, the bone barons waged a relentless battle over control of what turned out to be the richest dinosaur graveyard ever known. Marsh held the advantage. Through his arrangement with Carlin and Reed, the railroad men, Marsh was first to field crews who would find and exploit some of the choicest dig sites along the northern lee of the ridge, facing the plain across which the railroad ran by Como Station. Cope had to resort to a kind of guerrilla warfare with the entrenched Marsh forces. He dispatched agents to spy on the operation and eventually deployed his own digging crews to establish a beachhead on the fringes. A few Marsh workers defected to Cope. Some who did not defect could barely stand the sight of each other and kept their distance, digging separately in quarries at opposite ends of the ridge. Workers on both sides had to hunker down in blizzards, dig out of rock slides, bail out floods in their quarries, endure monotony and loneliness, and shrug off the inattention of their leaders.

After Samuel Williston's arrival at Como Station in November 1877, Marsh's forces began a systematic campaign of digging and collecting and in the first year recovered some thirty tons of dinosaur specimens. These were odd bones and partial skeletons of *Camarasaurus, Laosaurus, Diplodocus, Apatosaurus, Barosaurus,* and *Stegosaurus.* The cast of dinosaurian characters was getting larger. The new bones came from several quarries along the bluff, each one a paleontologist's joy and challenge. The fossils were many and jumbled.

Most quarries, Williston said, "are found containing remains of numerous individuals mingled together in the most inextricable confusion, and in every conceivable position, with connected limb bones standing nearly upright, connected vertebrae describing vertical curves, etc., precisely as though in some ancient mud holes these huge monsters had become mired and died, and succeeding generations had trodden their bones down, and then left their own to mingle with them."

Much of the digging was done by Reed and a hired assistant. Carlin turned out to be lazy and something of a conniver. Reed, in contrast, proved to be

Digging at Como Bluff, from drawing by Arthur Lakes

industrious and tenacious as well as unwaveringly loyal to Marsh. Each morning the spry, bowlegged Reed would walk out to a quarry, perhaps several kilometers from the station, swing a pick all day, and then trudge back with a heavy load of bones. His request to Marsh for money to buy a pack horse was ignored. (Marsh was often insensitive to the needs of his field hands and slow in paying wages. His failing was "not niggardliness, but carelessness," according to his biographers, Charles Schuchert and Clara Mae LeVene.) Reed pressed on winter and summer, working under a tent pitched over the excavation pit to afford some protection against the snow and sun. He endured all, for he had become an enthusiastic hunter of fossils. "I wish you were here," Reed wrote in a letter to Williston in March 1878, "to see the bones roll out and they are beauties."

It was not long before the Como fossil riches attracted the notice of Cope. In April 1878, Williston wrote to Marsh from Como telling of a visit by a sullen man who called himself Haines. He claimed to be selling groceries, but nearly all of his conversation and questions were of fossils. Carlin suspected that the man was Cope himself. When he told the visitor that Cope was a "damned thief," the man sneered. But Williston obtained a sample of the man's handwriting, and finding it to be "a very neat fine and legible hand," unlike

Cope's, which he knew to be messy and illegible, decided that this could not be Cope but perhaps was one of his agents. Any visitor to Como thereafter was viewed with deep suspicion.

Cope, however, made his first invasion of the Como deposits by subversion, not direct assault. Carlin became the turncoat. He and Reed had had a falling-out in the autumn of 1878. Carlin had not been bearing his share of the work, and Reed resented this. As their relationship deteriorated, Carlin, who was still acting as station agent, apparently forced Reed to move from Como. Reed set up a camp at Rock Creek near one of his quarries, enduring the wintry winds alone in a tent. He called the place Camp Misery. In one of his letters to Marsh in March 1879, Reed reported that Carlin had gone over to Cope. He had opened his own quarry and was making regular shipments to Cope.

Reed remained steadfast in his loyalty to Marsh. After he had extracted the best fossils from a quarry, he smashed the remaining bones so that Carlin would find nothing there to send to Cope. It was an inexcusable practice for a professional fossil hunter, but all was fair in this war. Reed was ever vigilant against spies and intruders. When two strange men appeared one day at one of his quarries, he hurried over and asked them what they had in mind. They said that they had come to dig bones. He responded that they could not get any bones there. They would try anyway, the strangers said. Reed then moved to the top of the pit and with a pick began digging dirt and rock and sending it in an avalanche down onto the men below. The strangers told Reed to leave. "But I was not quite ready to go yet," he said in a letter. Reed stayed with the trespassers four days and covered up their work with more dirt "than they will want to dig out."

Hearing of this invasion, Marsh ordered Arthur Lakes to leave the Colorado digs and lend Reed a hand at Como, but the two did not get along well. Reed had balked at being "supervised" by Williston and resented Lakes even more. It annoyed Reed that, while he dug and sweated that summer, Lakes often sat off from the quarry and drew sketches of the site and the bones being extracted. The sketches seemed like a waste of time to Reed. But John Ostrom and John S. McIntosh, in their book *Marsh's Dinosaurs: The Collections from Como Bluff,* wrote: "These drawings of course were of great value to Marsh and to posterity. Most of the quarries could be relocated in recent years and recorded in this volume chiefly because of Lakes's scenic sketches of the Como area and his geologic sections. Without them, much (if not all) of this information would now be lost." Moreover, the sketches preserved the flavor of early dinosaur hunting more faithfully than many of the letters, journals, and other written accounts. But the antagonism between Reed and Lakes deepened. Marsh instructed them to work separately at opposite ends of the bluff, which they did, to productive effect.

Both Marsh and Cope, who had been masterminding operations by mail and telegraph from their home bases, visited the scene of their bone war in the summer of 1879. Marsh made a brief visit in June and is credited with discovering a new quarry. Cope arrived in August to reinforce his tenuous position there. Carlin had quit him earlier in the summer to return to railroading and was replaced by two brothers from Michigan named Hubbel. F. F. Hubbel seems to have been responsible for obtaining the most important fossils collected for Cope at Como, which included a nearly complete skeleton of the large bipedal carnivorous *Allosaurus* as well as an *Antrodemus* skeleton and some *Stegosaurus* vertebrae.

Cope apparently stayed at Como only a day or two, and Reed and Lakes took elaborate precautions to make sure that the rival could not snoop around their most valued quarries. Each of the Marsh collectors and several of the assistants spread out along the bluff, occupying the sites and covering some of the more interesting bones with tenting or dirt. Their most carefully guarded site was Quarry No. 9, which had just been discovered to contain an abundance of mammal as well as dinosaur fossils. Of this quarry, Reed wrote Marsh, "I think it is the best yet found here." This was, it turned out, no exaggeration. Of the 250 Jurassic mammal specimens currently known from North America, according to Ostrom and McIntosh, all but three were collected at Como Bluff and, with few exceptions, they came from Quarry No. 9.

Cope came and went without incident. Lakes found him less of an ogre than Marsh had led him to expect. In his journal, Lakes wrote: "The Monstrum horrendum Cope has been and gone and I must say that what I saw of him I liked very much his manner is so affable and his conversation very agreeable. I only wish I could feel sure he had a sound reputation for honesty."

Despite their differences, Reed and Lakes continued to mine the bluff and maintain Marsh's lead in dinosaur discoveries there. In November 1879, Reed made his greatest discovery, the virtually complete skeleton of *Apatosaurus excelsus.* According to Ostrom and McIntosh, this is still one of the finest brontosaur skeletons ever found. (*Apatosaurus* is the proper generic name for what most people call brontosaurs.) It is a centerpiece of the Peabody Museum at Yale. In February 1880, Lakes braved freezing temperatures, snowdrifts, and cave-ins to extract a stegosaur skeleton from the quarry at Robber's Roost, at the western end of the bluff. With its small head, its stout body encased in large bony plates, the two rows of huge plates rising from its spine, and a tail bristling with spikes, the stegosaur is one of the most bizarre of the dinosaurs. Lakes had a devil of a time collecting all these strange fragments. Once, when he struck a spring during digging, he had to bail with one hand and dig out bone with the other. "It was more like fishing for eels than digging for bones," Lakes wrote. "Meanwhile snowing and freezing hard so what with water mud and slush it is no wonder if some small pieces are missing."

For another decade, throughout the eighties, the rival forces contended for bones along the slopes of Como Bluff. Arthur Lakes left to return to teaching. William Reed eventually grew weary of the struggle and took up sheep herding. Frank Williston, Samuel's brother and one of Marsh's better collectors, went over to Cope. Other bone hunters, from Harvard and the University of Wyoming, tried their luck. Some independent prospectors came poking around.

The battle of Como Bluff was over by 1889. Cope, his finances strained by unwise investments in silver mines, had already withdrawn his crews. Fred Brown wrote his last letter to Marsh in June 1889, which seems to mark the end of Marsh's digging operations at Como. Other expeditions showed up there from time to time in the next couple of decades and made some significant finds. But now only a vivid imagination can reconstruct the scene. The Union Pacific runs to the south of the bluff, leaving behind only faint traces of the old roadbed by Como Station. Away from the station site, across the sage, just two or three of the quarries are readily identifiable. The others have long since been eroded by wind and rain.

Paleontologists to this day are still sorting out and analyzing the specimens dug up by the Cope and Marsh teams. Marsh's collectors uncovered twenty-six new species of dinosaurs at Como Bluff and the revealing skeletal remains of several other previously discovered ones. Cope's crews, nearly always outmanned, came up with few new species at Como but were more successful at the Colorado site. Overall, however, Cope seems to have come out ahead in the contest to identify and describe new genera and species of life. He is credited with describing 1,282 genera or species of North American fossil vertebrates, compared to Marsh's 536.

Despite the pressures to collect bones in volume and rush them east for analysis and reconstruction, the men who worked for Cope and Marsh were encouraged to exercise care in describing the configuration in which the fossils were found and the geology of the beds and in preparing the brittle bones for shipment. Lakes's sketches and reports were models of field description.

The development of techniques for encasing fossils, much as doctors make casts for broken bones, led to methods of protecting specimens that are still practiced by field paleontologists today. On their 1876 expedition to the Judith River, Cope and Sternberg sought to minimize damage to fossils by leaving them in their rock matrix and, before shipment, coating the entire block in a cast. They improvised with materials at hand, rice and bags. They boiled the rice into a thick paste, dipped burlap strips into the paste, wrapped the material around the bones, and let it harden into a stiff cast. Williston, working in Colorado for Marsh, devised a similar method using flour paste and strong paper. Lakes employed plaster of paris for the same bandaging purpose. Soon all the field hands were taking such protective measures.

In this way the bones arrived east from the paleontological battlegrounds of the American West. Some of the bones represented the first complete skeletons of the giants of the Age of Reptiles. The skeletons, reassembled in awesome poses more striking than the Crystal Palace reconstructions, came to dominate the museums of the world. They were a source of wonder and the inspiration for an upsurge of interest in prehistoric life. The study of dinosaurs gained a firm footing as an important branch of paleontology. More is the pity that Cope and Marsh could not accept this as a sufficiently worthy achievement for a lifetime in science.

THE TWO ADVERSARIES grew even more vicious about each other. Despair and frustration drove Cope to abandon all restraint. Not only had he squandered his inheritance in played-out silver mines, but he had lost what little support he had been receiving from the government, a loss he attributed to the machinations of Marsh. He could no longer compete with Marsh in fielding fossil collectors. He could not even muster the finances to complete publication of the work that he felt would assure his immortality as a great naturalist. All the while, Marsh's star rose higher and shone brighter. Over Cope's strenuous objections, Marsh was elected president of the National Academy of Sciences. He also was appointed vertebrate paleontologist of the United States Geological Survey, which assured him funding for expanding his laboratory and hiring more assistants.

Cope had the misfortune to be allied with the losing side in the political struggle out of which the Geological Survey emerged in 1879. He had worked at different times with the western exploratory expeditions of Ferdinand Hayden and George Wheeler. But the new consolidated agency was controlled by Clarence King and John Wesley Powell, both of whom were rivals of Hayden and Wheeler and friends of Marsh. An arrangement was made, however, for Cope to publish his research stemming from the Hayden survey; this he did in the volume "Vertebrata of the Tertiary Formations of the West," which was so comprehensive that it is still used and known as "Cope's bible." Powell, as director of the Geological Survey, would not authorize money for Cope to bring out his concluding volume, and all attempts by Cope to lobby for a special appropriation were unavailing. Cope suspected that Marsh's hand was behind all this, as it very likely was. Then in December 1889 came the most stunning blow of all. The secretary of the interior demanded that Cope hand over to the United States National Museum his collection of vertebrate fossils because they were deemed to be government property. He had accumulated them while a member of the Hayden survey, though he was an unpaid "volunteer." This was too much for Cope. He could not publish, and now he was about to lose his fossils, which were not only a scientific treasure but also represented his remaining financial nest egg.

Cope decided on revenge. For several years he had been gathering ammunition to use against Marsh if the occasion arose. Much of it he obtained from Marsh's unhappy assistants at Yale. They complained of chronically tardy pay. They chafed at the restrictions Marsh placed on their own independent research and at their employer's practice of taking credit for work they had done. Samuel Williston told Cope that many research papers Marsh published on dinosaurs were "chiefly written by me." Marsh, it seems, interviewed his assistants, then took their information and dictated a research paper without so much as acknowledging any contribution by others. As Cope once wrote to Henry Fairfield Osborn, one of his few allies, Marsh was "simply a scientific-political adventurer who has succeeded, in ways other than those proceeding from scientific merit, in placing himself in the leading scientific position in the country." Since Cope had dissipated most of his influence in the scientific establishment, he chose to take revenge by exposing Marsh through the newspapers. "When a wrong is to be righted, the press is the best and most Christian medium of doing it," Cope wrote in another letter to Osborn. "It replaces the old time shot gun & bludgeon & is a great improvement."

On January 12, 1890, Cope paraded his accusations and pent-up anger in an article written by William Hosea Ballou, a reporter who was a friend of his, and published in the New York *Herald.* Nearly every scientific mistake and personal shortcoming of Marsh was itemized. Cope also charged that

Marsh had plagiarized some of his work on the evolution of the horse from a Russian paleontologist, Vladimir Kowalevsky.

Marsh had obviously been keeping his own file on Cope's vulnerabilities. In a response published in the *Herald,* he dredged up again the fact that Cope had once put the head at the tail of a fossil. He charged that Cope had been seen in Kansas breaking open crates of fossils that belonged to Marsh. As for the accusation that he had stolen the work of Kowalevsky, Marsh recalled that Kowalevsky was a reckless scientist—like Cope, he implied. "Kowalevsky was at last stricken with remorse and ended his unfortunate career by blowing out his brains," Marsh said. "Cope still lives, unrepentant."

Cope received some satisfaction when in 1892 his campaign, in alliance with a southern congressman who thought it a fiscal disgrace that an agency would support Marsh's writing about "toothed birds," brought about a sharp reduction in appropriations to the Geological Survey. Marsh was thereupon notified that his money had been cut off and that he must submit his resignation as the survey's paleontologist. Cope had little time to savor this minor victory. He made a few brief trips west in search of fossils, once looking for dinosaurs in South Dakota. To make ends meet, he sold many of his remaining fossils to the American Museum of Natural History in New York and became a professor at the University of Pennsylvania. In 1897 he died in Philadelphia of kidney failure, at the age of fifty-seven. Marsh by then must have run through much of his Uncle George's inheritance, for in later years he was forced to ask for a salary from Yale. But honors continued to flow to him, including the Cuvier Prize from the French Academy. Then, in 1899, Marsh developed pneumonia and died at the age of sixty-seven.

Edward Drinker Cope and Othniel Charles Marsh had in large measure been responsible for opening the American West to the exploration of the Mesozoic. With their passing, the men Cope and Marsh had hired and trained took up the exploration.

7 *Collecting Far and Wide: North America*

ONE OF COPE'S best investments in paleontology was $300 that he mailed to Charles H. Sternberg in the spring of 1876. Among the dinosaur hunters who went into the field for Cope or Marsh and then carried on the work after the two rivals were gone, Sternberg stood out. Like so many of these hunters, he was a Westerner and an outdoorsman who, but for an early fascination with fossils, might have settled into the life of a rancher. Instead, responding to the lure of fossils, he became more like a cowboy or prospector, a plain, sturdy man moved by a restless, questing spirit. Such was the nature of these men. They were stubbornly independent; even when they worked for institutions, the ties were loose, and they were never happier than when they roamed months and great distances away from their sponsors. They were resourceful; they drew on their frontier upbringing in learning to travel light, live off the land, seek water in a desert, manage balky mules, maintain equally balky wagons and equipment, and devise ways to get the bones out of the ground and overland to the nearest railroad. They also were infinitely patient; they thought nothing of living in the field for months, sometimes years, and combing endless rock exposures for a piece of bone that might draw them to the discovery, after days or weeks of digging, of another dinosaur new to science—or might lead to nothing. Somehow these hunters, the premier field hands in the exploration of time, could bear the rigors and solitude of the quest, seeing it as a challenge more than a discouragement, even finding it exciting. Charles Hazelius Sternberg was this kind of fossil hunter for sixty of his long life of ninety-three years. The early turning point in his career seems to have come in 1876 when he received money from Cope to outfit his first concerted bone-collecting expedition.

Sternberg had appealed to Cope for assistance because he had determined nearly a decade earlier that, as he wrote, "whatever it might cost me in privation, danger, and solitude, I would make it my business to collect facts from the crust of the earth; that thus men might learn more of 'the introduction and succession of life on our earth.' "

Charles H. Sternberg

He made this commitment in 1867, when he was seventeen years old and had just migrated to Kansas. He had been born in the Susquehanna River Valley of upstate New York. His father was a Lutheran minister and principal of Hartwick Seminary in Oneonta. A fall out of a barn loft left Charles with a crippled leg the rest of his life, but this did not keep him from limping through the woods of New York and seeing his first fossils or from plunging into the vigorous life of frontier Kansas. On their arrival at Ellsworth, in western Kansas, Charles and his twin brother Edward witnessed a skirmish between soldiers and Indians and saw the "dead cart" creak solemnly through the town to pick up corpses tossed out of the saloons after a night of gunfighting. When the brothers went hunting on the plains, they found rich deposits of fossil leaves in the Cretaceous sandstone and gathered an impressive collection, which they sent to the United States National Museum in Washington. These fossils of semitropical leaves, more evidence of the sublime Cretaceous climates that must have been the dinosaurs' happy lot, awakened Sternberg's imagination and set him on his course. His father counseled against such an impractical profession as paleontology. "He told me that if I had been a rich man's son, it would doubtless be an enjoyable way of passing my time," Sternberg wrote years later, "but as I should have to earn a living, I ought to turn to some other business." He could not keep his mind on farm work, however, not with all those fossils around waiting collection.

It was in 1871 that Sternberg first joined up with Cope, when the Philadelphian made his initial foray into Kansas and the "territory" of Marsh. The next year Sternberg accompanied Leo Lesquereux, a Swiss paleobotanist, who found many impressions of vines, ferns, figs, and magnolia flower petals from Cretaceous times. Slowly, with none of the fanfare associated with work in animal resurrections, scientists were reconstructing the vegetation that the dinosaurs must have known. Sternberg then studied for a year under Benjamin Mudge at Kansas State and in 1876 hoped to join Mudge on an expedition for Marsh. But there was no place for him in the party. So he wrote to Cope.

"I put my soul into the letter I wrote him, for this was my last chance," Sternberg recalled in his autobiography, *The Life of a Fossil Hunter.* "I told him of my love for science, and of my earnest longing to enter the chalk of western Kansas and make a collection of its wonderful fossils, no matter what it might cost me in discomfort and danger. I said, however, that I was too poor to go at my own expense, and asked him to send me three hundred dollars to buy a team of ponies, a wagon, and a camp outfit, and to hire a cook and a driver."

Cope responded promptly, and with the money Sternberg equipped himself and set out to hunt Cretaceous fossils. His description of this expedition recalls the hardships and excitement of these early days of dinosaur hunting.

In that summer, as in many years thereafter, Sternberg operated out of the frontier settlement of Buffalo Station, an oasis with a great windmill and a deep well of pure water. Mudge's collecting parties also came here from time to time and shared the water with Sternberg's crews. The animosities of their warring sponsors did not extend to these field hands. They were conscientious in serving their sponsors, competitive to the core, but civil toward each other. Sternberg was a gentle man who sought fossils more than fame.

In the trackless arid land beyond Buffalo Station, Sternberg faced constant danger from Indians. He made an effort at camouflage by using brown duck for tenting and the wagon-sheet, hoping this would blend in with the drab, brown buffalo grass all around. "I never carried a rifle with me," Sternberg said. "I left it in camp or in the wagon, for I soon decided that I could not hunt Indians and fossils at the same time, and I was there for fossils."

Hunting water seemed often to be the more consuming occupation. Sternberg gave the following description of a typical day of searching for water and fossils at the same time:

> Both sides of my ravine are bordered with cream-colored, or yellow, chalk, with blue below. Sometimes for hundreds of feet the rock is entirely denuded and cut into lateral ravines, ridges, and mounds, or beautifully sculptured into tower and obelisk. Sometimes it takes on the semblance of a ruined city, with walls of tottering masonry, and only a near approach can convince the eye that this is only another example of that mimicry in which nature so frequently indulges. . . .
>
> All this time I am wandering along the canyon in search of water. . . . I know that there is water at the river but it is so far from my work that I go on and on in the hope of finding some nearer at hand. Dinnertime comes, and the day is so hot that perspiration flows from every pore. A howling south wind rises and fills our eyes with clouds of pure lime dust, inflaming them almost beyond human endurance.
>
> Still no water. The driver, with horses famishing for it, makes frantic gestures to me to hurry. To ease my parched lips and swelling tongue, I roll a pebble around in my mouth or, if the season is propitious, allay my thirst with the acid juice of a red berry that grows in the ravines.
>
> After hours of search, I find in moist ground the borings of crawfishes; with line and sinker I measure the depth to water a couple of feet below in these miniature wells. The welcome signal is given to Will, the driver, and he digs a well, so that both man and beast may be supplied.

The water was harshly alkaline, which, Sternberg wrote, "has the same effect upon the body as a solution of Epsom salts, constantly weakening the system." Still, they drank the water, having no choice, and settled into camp for a meal of antelope meat, hot biscuits, and coffee. If Sternberg had seen any fossils along the route, he and the driver would return with pick and shovel to the discovery site and "trace the remains to where the rest of the bones lie *in situ,* as the scientists say, that is, in their original position in their rocky sepulcher."

Then came the really hard work of digging into the slope of the ravine. It is one thing to pick up a fossil or two while walking along a stream or trail; it is quite another thing, a test of patience, endurance, and devotion to the task at hand, to pursue the search down into resisting rock. Few men met the test as well as the plodding Sternberg or described the experience with such affecting prose. This is what he wrote:

> Every blow of the pick loosens a cloud of chalk dust, which is carried by the wind into our eyes. But we labor on with unfailing enthusiasm until we have laid bare a floor space upon which I can stretch myself out at full length. Lying there on the blistering chalk in the burning sun, and working carefully and patiently with brush and awl, I uncover enough of the bones so that I can tell what I have found, and so that when I cut out the rock which holds them I shall not cut into the bones themselves.
>
> After they have been traced, if they lie in good, hard rock, a ditch is cut around them, and by repeated blows of the pick, the slab which contains them is loosened.
>
> This is then securely wrapped and strengthened with plaster, or with burlap bandages that have been dipped in plaster of the consistency of cream. In the case of large specimens, boards are put lengthwise to assist in strengthening the material, so that it will bear transportation. . . .
>
> All day, from the first streak of light until the last level ray forced me to leave the work, I toiled on, forgetting the heat and the miserable thirst and the alkali water, forgetting everything but the one great object of my life—to secure from the crumbling strata of this old ocean bed the fossil remains of the fauna of Cretaceous Times.
>
> The incessant labor, however, had a weakening effect upon my system so that I fell a victim of malaria, and when a violent attack of shaking ague came on, I felt as if fate were indeed against me.
>
> I remember how, one day, when I was in the midst of a shaking fit, I found a beautiful specimen of a Kansas mosasaur. . . . Its head lay in the center, with the column around it, and the four paddles stretched out on either side. It was covered by only a few inches of disintegrating chalk.
>
> Forgetting my sickness, I shouted to the surrounding wilderness "Thank God! Thank God!" And I did well to thank the Creator, as I slowly brushed away the powdered chalk and revealed the beauties of this reptile of the Age of Reptiles.

Later in the summer of 1876, Sternberg left the Kansas chalk beds and, as we have seen, accompanied Cope on their trip to the Judith River of Montana. Over the years he continued to collect the bones of dinosaurs and other reptiles, supplying valuable specimens to the museums of Europe and North America. At least eighteen fossil species were named in his honor. Though he remained a freelance collector most of his life, he established a fossil-hunting dynasty that continued his kind of quiet, diligent exploration for years after his death in 1934. Sternberg's three sons, George, Charles, and Levi, became renowned dinosaur hunters and paleontologists themselves. Many seasons all four Sternbergs would work in the field together, and it was on one such expedition, in 1908, that they made one of their most sensational dinosaur discoveries.

The Sternbergs were digging that summer in southern Wyoming, far out from the town of Lusk. Their luck was low, as was their food. While the elder Sternberg and his son Charles took the team and wagon into town for provisions, a round-trip that would take five days, George and Levi subsisted on boiled potatoes as they picked away at the bones of a duck-billed dinosaur in a sandstone cliff. On the evening of the third day, they finally traced the skeleton to its breast bone. The skeleton lay on its back with the ends of its ribs sticking up.

"There was nothing unusual about that," George F. Sternberg wrote. "But when I removed a rather large piece of sandstone rock from over the breast I found, much to my surprise, a perfect cast of the skin impression beautifully preserved. Imagine the feeling that crept over me when I realized that here for the first time a skeleton of a dinosaur had been discovered wrapped in its skin. That was a sleepless night for me."

When his father returned to camp two days later, George told him the news, and without delay all the Sternbergs rushed to the site. The skeleton was by then fully exposed. "Traces of the skin were to be seen everywhere," George said. One glance was enough for the father to realize that they had made a major discovery.

The Sternbergs had discovered what was, in effect, a dinosaur mummy. It was one of the duck-billed dinosaurs known as trachodont. Technically, this was not a true mummy, since none of the original body was preserved. It was actually the fossil of what had once been a dinosaur mummy. When the dinosaur died some 65 million years ago, the body mummified under extremely arid conditions, in which moisture evaporated from it before significant bacterial decomposition could set in. Somehow it escaped the notice of scavengers and was quickly covered with sand and then fossilized. There it remained, lithified skin, tendons, and shreds of flesh, until the Sternbergs came along.

The American Museum of Natural History acquired the specimen from the Sternbergs and displayed it in a glass case with a label describing it simply as a "Mummy Dinosaur." This gave paleontologists their first look at the scaly texture and patterns of dinosaur skin. Charles Sternberg called it "the crowning specimen of my life's work." Whenever he was in New York, he would visit the trachodont mummy, which once inspired this son of a Lutheran minister to write: "My own body will crumble in dust, my soul return to God who gave it, but the works of His hands, those animals of other days, will give joy and pleasure to generations yet unborn."

IN THE SUMMER following his graduation from Yale in 1884, John Bell Hatcher arrived at Long Island, Kansas, to serve as an apprentice to Charles Sternberg. Hatcher was a protege of O. C. Marsh, and by now, with Cope no longer able to finance extensive fieldwork, Sternberg was digging for Marsh and having considerable success. His quarry near Long Island held an abundance of bones of a prehistoric rhinoceros. But within days of his arrival, the impetuous Hatcher decided that he was less than impressed with Sternberg and itched to work on his own. He thought the older man careless and unscientific in his excavations. There may have been some truth to this accusation, which he made in a letter to Marsh. Or it may have been an expression of the intolerance of an ambitious young man, very full of himself. In any event, the two men resolved the matter by working on different sides of the ravine. They ended the season with a prodigious output—117 large wooden crates of rhino bones shipped back to New Haven. Even though Hatcher must have been difficult to work with, as he always would be, the kindly Sternberg had nothing but praise for the "bright, earnest student." Hatcher, he wrote, "gave promise of a future even then by his perfect understanding of the work in hand and the thoughtful care which he devoted to it."

Hatcher thus burst on the paleontological scene in characteristic fashion. Though a small, unassuming man in appearance, he was hardworking and in a hurry. Scientists would speak later of his "unbounded enthusiasm and strenuosity" and of his "marvelous powers of vision, at once telescopic and microscopic," that contributed to his "unequaled ability in the field." Hatcher cut a heroic figure as the consummate fossil hunter.

His was a brief career. Hatcher was born in Illinois in 1861, but his family moved to Iowa when he was young. As a boy, he was sickly, but not coddled. Working in a coal mine to build up strength and earn money for college, he became interested in geology and fossils. He took fossils he found to Yale, and they brought him to the attention of Marsh. By the time he graduated, at the age of twenty-three, Hatcher had only twenty years to live. During that span, though, he searched for bones from Montana to Patagonia.

It was in the Judith River country of Montana, in 1888, that Hatcher made the first of his most important dinosaur discoveries. He found part of a dinosaur skull with horns, which Marsh decided represented a new family of dinosaurs, the Ceratopsidae, or horned dinosaurs.

That same year, Hatcher met a cowboy in the Lance Creek country of eastern Wyoming who told him of finding a skull with "horns as long as a hoe handle and eye holes as big as your hat." Marsh, hearing this tale, ordered Hatcher to broaden the ceratops hunt. Returning to Wyoming for four straight seasons, from 1889 through 1892, Hatcher pieced together the bones to create a picture of what these dinosaurs had looked like. Nothing like them had ever been seen by fossil hunters. The ceratopsians had tremendous heads. Together with the armor frill at the back of the skull, which protected the shoulders and throat, the skulls were two meters long. The ceratopsian bodies were unusually squat for dinosaurs. They stood less than three meters high at the hips and had relatively short tails, which brought their overall length to less than seven meters. The heaviest and most distinctive of these horned dinosaurs, Hatcher found, were those called *Triceratops,* a three-horned animal. They had the bulk of an adult elephant and the menacing horned appearance of a rhinoceros. Surely the ceratopsians were a plentiful breed in the last 5 million years of the Cretaceous. From the Wyoming sites Hatcher exhumed more than fifty individual ceratopsians, thirty-three of which had more or less perfect skulls.

All the while, Hatcher had his eye out for the more humble Cretaceous creatures, the little mammals. Scientific interest in them had spread since the discoveries at Como Bluff's Quarry No. 9. When Hatcher found a tiny mammal jaw during his second season in Wyoming, Marsh urged him to put more effort into such exploration. "They are very rare," Hatcher telegraphed Marsh, explaining his low output, "and about two teeth represents an average patient day's work."

Suddenly, without explanation, Hatcher's mammal fossil production rose sharply. "I broke the record yesterday by finding 87," he wrote in August. Before the summer was over, he was able to ship more than 800 tiny teeth to Marsh. Paleontologists were amazed. How did Hatcher do it? Not until 1896, as an afterthought in a report on horned dinosaurs and Cretaceous mammals, did Hatcher reveal the secret of his success. He was raiding anthills.

The plains west of the Mississippi are dotted with the mounds of the red western carpenter ant. In excavating their subterranean homes, the ants encounter bits of bone and stone and carry them outside. They heap the fragments on top of their mounds. It is also thought that these ants go out of their way to seek small, hard objects—some of the pieces are as big as the ants themselves—to drag back to their mounds. Scientists are not sure why the ants do what they do. Perhaps the coarse material protects the anthills from rain and wind erosion. Perhaps the stones and bones act as a solar-heat storage layer to help incubate the ant eggs and larvae that are inside the mound. All that mattered to Hatcher was that many of the anthills held an abundance of tiny fossil bones and teeth. The ants had done most of his work for him. Hatcher used an old flour sifter to separate the bones from the dirt. Paleontologists to this day welcome the presence of anthills and harvest them for thousands of mammalian bones that reveal much about the tiny contemporaries of the last dinosaurs.

Despite the Wyoming success, Hatcher became disgruntled about his working arrangement with Marsh. Like other Marsh field collectors, he felt underpaid and unappreciated. He wanted a chance to do more analytical laboratory work, in part because he was increasingly crippled by rheumatism so that he often needed assistance to mount his horse. In 1893, therefore, Hatcher left Marsh to become a curator of vertebrate paleontology at Princeton. In the next decade, at Princeton and later at the Carnegie Museum in Pittsburgh, he published extensively on the many fossils he had discovered. But to the end he remained, first and foremost, a field collector, and his last major undertaking, his most ambitious and arduous one, was three expeditions to Patagonia.

Hatcher was not after dinosaurs in South America, but the mammals of more recent prehistoric time. Still, his experience is worth recounting, for it is the stuff of which legends are made—and Hatcher is legendary in vertebrate paleontology. He and his party once spent five months in wild country without seeing any other human beings. He pushed himself beyond endurance, once suffering a recurrence of rheumatism that laid him up for six weeks. He had little money—or at least, as legend has it, he brought little money with him. When the expedition finances sank distressingly low, Hatcher had a knack for securing a supplemental "grant." His knack was poker.

This small, balding man, so unprepossessing, with deep-set eyes that kept their secrets, could spend an evening in a distant town and leave its hapless inhabitants poorer but wiser. One such moment was reported by James Terry Duce, an oil geologist, who wrote in *The Atlantic Monthly:*

> One trick Fate played on the Patagonians was to send a rather subdued-looking American scientist from Princeton to collect fossil bones. . . . The Professor passed through every hamlet from Bahia Blanca to the

> Straits; the lessons were always the same . . . but as a rule the loose change of the community passed on to the bone hunter to be spent on science. When the famous night finally arrived on which Hatcher was to leave San Julian the whole countryside dropped in to exact revenge. The game started early and was one of those friendly Western games with everyone's six-shooter on the table. The stacks of pesos in front of Hatcher climbed up and up until he was almost hidden behind them; the whistle of the steamer sounded down the harbor. Hatcher announced that he must go. Someone suggested that they would not let him. He picked up his gun and his pesoes and backed through the door with a "Good night, gentlemen." No one made a move. The wind whooped round the eaves and Patagonia went back to its sheep-shearing with a wry smile on its face.

The exertions of fieldwork caught up with Hatcher in 1904. He had returned to the American West the previous summer, written a three-volume document on his Patagonian findings (not mentioning poker), and was trying to complete his exhaustive report on the ceratopsians. But an attack of typhoid fever proved fatal to his overtaxed body. In tribute, William Berryman Scott of Princeton said that John Bell Hatcher "fairly revolutionized the methods of collecting vertebrate fossils, a work which before his time had been almost wholly in the hands of untrained and unskilled men, but which he converted into a fine art."

EARL DOUGLASS had been sure that he would find dinosaur bones in the sandstone slopes overlooking the Green River in northeastern Utah. Where the river emerges from Split Mountain Gorge, in the Uinta Range east of Vernal, the exposed rocks are from the same Morrison Formation in which the collectors for Cope and Marsh had found their fossils in Colorado and Wyoming. John Wesley Powell had noted the presence of fossil "reptilian remains" when he came through here on the way to exploring the Grand Canyon. Sheepherders told tales of great bones scattered over the arid land. Like Jim Jensen in later years, Douglass heard these stories and went to see for himself. In the summer of 1908, he had discovered a weathered-out femur of a *Diplodocus* lying at the bottom of a narrow ravine. He searched the slopes above the ravine but could not identify the stratum whence the bone had come. With high hopes, though, he returned in the spring of 1909 to continue the search, accompanied by George Goodrich, a local farmer. It was now August 19 and still no luck.

In the shade of a juniper a hot, weary Douglass rested, fighting off despair, and cast his eyes over the crest of a nearby ridge to the steeper slope beyond. He was trying to decide where to look next. Recognizing in the distant slope the same gray sandstone that cropped out near where the *Diplodocus* femur had been found, Douglass scrambled over the ridge to it. He saw far above him a fossil bone, and fired his gun twice as the signal of discovery to his partner. By the time Goodrich came over the ridge, Douglass was certain that his discovery was something major. For in the wall of sandstone, etched in relief, were eight immense tail bones of a giant dinosaur. Even more impressive to Douglass was the fact that the bones were in a line, separated only by the space taken up by normal cartilage. This order, or articulation, was a strong clue that quite possibly he had come upon a complete skeleton of a dinosaur, something far more important than some isolated or scattered bones.

Douglass immediately got down to the work that would consume the next fifteen years of his life. This was a man who had known the peripatetic side of fossil hunting and seemed ready to settle down to one quarry. He had been born in Minnesota in 1862, educated in South Dakota, and had taught school for some years in Montana, where he also dug some fossils. He once went with a botanist on a collecting trip to Mexico and spent a year cataloguing specimens for the Missouri Botanical Gardens in St. Louis. In 1902, after studying under Scott at Princeton, Douglass joined the staff of the Carnegie Museum as an authority on early mammals. But Andrew Carnegie, the museum's wealthy patron, wanted something "big as a barn" for the new wing of the museum in Pittsburgh, and this was why Douglass had been looking for dinosaurs in Utah. He reported his discovery in a letter to William J. Holland, the museum's director, who went out to Utah to have a look. Douglass and Goodrich had been busy chipping away at the sandstone cliff. They had now exposed the better part of the entire skeleton, which Holland, after a close examination, designated *Apatosaurus louisae.* The species name honored Carnegie's wife. The steel magnate, not surprisingly, gave generously to support Douglass in his ambitious excavations at the "Carnegie Quarry."

This was to be no seasonal, expeditionary operation. Douglass planned to dig winter and summer. His wife, Pearl, and their baby son joined him in September, and together, with a fortitude inconceivable to us today, they faced and endured the blowing, freezing winter. They cut a wagon road through to the discovery site and their camp below it. Their main shelter was a frame of wooden two-by-fours covered with canvas in which they kept warm by an iron cookstove. The family slept in a nearby tent and stored their equipment in another tent. The three hired workmen slept in a sheepherder's wagon. In all except the worst gales, Douglass and the men went out each morning to blast away at the cliff, exposing more of the skeleton. The tail alone measured some nine meters. The entire animal must have been about thirty meters long, the largest and most complete dinosaur skeleton ever found.

Earl Douglass standing in front of partially exposed skeleton of Diplodocus

Over the weeks of arduous work Douglass and his men exposed the skeleton piece by piece. They found the pelvis, the limbs, the shoulders, all in their proper places. The form of the long, bulky creature became increasingly clear, except for the neck and head. Nothing from above the shoulders could be found. Douglass had a hunch, though, that the neck and head might be twisted back behind the rest of the body. Eventually, he found the bones of the long neck where he suspected they would be, doubled back along the body. But the skull was lost forever.

Where there was one skeleton so grand, Douglass believed, there must be others waiting to be exhumed. With the museum's approval, he settled down to make the quarry his life as well as his career. The camp became a homestead.

He built a solid log cabin near the site, bought a cow and some chickens, and cultivated a large vegetable garden. But he never lost sight of his reason for being in the Green River sandrock country. He was a scientific collector. He searched for plant, insect, and fossil specimens. He kept detailed journals of his observations, his discoveries, his disappointments. And, through it all, he and some workmen scraped, chiseled, dug, and blasted into the slope where they had found the *Apatosaurus.*

The Morrison Formation here was upturned. The fossil beds, once sediments of an ancient river basin, had been tilted by the earth's contorting forces from a horizontal plane to an almost vertical wall, some of which was exposed on the slope but much of which disappeared into the newer sediments laid down by the Green River. As he finished with the exposed parts of the bed, Douglass dug a trench into the layers of rock to one side of the fossil-bearing wall. The trench got longer and deeper with the years, as much as 200 meters long and 25 meters deep. Workers laid the track of a mine railroad along its floor to haul off the debris in dump cars. Few fossil hunters were ever more methodical or industrious than Earl Douglass.

One of his rewards was another remarkably complete articulated skeleton of a giant dinosaur, a *Diplodocus.* Douglass shipped tons of bones of this creature, skull and all, back to Pittsburgh for cleaning and analysis. It was the best example of a *Diplodocus* ever found. These herbivorous animals were almost as large as the *Apatosaurus,* but more streamlined and graceful in appearance. Holland, in his analysis, decided that this particular specimen represented a different species, which he named *Diplodocus carnegii.* Its namesake, Andrew Carnegie, was so pleased that not only did the *Diplodocus* become a centerpiece of the museum but he also had complete plaster casts of the skeleton made and distributed to many museums around the world.

From 1909 through 1923, Earl Douglass uncovered many other dinosaurs and shipped more than 350 tons of rock-encrusted bones to Pittsburgh. He had found more than a dozen species, including the remains of *Stegosaurus, Allosaurus, Laosaurus,* and *Camptosaurus.* One of his discoveries was the rare specimen of a juvenile, a *Camarasaurus.* Nearly all specimens of dinosaurs, until then, had been of fully grown adults.

In 1924, the Carnegie Museum had a surfeit of dinosaur bones and decided to suspend digging operations at the quarry. Douglass would not think of returning to Pittsburgh. His home was in Utah. But his homestead had not prospered to match his fondest dreams. He was unable to get enough water to irrigate anything more ambitious than his vegetable garden and could not support his family without the museum salary. So he arranged to dig some bones for the University of Utah, and for the next two years lived in Salt Lake City, where he prepared the bones for mounting in the university museum. It was not a happy arrangement. Douglass received no credit for the work, being regarded as no more than a menial assistant, and was denied a permanent position at the university. Years later, writing about Douglass in a chapter of *Mormon Country,* Wallace Stegner found that the fossil hunter's name had been "blotted . . . from the university's memory." He died in 1931 in comparative poverty.

The old Carnegie Quarry itself remains as a monument to Earl Douglass. In 1915, with the help of Holland, Douglass had persuaded the federal government to set aside the site as a national monument. Writing in his diary, Douglass said: "I hope that the Government, for the benefit of science and the people, will uncover a large area, leave the bones and skeletons in relief and house them in. It would make one of the most astounding and instructive sights imaginable." This was the genesis of Dinosaur National Monument, situated east of Vernal, Utah. Visitors can now walk along an enclosed gallery and, as if looking through a window on the past, see the fossils still embedded in the tilted sandstone stratum where Douglass discovered some of the most awe-inspiring Jurassic giants.

OF BARNUM BROWN it has often been said that he dug up more dinosaurs than any man who ever lived. Henry Fairfield Osborn, who as president of the American Museum of Natural History perhaps oversaw more field paleontologists than any other museum leader, once said: "Brown is the most amazing collector I've ever known. He must be able to smell fossils. If he runs a test-trench through an exposure it will be right in the middle of the richest deposit. He never misses."

The record shows that Osborn could be excused the hyperbole. When Barnum Brown arrived at the American Museum in 1897, it possessed not a single dinosaur fossil. When he died in 1963, one week short of his ninetieth birthday, the museum had one of the largest and most important collections in the world, the result in no small part of Brown's wide-ranging explorations over sixty-six years. His most imposing discovery was the first skeletons of *Tyrannosaurus rex,* the largest carnivore that ever preyed over the land.

Brown joined the museum in New York when he was a young graduate student in paleontology at Columbia University. He had been born in Carbon-dale, Kansas, in 1873. His parents named him after P. T. Barnum, the circus impresario, to give an alliterative flourish to his common surname. It was not an entirely inappropriate name, a museum writer once said, because Barnum Brown "put on one of the greatest animal shows on earth." He began rehearsing as a boy by picking up the fossils of extinct animals and at the University of Kansas came under the tutelage of Samuel Williston, who had settled into academia. Brown never completed work for his doctorate at Columbia because, as he said, he "tried to cover too much and was swamped." Mostly, the lure of the field was more compelling than that of the classroom and laboratory. In this Brown was like many of the dinosaur hunters of his time.

Yet in dress and carriage, he looked more like a scholar or church elder than a field explorer. One colleague spoke of Brown's "grave, sometimes melancholy countenance." His dress was usually impeccable, his bearing stiff and proper. He viewed the world and fossils through a gold-chained pince-nez. But women, it seems, found him utterly charming. He was an accomplished ballroom dancer and an engaging dinner guest. When he returned to excavation areas, the people of the towns, the women in particular, would meet his train and compete for the honor of driving him from the station to their homes for dinner.

Soon after he went to work for Osborn, Brown found himself with an American Museum expedition that was reopening the quarries at Como Bluff. At first, in the summer of 1897, the party had reason to feel that the Marsh hunters had picked the bluff bare. But Osborn and Brown eventually discovered a dinosaur skeleton, and Jacob L. Wortman, the expedition leader, came upon a second one—enough work for the rest of the summer. They struck it rich the following summer. Moving well north of the bluff, the party, under Wortman's leadership with the assistance of Walter Granger, came into a small valley littered with the bones of dinosaurs. Not far away, near the Medicine Bow River, stood ruins of a sheepherder's cabin. It had been constructed almost entirely of dinosaur bones, which were seemingly more abundant and accessible than timber. This became known as the Bone Cabin Quarry, which the museum's expeditions mined for all it was worth for seven more seasons.

By this time, Brown had moved on to more distant hunting grounds. In the winter of 1899, as Brown enjoyed telling the tale in later years, Osborn called him into his office early one day and told him that the Princeton University expedition was leaving for Patagonia at eleven o'clock that morning. "I want you to go along to represent the American Museum," the imperial Os-

Barnum Brown (left) with H. F. Osborn at Como Bluff

born directed the twenty-six-year-old Brown. The young paleontologist made the ship and remained in Patagonia for nearly two years, working with Hatcher's group.

Brown came into his own as a fossil hunter in the summer of 1902. He went by train to Miles City, Montana, and scouted the surrounding badlands south of the Missouri River. "This country promises well and has never been examined," he wrote Osborn in June. Here was a chance to explore fossil beds of the late Cretaceous, a period that had been relatively neglected in the rush by most dinosaur hunters to exploit the Jurassic fossils of the Morrison Formation. Hiring a wagon and team, Brown journeyed five days north to the little settlement of Jordan, then proceeded into rougher country still, at the head of Hell Creek. Cowboys and sheepherders had reported finding strange bones in these parts. Brown set up camp in a narrow valley near a stockman's cabin. Before dinner the first night, July 12, he picked up some *Triceratops* fossils. A few days later, Brown made his most sensational discovery. In the hard yellow sandstone bluff across the creek he found the first bones of what turned out to be an almost complete skeleton of *Tyrannosaurus rex.*

Brown spent the rest of that summer and most of the following one excavating the pieces of the skeleton. He blasted away the sandstone matrix, then worked out the bones with pickaxe and chisel. He applied shellac to harden the fragile pieces and wrapped others in burlap dipped in plaster of paris. The largest part of the skeleton, the stone-encrusted pelvis that weighed two tons, presented Brown with the sternest logistical test. Since it was too heavy to be carried by the wagon, he had a sturdy sled built and to it hitched a team of four horses. It took all day just to drag the pelvis out of the Hell Creek Valley to the road. Then began the 200-kilometer haul to the railroad at Miles City.

Five years later, in 1908, Brown made his second tyrannosaur discovery. Working north of the Hell Creek site, in an area now submerged by the Fort Peck Reservoir, he made a "ten strike," as he exclaimed in a letter to Osborn. Brown reported finding "15 caudals [tail bones] connected, running into soft sand." He dug a trench with pick and shovel and found the bones continuing into hard sandstone. "I have seen nothing like it before," Brown told Osborn, commenting on the apparent completeness of the skeleton. Osborn responded: "Your letter . . . makes me feel like a prophet and the son of a prophet, as I felt instinctively that you would surely find a Tyrannosaurus this season." The more he dug, the greater was Brown's excitement. "Magnificent specimen," he wrote in another letter. "This skull alone is worth the summer's work, for it is perfect."

Back at the museum in New York, the bones of the two tyrannosaur specimens were assembled with much care so that the world could gaze upon the fearsome aspect of the mightiest carnivore that ever lived. These creatures, which lived in the final millions of years of the Cretaceous, had enormous heads, more than one meter from front to back. The jaws were only slightly shorter and filled with saberlike teeth fifteen centimeters long and two and a half centimeters wide. The animals stood on stout hind legs that ended in huge birdlike feet with three forward-pointing toes armed with sharp talons, their weapons of prey. Brown's 1902 tyrannosaur was sold to the Carnegie Museum in Pittsburgh during World War II as a precaution against the creatures' second extinction, for there were widespread fears that New York might be bombed. (Some dinosaur bones were lost in World War I when a Canadian ship, bound for Britain, was torpedoed by a U-boat.) The 1908 tyrannosaur has stood its ground all these years at the American Museum, a menacing presence to wide-eyed children and the pride of Barnum Brown, who enjoyed introducing the skeleton to visitors as "my favorite child."

In 1910, acting on a tip from a Canadian rancher, Brown looked northward for new adventure and even more Cretaceous discoveries. He would spend six seasons exploring the Red Deer River country of central Alberta. Several Canadian geologists, starting with George Dawson in the 1870s, had called attention to the dinosaurs waiting to be unearthed in the western provinces, especially Alberta. Lawrence Lambe, of the Geological Survey of Canada, focused in particular on the sediments along the Red Deer. But it was Brown who mounted the most innovative and successful foray.

After reconnoitering the country, Brown decided on a water-borne approach to dinosaur hunting. A river barge would be his floating camp, and he would thus proceed downstream, tying up from time to time to dig and hauling the fossils out on the barge. A flatboat was duly constructed. Ten meters long and almost four meters abeam, the boat had ample room on deck for a fully established camp of wall tents and a cookstove. Brown knew how to travel: no time wasted looking for water, no troubles with contrary mules and wagon breakdowns. By the end of each season, the boat was piled high with plaster-coated fossils as it docked near a railroad. Among the prized specimens were virtually complete skeletons of the horned dinosaur *Monoclonius* and the crested duck-billed dinosaur *Corythosaurus.* Of even more interest to paleontologists, Brown had been able to dig fossils out of several different strata of the Cretaceous and thus bring back revealing evidence of the evolutionary development of dinosaurs in the last several million years of their existence.

Brown's impressive results proved embarrassing to Canadians. Why was this Yankee permitted to poach on Canadian dinosaur-hunting grounds? In response, the Geological Survey of Canada, having no sufficiently experienced bone hunters of its own, enlisted the services of Charles H. Sternberg and his three sons. Some of the Sternbergs had already done work in Canada, but in 1912, they were told to find some Red Deer dinosaurs before Brown could get them all. In their first season, the Sternbergs operated a traditional expedition, setting up a base camp near Drumheller and making trips downriver by wagon or rowboat. In 1913, however, they paid Brown the compliment of copying his floating-camp technique, and they, too, put in several productive years among the late Cretaceous beds. They provided Canadian museums with skeletons of many duck-billed, armored, and carnivorous dinosaurs as well as a specimen of the spiked-skull *Styracosaurus.*

The rough sandstone country of the Red Deer held enough dinosaurs to satisfy the competing Brown and Sternberg teams and the museums of two nations. (The area, part of which has been set aside as Dinosaur Provincial Park, is still being explored with fruitful results.) The dinosaur hunters had by now expanded their scope and skill and in the process gained a welcomed maturity. They could be rivals and, in response to tips and hunches and an informed reading of the landscape, race to be the first to resurrect some great beast from its lithified grave. And they demonstrated, to the relief of the paleontological profession, that you did not have to be a Cope or a Marsh to leave a legacy of accomplishment.

8 *Collecting Far and Wide: Europe and Africa*

A YEAR AFTER those amazing 1877 discoveries in the American West, workers opening a new gallery more than 300 meters down in a Belgian coal mine struck a rich seam of bone. They had tunneled into a bed of Cretaceous marl that dipped down through the deposits of coal formed out of the swamps of the more ancient Carboniferous period. A deep ravine must have cut through the coal there some 100 million years ago, and into this ravine fell many hapless dinosaurs whose bodies were soon covered in mud borne by flood waters. The mud turned to stone and the dinosaur bones turned to fossil. And there the fossils remained until humans in an industrial age had need of coal. The miners destroyed one skeleton before they realized that they had happened on a prehistoric graveyard. Then for the next three years paleontologists from the Royal Museum of Natural History in Brussels worked in the gloom of the coal mine gallery at Bernissart, near the French border. They extracted more than thirty virtually complete *Iguanodon* skeletons. Never before had so many specimens of a single dinosaur genus been found in one place, a circumstance affording scientists the rare opportunity to study the variations within a species and to re-create the lives and habitats of dinosaurs.

Louis Dollo was the paleontologist who made an illustrious career out of these iguanodonts of Bernissart. He was, in a sense, the first modern scientist of dinosaurs. Unlike most of his contemporaries, Dollo spent little time in the field hunting bones; they were brought to him in abundance. He felt no urge to compete in finding new species, larger species, or more species; he was a retiring man of the laboratory content to spend a lifetime drawing every possible inference from the bones of one species, the *Iguanodon.* In both respects, Dollo anticipated the working styles of many of today's outstanding dinosaur scholars. They may dig some, and many are anything but retiring, but the emphasis today is less on the hunt than on analysis. The battles are over ideas, not quarries.

Louis Antoine Marie Joseph Dollo was born in 1857 in Lille, France, and earned a university degree in civil and mining engineering. When he moved to Brussels in 1879, he worked as an engineer in a gas factory, but his interest in geology and zoology drew him to paleontology. He joined the staff of the Royal Museum of Natural History in 1882, which was when he first became acquainted with the iguanodonts of Bernissart.

Louis Dollo

Within a year, Dollo assembled and mounted his first skeleton and began to issue succinct interpretations of what these animals must have been like. Such pronouncements used to be based on little more than a tooth or a few isolated bones, and so their credibility derived more from the stature of the scientist than the facts at hand. Dollo, at first, had no stature—only an abundance of bones, the first skeletons of dinosaurs to be found with almost all of their bones in place. This gave him all the authority he needed to create a sensation in the world of paleontology and shape scientific thinking about dinosaurs.

The effect was to confirm or revise earlier ideas. Working with whole skeletons, Dollo could report with confidence that the *Iguanodon* stood and moved about on its hind legs, with its front limbs free to grasp leaves and branches from trees and other edible vegetation. It was not quadrupedal, as characterized in the Crystal Palace exhibit, but bipedal, as Huxley had postulated. A fully grown *Iguanodon* was strong and bulky, probably weighing seven tons, with a length of about ten meters and a height of five meters. Dollo also showed that the bony spike, which Mantell had taken for a rhinocerine nose horn, belonged instead as a claw at the end of the iguanodont's thumb. This was presumably one of the herbivore's weapons of defense.

Examining the *Iguanodon* tail, Dollo discovered an arrangement of ossified tendons crossing the vertebrae and surmised that this must have given the tail a stiffness and strength not previously supposed. A stiff tail, he concluded, could also have been one of the dinosaur's most effective weapons in combat. Long afterwards, scientists would determine that such a tail also served as a balance when some dinosaurs ran about on their two hind legs.

In his studies of dinosaurs, Dollo was venturing into what he called ethological paleontology. He looked beyond the bones to see how the dinosaurs had lived. One important clue, of course, was their anatomy, from which he inferred their posture, possible feeding habits, and defenses against predators. Dollo sought also to re-create the environment in which the dinosaurs had lived—a standard practice of paleontology now, but not then. He documented the fossils of animals, insects, and plants that shared the world of the iguanodonts. He studied the sediments for intimations of the ancient climate and landscape. Dollo was pioneering methods that would be developed with increasing sophistication in the twentieth century, giving us incredible visions of the past.

As for the iguanodonts of Bernissart, according to Dollo's educated re-creation, they must have browsed over a large river delta that covered Belgium, northern France, and southern England—contiguous then, 100 million years ago in the Cretaceous. The delta opened into a shallow sea that spread across southern Europe into Asia, the Tethys Sea. The climate was tropical. Conifers rose above the fern-covered ground. Among the crocodiles, turtles, frogs, and large flying insects the iguanodonts in great number lived and grazed, always alert to the sound and sight of predacious dinosaurs. The iguanodonts might fight off the predators with claw or flailing tail, or they might flee into the water. Some of them, for some reason, found themselves trapped in a deep ravine that became their tomb.

Dollo devoted more than twenty-five years to the study of those particular iguanodonts. He suspected that the bones represented two species: a large species, *Iguanodon bernissartensis,* and a smaller one, *Iguanodon mantelli,* in honor of Gideon Mantell. In this Dollo may have been mistaken. According to Edwin

Colbert, other scientists believe that the skeletons were from one and the same species. The anatomical differences, Colbert said, are probably those separating the two sexes.

Louis Dollo became a professor at the University of Brussels and extended his studies to other dinosaurs, including *Triceratops* and *Stegosaurus.* By the time he died in 1931, many other dinosaurs had been unearthed in Europe, from Scotland to Transylvania, from the Netherlands to Spain and Portugal. But no European discovery before or since has matched the iguanodont skeletons found in the coal mine at Bernissart.

IN THEIR PURSUIT of dinosaurs, as in other quests, Europeans could not confine themselves to their own continent. Dinosaur hunting, it seemed, followed the flag, which is how the first discoveries occurred in the Southern Hemisphere. British colonists in South Africa often sent mysterious bones to London for identification. The first of these to be documented as dinosaurian was a specimen from a Triassic prosauropod. Owen in 1854 described it and gave it the name *Massospondylus.* These animals, whose typical length was about four meters, were thought to be direct ancestors of the large Jurassic sauropods, the gigantic quadrupeds such as the brontosaurs. But, according to Alan Charig, many authorities now believe that the prosauropods were a side-branch of the sauropod family tree that died out at the end of the Triassic. "The Triassic ancestors of the largest beasts that ever trod the earth have yet to be discovered," Charig said. Other relics to reach London from South Africa in 1866 were identified by Huxley as another new Triassic prosauropod species, *Euskelosaurus.*

Little was heard again about African dinosaurs until Robert Broom began reporting on his explorations in the early 1900s. A Scottish doctor and student of mammalian origins, Broom had worked years in Australia investigating the anatomy of such primitive mammals as the egg-laying monotremes and the marsupials before moving to South Africa. His interest there was primarily in the fossil remains of some odd creatures known as mammal-like reptiles. From some of these animals, which thrived in the Permian and Triassic, evolved the tiny mammals that struggled to survive through the Age of Reptiles. Years before Africa was established as the birthplace of the human species, Broom found in the Great Karoo, an arid basin at the southern tip of the continent, ample evidence of the early ancestors of the first mammals. While tramping through the Karoo, he also came upon dinosaur bones, about which he delivered his first report in 1904. Broom described the bones of a brontosaurian creature, *Algoasaurus,* that lived in the early Cretaceous period. This encouraged paleontologists to step up the hunt for dinosaurs in Africa.

They soon found all the bones they could hope for at a place called Tendaguru. The fossil beds there proved to be the richest ever worked in the Southern Hemisphere.

In 1907, a German mining engineer, W. B. Sattler, was working 110 kilometers inland from Lindi, a seaport of German East Africa (later, under the British, Tanganyika; now, Tanzania). Near Tendaguru, a hill overlooking a rolling plain of grass and low trees, Sattler came upon several pieces of large bone lying on the ground and recognized them to be fossils. Eberhard Fraas, an authority on fossil reptiles who happened to be in the colony on a visit, was brought in to inspect the bones. Everywhere he looked in the tall grass he saw more bones that had weathered out of the hill. After collecting several specimens, he went home to Stuttgart and spread the word of a fabulous dinosaur site just waiting the pick and shovel. Money was raised to mount the Tendaguru Expedition.

Under the leadership of Werner Janensch, the young curator of fossil reptiles at the Berlin Museum, German paleontologists and hundreds of local people worked the site for four years, beginning in 1909. It was a monumental undertaking, more so than any of the dinosaur expeditions into the American West. There were no railroads, for one thing. It was two days by coastal steamer from Dar es Salaam south to Lindi, a torpid settlement with little to recommend it to visiting Europeans. Some years later, a British paleontologist, John Parkinson, wrote: "It is wise to land at Lindi self-contained; it is presupposed you have your bed and mosquito-net with you, also a cook and a boy. Quinine can be bought at the post office." From Lindi it was a four-day tramp in the tropical heat inland to Tendaguru. An infestation of flies precluded the use of donkeys and mules. Everything had to be hauled in on the heads and backs of local porters. The Germans hired 170 laborers the first year, increasing the number to 500 in subsequent seasons. Since many workers were accompanied by their families, the encampment below Tendaguru Hill was probably the largest ever associated with a dinosaur dig.

The excavation strategy was different here than at most other sites because the fossil-bearing strata were not readily accessible. Nowhere were they exposed in cliffs or ravines, places where erosion has done much of the preliminary work for paleontologists. So, once they had collected the scattering of surface fossils, Janensch and his workers had to dig pits deep into the plain and the hill. Their pits extended over an area of several kilometers, some of them being an hour's walk from camp. But all the labor bore voluminous and spectacular results.

Trains of porters carrying the ancient bones must have worn a bare-earth path from Tendaguru to the sea at Lindi. According to expedition reports, porters made 5,400 trips to Lindi during the first three years, taking out bones and bringing back supplies. They carried boxes of small bones on their heads and backs. Heavier bones, the femurs and intact vertebrae, were slung on a pole borne by two men. At Lindi, the bones were packed for shipment to Germany, with more than 1,000 boxes, or 250 tons, going out in the four years of digging.

The most prized trophy of the hunt was a Jurassic giant, *Brachiosaurus*—the "arm lizard." When Janensch assembled the bones of this creature back in Berlin, the result was truly impressive. This was apparently the largest of all quadrupedal, herbivorous sauropods, the formidable dinosaurs so familiar now. Unlike most dinosaurs, the brachiosaur's front legs were much longer than the hind legs. Its back sloped steeply upward and merged into a long neck at the top of which was a relatively small head. The head was 12.6 meters above the ground, high enough for the brachiosaurs to have peered over the top of a four-story building. Janensch estimated the animal's live weight at eighty tons, twenty times as heavy as a large African elephant. The brachiosaur skeleton now stands on display at the Natural History Museum of Humboldt University in East Berlin as the most visible result of the Tendaguru Expedition and of the long scientific career of Werner Janensch, who was born in 1878 and died in 1969.

Until recently, *Brachiosaurus* was judged to be the largest land animal that ever lived. But another dinosaur, perhaps a distant brachiosaurian relative, may have surpassed it in height and weight. This is the so-called ultrasaurus Jim Jensen found in Colorado in 1979. On the basis of the shoulder blade, the only major skeletal piece uncovered, Jensen estimated that this dinosaur stood at least one story higher than the Tendaguru brachiosaur.

The Germans never returned to Tendaguru after the 1912 season. With the colony passing into the hands of the British after World War I, the next expedition to the site was led in 1924 by W. E. Cutler, a University of Manitoba paleontologist with experience in the Canadian fossil beds. He was accompanied by Louis S. B. Leakey, the Kenya-born paleontologist who would become famous for his early-man discoveries. Cutler died in Lindi in 1925, and in subsequent years the digging was carried on by Parkinson and Boheti bin Amrani, a local man who had been an overseer in the German expedition. In his 1930 book, *The Dinosaurs in East Africa,* Parkinson attributed the concentration of dinosaurs at Tendaguru to the probable conditions there in the late Jurassic. The dinosaurs were living along the mouth of a river that emptied into a lagoon separated from the ocean by a bank of sand. "Doubtless many animals were caught and entombed in the lagoons," Parkinson wrote, drawing a not very pretty picture. "The rotting carcasses, buoyed up by the gases of decomposition, float onwards to slow dismemberment," he continued. "The sands in which the bones are found are invariably fine-grained, and for such weights to be transported by water having therefore necessarily a small velocity, argues that the whole was a mass of mud and sludge."

The British, mostly, continued the work of the Germans. But, before concluding operations in 1929, they extended them a little north to a place called Kindope, which had not been exploited by the Germans. There the British found, among other fossils, a dinosaur resembling the plated stegosaurs of North America, though slightly smaller at lengths of about five meters. They were named *Kentrosaurus.*

Fossil hunters had by now established the global distribution of dinosaurs. Their bones had been unearthed in England first; then in the rest of Europe, most notably at Bernissart. They had been found in profusion in North America, most notably in the western states and provinces. In 1882, the first bones were identified in South America, in Argentina. In 1924, some dinosaur specimens came to light in Australia. And a treasure of fossil remains in Asia had inspired a new adventure in dinosaur hunting.

9 *Gobi: The Stuff Is Here*

EARLY ON THE MORNING of April 21, 1922, a party of men left the frontier town of Kalgan, north of Peking, and made for the gate in the Great Wall beyond which lay Mongolia. Caravans without number had taken this route before, travelers of all descriptions, but this was one of the oddest. Three sturdy Dodge motorcars and two Fulton trucks bounced over cart tracks and churned up the steep grade to the north of Kalgan. In them were several adventurous American scientists, naturalists and paleontologists and geologists, and their retinue of mechanics, cooks, and helpers. They had been preceded days earlier by a caravan of seventy-five camels bearing cans of gasoline and boxes of other supplies (180 kilograms on the back of each camel) to be dropped off at designated caches along the intended route out through the Gobi, the great desert that spreads east and west for 3,000 kilometers through the center of Mongolia. These forty men, five motor vehicles, and seventy-five camels formed the Central Asiatic Expedition, organized and led by Roy Chapman Andrews. He described the undertaking as "the biggest land scientific expedition ever to leave the United States." Nothing like it had ever been seen in Asia, or in the annals of dinosaur hunting; though, strictly speaking, this expedition was not supposed to have anything to do with dinosaurs. Its primary objective was nothing less than a search for the origins of man. Such an ambitious aim had aroused suspicion among incredulous Chinese and Mongol bureaucrats. They could hardly believe that sane men would risk the Gobi solely to dig up some old bones; it must be a cover story. They suspected the lure was more likely gold or oil, or else the country itself, and that these men who called themselves scientists were in fact prospectors or, worse, agents of American imperialism. This they could understand, if not condone, for such were the motives that had long attracted outsiders to China and now Mongolia. Nonetheless, through letters of introduction from American officials and with the intervention of influential people in Peking, Andrews had obtained the necessary permits and set forth as the snows melted and the warmth of spring returned to the Gobi. Passing through the gate of the Great Wall, Andrews looked back on the blue haze of the Shansi Mountains of China and ahead to the undulating plain and rounded hills of Mongolia. It is a wonderful thing to be in an exotic land and alive with romantic energy.

In the year he had spent in Peking preparing for the expedition, Andrews had listened to the counsel of many who warned against driving from Kalgan to Urga (now Ulan Bator), the capital of Mongolia. "We were little less than fools," he recalled being told. The Gobi was a wasteland of gravel, camel sage, and thorny bushes. In the summer the searing heat of day could be unbearable, but nothing compared to the freezing winds they would face if they should overstay and be stranded there in the winter. The human elements might be no more hospitable. Brigands menaced the caravan routes and political warfare rent the countryside. While Andrews was wintering in Peking, armies of Mongols succeeded in driving the Chinese out of their land. Many times in its travels the expedition would come upon evidence of unrecorded battles fought in the dark night of isolation: heaps of spent rifle shells, cartridge clips, and tattered uniforms. No sooner had the Mongols rid themselves of the Chinese than they found their land infiltrated by Russians from the north and west. Bolshevik troops had entered Mongolia in pursuit of unrepentant White Russians and, after taking care of them, stayed on to take advantage of the political chaos in the aftermath of the Chinese wars. Mongolia gradually came under Russian control during the 1920s, that is to say during the time Andrews was there looking for the origins of man and whatever else he might find in the way of old bones.

In Peking there were those who scoffed at the idea of hunting fossils in the Gobi. "We might as well search for fossils in the Pacific Ocean," Andrews said he was told. It was, indeed, a speculative venture. "Gamble" was Andrews's word for it. The fossil history of the remote parts of Asia, including Mongolia, was completely unknown. The Gobi had been crossed and recrossed by several explorers and naturalists in the late nineteenth century, but having no time for intensive exploration, they had satisfied themselves with sweeping surveys. If they found any fossils, these were unreported, with one exception. In 1892, a Russian geologist, Vladimir A. Obruchev, picked up a single fossil rhinocerous tooth along the caravan route from Kalgan to Urga.

Not much to go on, to be sure, but the genesis of the Andrews expedition lay in a prophecy, not in any one fossil. In 1900, Henry Fairfield Osborn had prophesied that in Central Asia paleontologists would find the birthplace of primitive man. In the absence of facts—the great hominid discoveries in Africa were yet to be made, and Central Asia remained a virtual blank on the map of natural science—Osborn's speculation could not be refuted and, given his considerable influence, could not be ignored. The idea gained some scientific respectability a decade or so later when William Diller Matthew, curator of vertebrate paleontology at the American Museum of Natural History, postulated in a study of climate and evolution that Central Asia might well be the Garden of Eden of most mammals, if not of man himself. From there they would have migrated to Europe and Africa and to the Americas. It was a hypothesis begging to be investigated in the field. This was where Andrews entered the picture, a man looking for adventure and determined to find it.

Andrews believed with all his heart that he had been born to be a naturalist and explorer. "Nothing else ever had a place in my mind," he wrote in *Ends of the Earth,* published in 1929. "Every moment that I could steal from school was spent in the woods along the banks of Rock River or on the water itself. . . . To enter the American Museum of Natural History was my life ambition." He left the banks of the Rock River near his hometown of Beloit, Wisconsin, in 1906, after completing college, and headed straight to New York and the American Museum. His first job there was scrubbing floors in the taxidermy department. He would have done anything to get his foot in the museum door. In only seven months he was off on his first "expedition"—to Amagansett, on the south fork at the end of Long Island. A right whale had been harpooned and beached, and Andrews accompanied one of the museum taxidermists to buy it and bring back the bones. Thus began his interest in cetology, and over the next several years he collected and studied whales in Alaska, British Columbia, Korea, and Japan, all with unflagging enthusiasm. There was in his approach to natural history a Teddy Roosevelt zest. Writing about his work with whales, Andrews said: "I even went so far as to crawl into the tummies of several just to see what sort of apartments Jonah had rented."

A flair for writing and lecturing proved to be his forte. With lantern slides and language evocative of faraway places and uncommon creatures, the flamboyant Andrews commanded the rapt attention of audiences across the country. Men of wealth who heard him wrote out generous checks to the museum and to his expeditions. In his twenty-two books, all full of thrilling tales written in a popular vein, Andrews shared the excitement of paleontology and natural history with millions of people, especially the young. Speak of dinosaurs and other great fossils to anyone whose childhood ended before the 1950s and he or she is likely to recall only one person's name: Roy Chapman Andrews. "As a kid," said Malcolm C. McKenna, an American Museum curator today, "I got interested in paleontology because of Andrews and his books."

Andrews got interested in exploring the Gobi because of Osborn and Matthew. The idea of searching for the origins of man in a strange and remote land fired his imagination; looking for dinosaurs had not crossed his mind. By 1920, he had made a couple of reconnaisance trips along the border of China and Mongolia, near Tibet and Burma, and then briefly into Mongolia itself. Having got a feel for what had to be done, he personally raised most of the money from wealthy patrons to finance the undertaking and traveled to Peking in April 1921 to get everything ready. Andrews proved to be a master field-trip organizer.

As he essayed the situation, the problem was to transport a group of specialists from several fields of science, such as paleontology, geology, and botany, deep into Mongolia, give them ample time for intensive exploration at promising sites, and get them out before the snows of October. But how? No railroad existed in the whole of Mongolia. Camels, which previous explorers had used, averaged only 16 kilometers a day (10 miles). At that rate, he realized, the expedition would be severely limited in how far it could penetrate into Mongolia and how much time could be devoted to digging. The solution, it seemed to Andrews, was to rely on a combination of camels and, for the first time in a major scientific expedition, automobiles. An advance caravan of camels would haul in the gasoline; for one field season, 125 camels carried 4,000 gallons of gasoline, 100 gallons of oil, 3 tons of flour, 1 1/2 tons of rice, and stores of other food. The scientists would follow two weeks later in the automobiles, laden with spare parts, digging tools, tents, and rations of food, water, and more gasoline. Andrews figured that, since the autos should make 160 kilometers (100 miles) a day, compared to the camels' 16, the expedition should therefore be able to accomplish ten years of work in one season. The automobiles, equipped with extra-strength springs, were shipped from the United States to Andrews in Peking.

There could be no thought of living off the land in a place as desiccated as the Gobi. The expedition might purchase a sheep here, shoot an antelope there, or stock up in Urga, but nothing could be counted on. All their needs had to be anticipated, and the necessary provisions carried with them. And Andrews, though brave and hardy, did not believe in skimping on creature comforts. "Eat well, dress well, and sleep well is a pretty good rule for everyday use. Don't court hardship," he wrote in his summary report on the expedition. "Neither do I believe in adventure." On this point Andrews quoted the motto of the Arctic explorer Vilhjalmur Stefansson: "Adventures are a mark of incompetence." Even so, to stay-at-homes, the travels of Andrews qualified as incomparable adventures, particularly given the way he would describe them.

While in Peking, Andrews gathered as supplies tents of blue cotton cloth and felt-covered yurts (the dome-shaped Mongol tents), flannel shirts and khaki breeches, sheepskin coats and trousers for the cold nights, sheepskin sleeping bags, dried vegetables from New York, dried milk and powdered eggs, some canned food and cured meat, and weapons for shooting any game (or attacking bandits) along the way. He also laid in "a few bottles of whiskey for birthday celebrations."

All this having been moved up to Kalgan by rail, Andrews waited until the lilacs bloomed in the courtyard of his Peking headquarters and then journeyed there himself with his party of scientists and helpers. These included two geologists, Charles P. Berkey and Frederick K. Morris; Davidson Black, a physician and anthropologist from the Peking Union Medical College; Bayard Colgate, a wealthy young man who interrupted an around-the-world trip to serve as the expedition's chief of motor transport; and J. B. Shackelford, a photographer. They were accompanied by a representative of the Mongolian government, who served as a guide, interpreter, and emissary to the local officials. But the most important scientific member of the expedition was Walter Granger, the chief paleontologist and second-in-command.

Andrews was the promoter, organizer, and leader, an adventurous explorer of the Victorian school, but he was not the scientist of the expedition. He lacked the training and experience of a professional paleontologist, and the patience as well. He admitted as much, calling himself a "restless spirit" temperamentally unsuited to be a paleontological collector. "Disappointments and successes," Andrews said, "send me too easily into the blackest depths or to the pinnacle of happiness, and particularly I cannot curb my impatience sufficiently when a specimen has been found." His carelessness with specimens became a museum legend; for years museum people spoke of a specimen being "RCAed" if it had been badly broken up through mishandling. Andrews's restlessness seemed to leave him too little time for study. "Roy was a peculiar fellow," Robert Cushman Murphy, an ornithologist at the American Museum, once told a writer for *The New Yorker.* "He was full of hiatuses in his knowledge. He was exposed to a great many things that never took." Granger, however, made up for many of Andrews's scientific deficiencies. The two men had similar beginnings. Granger, too, had grown up with a keen interest in wildlife and a desire to work for the American Museum. He was not quite eighteen years old when he left his native Vermont, in 1890, and found a job as a janitor and helper in the same taxidermy department where Andrews would work on his arrival. In a brief time, Granger learned about dinosaurs at Como Bluff and Bone Cabin Quarry and became an authority on primitive mammals. Colbert remembers him as a "big, jovial person with a hearty laugh" whose very presence contributed to the smooth operation and success of an expedition, and seldom in the forty-five years of his career did a season pass without his presence in the field somewhere.

In the season of 1922, Granger joined Andrews on the first of what would be five journeys into Mongolia undertaken by the Central Asiatic Expedition between then and 1930. The expedition was misnamed; Mongolia, which turned out to be the only destination, lies in northeastern Asia. And for all anyone knew, their efforts might prove to be foolish and in vain, as they had been warned; as futile as searching for fossils in the Pacific Ocean. Still, they hoped to find fossils of primitive man—though, in truth, they had no reason to know what they would find and no presentiment that they were entering one of the world's richest prehistoric boneyards.

THE ANDREWS EXPEDITION made good time after passing through the gate of the Great Wall, and in four days the motor caravan had traveled 425 kilometers from Kalgan, approximately halfway to Urga. The men had reached the basin known as Iren Dabasu, and if anything could be more bleak than the terrain they had already traversed, this was it. Conical mounds of sand rose like giant anthills out of the basin floor. Salt marshes covered the lowest part of the basin. In more peaceful times, Chinese laborers, recruited in Kalgan, collected the salt and shipped it south in caravans of oxcarts. But these were not peaceful times, and Andrews came upon a scene of stark desolation. No salt workers or caravans camped at the wells, a lama temple nearby was abandoned, and the mud huts of the telegraph station were all but deserted. The cache of gasoline was there, however. His camel caravan, Andrews learned, had passed that way two weeks earlier.

He decided to make camp a little to the west at the base of some gray-white ridges. While he supervised the pitching of tents, Granger, Berkey, and Morris drove about reconnoitering the area. At sunset, the scientists' two cars swung around a brown bluff and roared into camp. Andrews looked at Granger and

Towing one of the Fulton trucks in sand of the Gobi Desert

saw that his eyes were shining with excitement. Berkey was "strangely silent." Granger dug into his pockets and pulled out a handful of bone fragments. Berkey and Morris did likewise. "Well, Roy, we've done it," Granger exclaimed, between puffs on his pipe. "The stuff is here."

While dinner was being cooked, Granger wandered off along the ridge near the camp and found more fossils. The following morning, before breakfast, the scientists were off looking again. Berkey picked up a fragment of the femur of something. To Granger it appeared reptilian. Presently, Granger walked up to the crest of the ridge and fell to his knees. He began brushing the sand away from something embedded in the ground. It was the tibia of a large reptile.

Any doubt that Granger might have harbored was now dispelled. This was the bone of a dinosaur, the first known in Mongolia and one of the first known anywhere in eastern Asia. A jubilant Andrews could forget the skeptics back in Peking, for there were fossils in Mongolia and he had found them. The fossils were much older than humans or anything he had had reason to expect to find.

Granger and a few others remained for a week at Iren Dabasu. The setting might be foreign, but Granger's work habits were the same as at Como Bluff: he collected bones, soaked them with shellac to harden all the loose particles, and encased them in burlap and flour paste for the long journey to the laboratory. Granger's group would catch up with Andrews and the others at Urga, where Andrews had proceeded straightaway to conclude travel arrangements with Mongol officials. Urga was a rough, polyglot city strung along the north bank of the Tola River; he came first to the teeming Chinese quarter, then the Russian quarter, and finally the city proper, where unrest and political intrigue were epidemic. It is amazing that Andrews succeeded in obtaining the necessary passports. While he was there, a friend on whom he had counted, a former interior minister, was dragged out of his house and shot. Nonetheless, Andrews managed by the middle of May to satisfy the wary officials that his expedition represented no threat to the country's uncertain security.

The expedition, now regrouped, headed back into the Gobi, this time to the southwest of Urga and to their major discoveries. The day after their arrival at Wild Ass Camp, so named by the expedition because there they had happened on and given futile chase to three dun-colored asses, Shackelford, the photographer, found a beautifully preserved foot bone of some kind of ancient rhinoceros. "In some uncanny way," Andrews wrote with a touch of envy, Shackelford the amateur collector "seemed to know exactly where the best specimens lay." Not to be outdone, Andrews scratched around and uncovered some crumbling teeth. It took four days of meticulous work for Granger to extract the teeth from the ground and to expose the skull to which they belonged. Shackelford's foot bone and the skull proved to be the most scientifically interesting finds of the expedition. Back in New York, in 1924, Osborn determined that these had belonged to the giant extinct fossil rhinoceros *Baluchitherium,* previously known only from Baluchistan. This was the largest land mammal ever known to exist.

Turning back east to begin the return journey to China, the expedition followed an old caravan route that brought them one afternoon to the edge of a vast basin bordered by walls of red sandstone. The sight was breathtaking. The setting sun seemed to turn the rock into a bank of glowing embers. The dazzled men named them the "Flaming Cliffs" of Shabarakh Usu (now called Bain-Dzak), and Andrews the writer was ecstatic. "From our tents, we looked down into a vast pink basin, studded with giant buttes like strange beasts, carved from sandstone. One of them we named the 'dinosaur,' for it resembles a huge *Brontosaurus* sitting on its haunches. There appear to be medieval castles with spires and turrets, brick-red in the evening light, colossal gateways, walls and ramparts. Caverns run deep into the rock and a labyrinth of ravines and gorges studded with fossil bones makes a paradise for the paleontologist."

Shackelford once again made the first and most significant discovery. On the first day at Flaming Cliffs, "as though led by an invisible hand," said Andrews, who was amazed now as well as envious, Shackelford walked straight to a small pinnacle of rock on the top of which rested a white fossil bone. Granger, examining it, concluded that this was a piece of a reptilian skull. It was packed away with care. (The hair the camels shed in June and July made excellent packing material.) Then, going down into the basin, all the men fanned out, combed the sand and rock, and returned with all the fossils they could carry. Granger brought in, among other things, a piece of eggshell. The men scarcely gave it a thought, believing it was merely the shell of some fossil bird. They would learn the truth the next year.

With reluctance Andrews departed Flaming Cliffs, vowing to return. "We could hardly suspect that we should later consider it the most important deposit in Asia, if not in the entire world," he wrote. But the wind blew cooler with each day and the expedition had to reach China by October. Fortune had favored them so far: they had found their first fossils early in the journey, they had successfully negotiated their way through the bureaucracy at Urga, they had been overwhelmed by the splendor and paleontologic promise of Flaming Cliffs, they had been spared anything more than minor trouble with the cars (worn clutches and gears, immobilization in soft sand or wet soil), and they had somehow avoided any traffic with bandits or civil warriors.

Andrews brought the expedition safely back to Kalgan in the last days of September, just ahead of an early winter. Directly they reached Peking, one man was dispatched to New York with a preliminary report and the reptilian skull found by Shackelford at Flaming Cliffs. In due course that winter, Osborn cabled: "You have made a very important discovery. The reptile is the long-sought ancestor of Triceratops. It has been named Protoceratops andrewsi in your honor. Go back and get more."

This was exactly what Roy Andrews intended to do, when spring came again to Mongolia.

ANDREWS SAW many changes on the great plateau when he entered Mongolia in April 1923. Robust life had returned along the caravan route from Kalgan to Urga: yurts clustered near almost every well, flocks of sheep and goats grazed on the southern grassland, more land had come under cultivation, and many camel caravans moved ponderously in each direction with skins and furs bound for Kalgan and merchandise headed for Urga. A few other motorcars joined the traffic this year, and quite a sight some of them made.

Andrews remarked on seeing ten to fourteen Chinese merchants, and as many bedrolls, squeezed into a five-passenger Dodge car and headed for the big deals in Urga. Now, more than a year after the cessation of hostilities between Mongolia and China, the country was open for business.

This is not to say that hazards were now few. Even more than the year before, bandits were a scourge of the travelers along the caravan routes, particularly just north of Kalgan. Andrews had heard the disquieting news while he was in Kalgan. A week or so before he left, two Russian cars were stopped and looted by Chinese soldiers; one man was killed. The soldiers were to be feared almost as much as the bandits. Charles Coltman, who had been on the 1922 expedition, was murdered in the winter by Chinese soldiers at the border near Kalgan. Caravans were attacked with impunity. A common occurrence in Kalgan was the "trial" of some bandits and their execution in the dry river bed that runs through the city's center. The Andrews expedition took the precautions of spending its first night on the road at a Chinese inn guarded by soldiers and of obtaining a reliable military escort through some of the more dangerous territory. Days later, though, when Andrews led a small party back to Kalgan to pick up some equipment that had been late in arriving, he had an encounter with three mounted bandits. He escaped harm by charging them with his car, causing their horses to buck and rear with fright. The bandits, he said, "fled in a panic."

The expedition made for Iren Dabasu, reoccupied its campsite of the previous year, and settled down to a month of fossil collecting. At the request of Andrews, the American Museum had assigned three additional fossil collectors to the new Central Asiatic Expedition. They were George Olsen and Peter C. Kaisen, longtime museum staff workers, and Albert F. Johnson, who had worked with Barnum Brown in Alberta. One young Chinese who had been on the 1922 journey was promoted from mess boy to paleontologic assistant to Granger.

Twelve men could have worked twelve months without exhausting the fossil treasures of Iren Dabasu. Johnson developed the richest quarry, a source of bones of both carnivorous and herbivorous dinosaurs of several species; many were duckbill dinosaurs. He also found some smooth curved fragments, which remained so many odd pieces of a lost jigsaw puzzle until the end of the season—after the big discovery at the Flaming Cliffs of Shabarakh Usu.

Flaming Cliffs was this expedition's ultimate destination. Following their tracks of 1922, the men reached Shabarakh Usu on July 8 and remained five weeks. By dinner the first night, each collector had found and begun to excavate a dinosaur skull. Fossils were everywhere, but the discovery that would bring worldwide fame to the expedition occurred five days later, on July 13.

George Olsen returned to camp that afternoon to report seeing three fossil eggs in the sandstone. He could have been mistaken, of course. The stone was Cretaceous and probably too early to be containing eggs of large birds. They might not be eggs at all, merely some odd geological phenomenon in which stone is shaped like eggs. But when Granger, accompanying Olsen to the site, inspected the brown striated shells, he had to conclude: "These must be dinosaur eggs. They can't be anything else."

George Olsen (left) and Roy Chapman Andrews at nest of dinosaur eggs in Mongolia

Dinosaurs were reptiles and reptiles, with rare exception, lay eggs. The hard-shelled egg, in fact, was the evolutionary invention, along with scales, by which reptiles won the land. The early amphibians, like frogs and salamanders today, had to lead a double life: they could leave the water, but had to return to it frequently not only to keep their soft skin moist but to lay their eggs. The ordinary amphibian eggs were specks of embryo in jelly, which would quickly dry up out of water. Reptiles in time developed a way to sever their aquatic ties. They pioneered the amniote egg, a self-contained capsule that could be laid anywhere. The embryo, developing inside the firm porous shell, was surrounded by the amnion, a sac filled with albumin as a substitute for water and yolk as the food supply. This egg, which reptiles evolved 300 million years ago in the Carboniferous, serves as a telling reminder of the reptilian ancestry of mammals and birds. Humans, as mammals, share this kinship. Though we do not lay eggs, the human egg, when fertilized, becomes surrounded by a sac of amniotic fluid much like that of the reptilian egg. (The covering of the human egg also contains a tiny yolk sac; the embryo, however, is nourished through the placenta from the mother's blood.) And the fluid in this sac is salty. Evolution has yet to eradicate this vestige of our origins in the sea, whence came the first fish to crawl on land, the amphibians that lived in both worlds, and then the reptiles that, with the advent of the hard-shelled egg, were able to make a permanent home on the land and give rise to mammals.

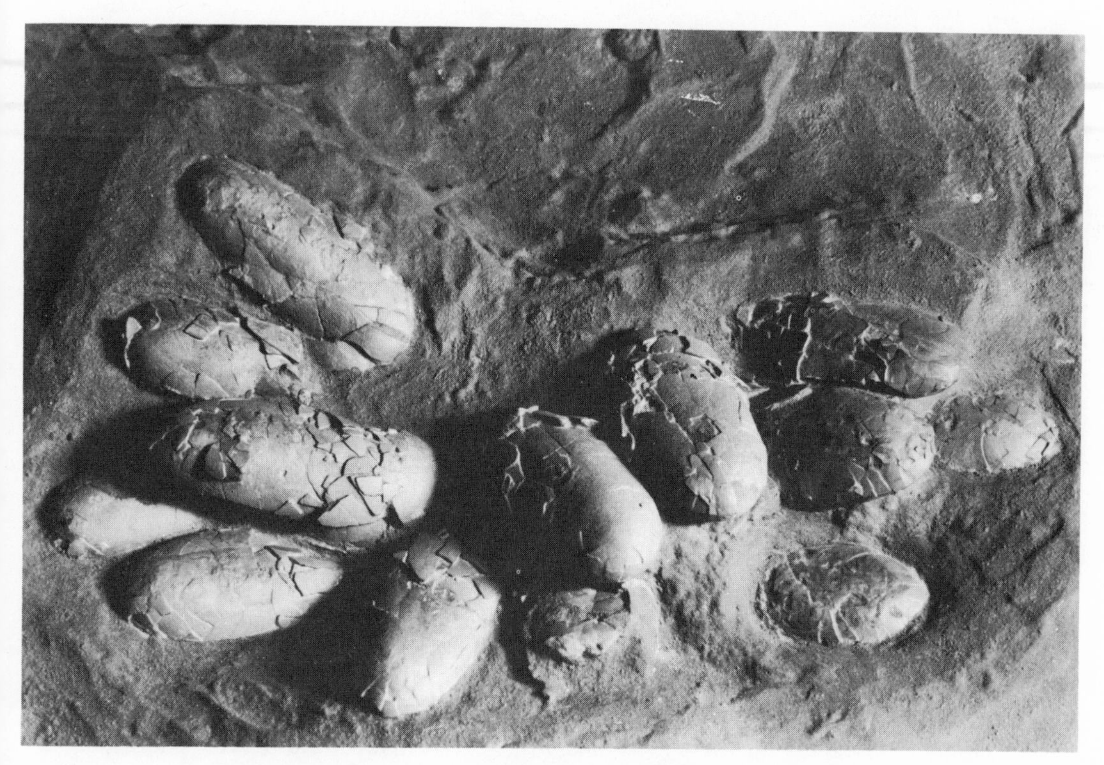

Nest of thirteen Protoceratops *eggs*

So it was not really surprising to discover that dinosaurs had been egg-laying animals; the greater surprise would have been to find that dinosaurs did not lay eggs. But until this moment no one could be sure about this aspect of dinosaurian life. No fossilized eggs had ever been found intact. There had been those enigmatic flakes of shell picked up at Flaming Cliffs in 1922 and at Iren Dabasu just a few weeks before; clues no one could appreciate until Olsen's discovery.

In camp the scientists and collectors studied the three eggs. Each was 20 centimeters long and 17 centimeters in circumference, rather more elongate and flattened than those of modern reptiles. The shell was a mere millimeter thick, the outer surface being roughly corrugated and the inner surface smooth. Try as they might, not wishing to commit some foolish mistake, the men could not think of what these reddish-brown objects could be other than eggs—and dinosaur eggs at that.

The expedition presently uncovered more eggs, twenty-five in all, some in clusters, some in nests. Granger found five eggs in a cluster. Johnson discovered a group of nine, two of which were broken, exposing the tiny skeletons of embryonic dinosaurs. A section of egg-bearing sandstone was removed and shipped whole back to the American Museum, where it was found to contain thirteen eggs in two circles; their ends pointed toward the center exactly as they had been left in a sandy nest tens of millions of years ago. The dinosaurs must have dug pits, filled them with as many as twenty eggs in three concentric circles, and covered the eggs with a thin layer of sand, leaving them to incubate in the warmth of the sun. Somehow, for all this care, these particular eggs never hatched. Perhaps a sudden cold spell interrupted incubation, or a windstorm buried the nests in sand too deep for the sun's heat to penetrate. In any event, the eggs cracked, fine sand sifted into their interiors, and the slow process of fossilization set in.

Granger assumed that the eggs at Flaming Cliffs were those of *Protoceratops,* the dinosaurs discovered by Shackelford there in 1922. Of the seventy skulls and fourteen skeletons collected by the expedition there in 1923, most were identified as the remains of this supposed ancestor to the horned, or ceratopsian, dinosaurs. Granger was probably correct. But other dinosaurs lived at Flaming Cliffs at the time; it was a popular nesting ground.

Olsen came upon one small dinosaur skeleton when he was brushing soil off the top of a clutch of eggs. This seemed to have been a toothless animal. Perhaps it lived by sucking *Protoceratops* eggs. Whatever the truth, Osborn later was swayed by the circumstantial evidence into assigning the animal the name *Oviraptor philoceratops. Oviraptor* signifies "egg-seizer"; *philoceratops* means "fondness for ceratopsian eggs." Imagination, often more than hard evidence, suggests the names eventually applied to dinosaurs. The position of the skeleton on a nest of eggs, Osborn said, "immediately put the animal under suspicion of having been overtaken by a sandstorm in the very act of robbing the dinosaur egg nest."

From the other bones and skulls scientists identified another alleged thief, *Velociraptor* ("fast-running robber"); a large armored dinosaur that was given the name *Pinacosaurus;* and the birdlike dinosaur *Saurornithoides.* The latter had almost winglike hands and a lightly built skull; but, as Andrews noted, it was much too late in geological time to be ancestral to birds. All these, and many more protoceratopsian fossils, were new to paleontology.

At the end of the 1923 expedition, Andrews returned to the United States, but news of the egg discovery had preceded him and prompted a flurry of newspaper and magazine publicity. Reporters boarded Andrews's ship when it docked in Seattle and bombarded him with questions and offers of money for the exclusive use of the egg photographs. An egg is a fragile thing, and to think of eggs laid by dinosaurs millions of years ago somehow surviving in fossil form seemed incredible; pictures of these large objects, as much or more than bones, seemed to document the reality of dinosaurs as living, breathing, reproducing creatures of long ago. Andrews declined the offers, but proceeded to capitalize on the public interest by raising $280,000 to support the next expedition. Altogether, more than $1 million was spent on the decade of Gobi exploration. As a publicity ploy, one egg was auctioned, bringing a price of $5,000 from Bayard Colgate's uncle, Austin Colgate, who presented it to Colgate University.

Andrews came to regret this sale. Chinese and Mongol officials, hearing of the Colgate purchase, got the idea that dinosaur eggs were worth $5,000 each on the world market; so it was not gold or oil these people were after but valuable stone eggs. "They never could be made to understand," Andrews said, "that that was a purely fictitious price, based on carefully prepared publicity; that actually the eggs had no commercial value." Future expeditions were watched with increasingly suspicious eyes.

NO EXPLORATION was pursued in 1924, giving Andrews time to raise money and the scientists time to study the fossils gathered on their two trips, but in the spring of 1925 the largest of all the expeditions set out from Kalgan. It had not been easy to win permission, what with the misunderstanding over the price of eggs. The government insisted that observers accompany the party. Andrews, to mollify Mongol officialdom, visited Urga with gifts of an accurate cast of dinosaur eggs and a cast of the *Baluchitherium* skull. While there, he received word from New York that one of the small fossil skulls collected at Flaming Cliffs in 1923 was that of a Cretaceous mammal, a paleontological rarity of great import.

Until then, only one skull of a mammal from the Mesozoic had been discovered. It was found in South Africa and identified as belonging to the group known as Multituberculata. These were small insect-eating rodentlike mammals related distantly to modern shrews and hedgehogs. Some of their kind survived the extinctions that wiped out the dinosaurs and lived on for a time before their world, too, came to an end. They left no direct descendants, but their fossils there in the sandstone of Mongolia attested to a widespread mammalian presence among the reptilian giants of the Mesozoic.

In his letter to Andrews, Matthew wrote: "Do your utmost to get some other skulls." Andrews so instructed Granger, who was already back digging at Flaming Cliffs, and in a week the men had collected seven tiny mammalian skulls. Subsequent analysis showed that these animals were scarcely larger than a rat and had furry bodies and pointed snouts. Not all were multituberculates, which were a side branch in mammalian evolution from reptiles. The specimens revealed to William K. Gregory and George Gaylord Simpson, American Museum paleontologists, that in the Cretaceous mainstream mammals as a class had already separated into marsupials and placentals—those that, after giving birth, nurture their fetuses in the mother's pouch and those that give birth to fully formed infants. This confirmed earlier speculation by Huxley and Osborn that the remote ancestors of placental mammals would be found as long ago as Cretaceous times in the form of small rodentlike creatures that scurried under the feet of the mighty dinosaurs.

Andrews led two other Mongolian expeditions in 1928 and 1930. The scientists confined their fieldwork in 1926 to Yunnan Province. Civil war and rampant antiforeign sentiment kept them out of the field in 1927. An ultranationalist group known as the Society for the Preservation of Cultural Objects so intimidated Chinese officials that they dared not grant permission for explorations lest they be called pro-foreign. An Andrews expedition did go forth in 1928 and make a few dinosaur discoveries—some eggs from Iren Dabasu—but it was waylaid by soldiers who seized boxes of specimens. The cultural society charged that the Americans in the expedition were "spies

MIDDLE TRIASSIC, NEW MEXICO UPLANDS

Diplodocus

LATE JURASSIC, COLORADO SWAMP

Velociraptor

EARLY CRETACEOUS, GOBI DESERT

Iguanodon

LATE CRETACEOUS, EUROPEAN FOREST

Albertosaurus

LATE CRETACEOUS, FRESHWATER LAKE, MONTANA

Triceratops

LATE CRETACEOUS, NORTH AMERICAN SWAMP

POST MESOZOIC, SURVIVORS OF THE MASS EXTINCTION

against the government" and had "stolen China's priceless treasures." Only after six weeks of negotiations, involving the American legation and going as high as the minister of foreign affairs in Nanking, were the fossils returned to Andrews and his scientists. The fifth and final expedition was mounted in 1930, but it did not travel deep into Mongolia. Then, conditions having become so unsettled, Osborn instructed Andrews to close the expedition headquarters in Peking and make no further journeys to the fossil beds of Mongolia.

MORE THAN ANYONE realized at the time, this was the end of an era. Childs Frick, son of the steel magnate and a patron of the American Museum, as well as an avid fossil collector of no mean standing, hired Chinese to bring in bones from Mongolia in succeeding years. But no more major expeditions left Kalgan, or anywhere else. Economic depression and world war drove paleontology from the field. The present was too consuming in its demands to allow time for reflection on the prehistoric past.

Moreover, the old order in paleontology was passing, and symbolic of its passage were the retirement of Osborn from the presidency of the American Museum in 1932 and his death in 1935. His life and career spanned the headiest expansionary period of paleontology. It is tempting today to dismiss Osborn as a wealthy autocrat who moved through and above paleontology as his personal fiefdom. The son of the president of the Illinois Central Railroad, he was born in 1857 to a substantial fortune, and his initial forays into paleontology had all the marks of dilettantism. The young Osborn, fresh out of Princeton in the late 1870s, made field trips to the Wyoming sites that were being opened and fought over by Cope and Marsh. He spent time in London, studying comparative anatomy under Huxley and meeting the great Darwin. But paleontology was not to be merely a pastime for him. He produced his share of scholarly tomes, founded the zoology department at Columbia University, and went on to the American Museum to launch its vertebrate paleontology department and establish the museum as a major research institution. Harry L. Shapiro, a museum paleontologist who recalled him in recent years, said: "The whole Museum was an extension of Osborn." But his reputation suffered a posthumous decline because he shared and espoused many of the prejudices of his time. He believed that women lacked the "virile quality" to make good teachers. He wrote an approving preface to a book on the superiority of the "Nordic races." Still, he was a giant of paleontology because of his own scholarship and his encouragement of Cope, Barnum Brown, Andrews, Granger,

Simpson, and many other fossil hunters. Osborn was a showman, too. The more spectacular bones brought back by the hunters were not allowed to languish in crates and storerooms. He saw to it that the bones, especially those of the large dinosaurs, were assembled and displayed in "real-life" poses. He hired Charles R. Knight, a freelance painter and sculptor, to produce vivid murals of dinosaurs in action against the backdrop of the Mesozoic landscape. Following Osborn's example, said Charles Schuchert of Yale, "There began to appear in one museum after another articulated fossil skeletons standing in lifelike poses, which fascinated the interested visitor, and which were great educators not only for the general public but even more for the paleontologist." Dinosaurs, more than ever, became imprinted in the human imagination, in no small part as a legacy of Henry Fairfield Osborn.

But paleontology in these years was beginning to resurrect a past of more immediate interest to humans, our own fossil roots. The Neanderthal man had been found in the 1850s; the Java man, *Homo erectus,* in the 1890s. Then in 1924, Raymond Dart discovered in southern Africa the Taung child, the fossil skull of *Australopithecus africanus.* This seemed to be the creature Darwin had foreseen, midway between ancient apes and modern man. Andrews, acting on Osborn's hunch, had apparently been looking in the wrong place for the origins of man. The Taung discovery brought paleoanthropology into its own, and in the decades to come *Australopithecus* and *Ramapithecus* would compete for scientific and public attention with *Tyrannosaurus* and *Brontosaurus.* Places like the Great Karoo and Olduvai Gorge, Laetoli and the Afar Valley, would evoke the romance of fossil discovery once associated with Bernissart and Como Bluff, Hell Creek and Flaming Cliffs.

The changing circumstances left Roy Andrews a frustrated man; how sad to be full of romantic energy and have no more exotic lands beckoning. He became deskbound, an unhappy fate for an outdoors man with a taste for adventure and little aptitude for administration. He served seven years as director of the American Museum, until he was eased out of the job in 1941. Andrews found himself to be something of an anachronism. With a war on, the world had no need for adventurers and the vicarious thrills they could provide. Even if there had not been a war, it is unlikely that Andrews would have been given an opportunity to mount any new explorations on the scale of the Gobi expeditions. The modus operandi of paleontological discovery was changing. Much of the world, except for the polar regions, had now been scouted by the hunters of vertebrate fossils. Dinosaur bones had been identified in Europe and North America, in Africa and South America, in Australia and also in Asia from India through China and up as far as Mongolia. The practice of making broad, sweeping reconnaissance expeditions gave way in paleontology, as it already had in most geographic exploration, to fieldwork of a more narrow scope: digging in one small area, examining in depth one period of geologic time, searching not so much for new species of dinosaurs as for a better understanding of the lives and times of the dinosaurs whose bones had already been disinterred. This was not the kind of work for restless men like Andrews. Air transportation and improved communications were beginning to simplify the logistics of paleontological operations; with few exceptions, there was no longer any need of raising what amounted to a small army to sustain a few scientists for months and months in the field. This was the kind of work Andrews did so well, in the manner of the Victorian explorers, but for which there was not much demand any longer.

For the next nineteen years, after he was cast out by the museum and until he died in 1960 at the age of seventy-six, Andrews relived the glories of his explorations through the books he wrote, books that fed the minds of paleontology's next generation.

III

10 *Revival and Revisionism*

SCIENCE PROCEEDS first by open exploration, the time of the initial discoveries. Then follows reconnaissance, gathering evidence on a broad front, pursuing leads to the far corners of the problem, and generating preliminary hypotheses. Finally, if warranted by the results of the exploration and reconnaissance, there comes the time for detailed studies and the testing of more informed hypotheses. After the lull following the final Andrews expedition, dinosaur studies in many respects entered this third phase, revived by new discoveries in the field and a ferment of inspired thinking about the life and times of these wondrous reptiles. Old assumptions were challenged, and often overturned. Other scientists, physiologists and physicists, geologists and anatomists and climatologists, not only paleontologists, turned their attention to dinosaurs, in a sense rediscovering them, and sometimes with startling effect. Their hypotheses, based on stronger evidence, became more novel and revolutionary. There was more excitement in dinosaur research than at any time since the heroic explorations of the Victorian era.

Paleontologists still went into the field each summer looking for bones. Digging fossils is, after all, the sine qua non of paleontology. These new explorers of time probed the Jurassic and Cretaceous beds of North America with a zeal not seen since Barnum Brown. "Dinosaur Jim" Jensen, who excavated the bones of what may have been the biggest dinosaurs of all, became a minor celebrity to children. Scientists found a possible early ancestor of *Tyrannosaurus rex* in west Texas. Vast quarries of dinosaur fossils were opened in Alberta. Polish, Russian, and Mongolian scientists returned to the haunts of Andrews in the Gobi and made spectacular discoveries. The quest extended deeper into the Triassic. In 1984, a team led by Robert Long of the University of California discovered in Arizona's Painted Desert what is believed to be the earliest known dinosaur. There, in rocks estimated to be 225 million years old, Long's team excavated the skeleton of a creature the size of a small ostrich. Slightly older than the staurikosaurids found in South America in the 1960s, which were previously thought to be the oldest known dinosaurs, this creature may represent an entirely new family of plant-eating dinosaurs (as yet unnamed), which could be related to the later plateosaurs and perhaps were very early ancestors of the brontosaurs. The occasional amateur still came upon important discoveries, too. Marj Averett, an amateur geologist, found the fossils of jaws and teeth in a block of sandstone near Grand Junction, Colorado; they were identified in 1985 as remains of a primitive iguanodont, the first of these dinosaurs to be unearthed in the Americas and perhaps the original ancestors of the species initially identified by Gideon Mantell and so common throughout Europe.

But the successes of the dinosaur hunters, the professionals in particular, were no longer measured by the tonnage of their haul or the number of new species they could identify. The museums had more bones than they knew what to do with. Rather, the emphasis was on finding clues to the anatomy, behavior, and physiology of dinosaurs and answers to the big questions. Were the dinosaurs examples of evolutionary misdirection, anomalous creatures plodding toward a dead end? How did their success and ultimate extinction shape the course of life thereafter? Why were they so successful for so long, for 160 million years? Why did they eventually disappear with such apparent suddenness? Did they really die without heirs? The new generation of paleontologists concerned themselves with these questions as they sought to determine the place of dinosaurs through time.

Symbolic of the shift in dinosaur research was the change of heads on the brontosaur skeleton on display at the Carnegie Museum of Natural History in Pittsburgh. It was not a matter of much scientific importance, only a little anatomical tidying-up and the acknowledgment that some previous work in the field had been haphazard.

When Marsh's collectors discovered the first two specimens of *Brontosaurus* (or *Apatosaurus*) in Wyoming in the 1870s, the skeletons were headless. Marsh looked about—far about, it seems—and found a couple of skulls to go with the skeletons. One was picked up 6 and the other 650 kilometers away. These were squat, snub-nosed skulls uncovered with the bones of *Camarasaurus,* not *Brontosaurus.* This carelessness, or sleight-of-head, was documented in 1975 by John S. McIntosh, a physicist and dinosaur specialist at Wesleyan University, and David S. Berman, associate curator of the Carnegie Museum. McIntosh said: "Marsh needed a head, so he guessed."

Earl Douglass, digging for the Carnegie Museum, had suspected back in 1915 that something was amiss. He excavated a very complete *Brontosaurus* skeleton in Utah, and its head looked more like that of *Diplodocus* than the *Camarasaurus*-like skull on the Marsh specimens. William J. Holland, the museum director at the time, wanted to mount the new head on the brontosaur skeleton. He said that Osborn "dared" him to. Marsh's judgment still carried weight, and no one swung his own weight around in paleontology more than Osborn, who had also studied *Brontosaurus* and accepted its likeness to *Camarasaurus.* Under the pressure, Holland decided to leave the skeleton headless, which it remained until a later director, in 1932, crowned it with the Marshian skull of dubious provenance.

After studying the field notes and museum records, McIntosh and Berman decided that Douglass and Holland had been right. In October 1979, the authentic skull took its rightful place on the brontosaur skeleton at Pittsburgh. Other museums followed suit. The new skull was longer and slimmer than the snub-nosed one Marsh had collected. The replacement brought about no major reinterpretation of dinosaurs, not even of *Brontosaurus.* These huge animals were found to be more closely akin to *Diplodocus,* in the same family, but that came as no surprise to scientists who had long noted the anatomical similarities. Of more importance, the change of heads symbolized dinosaur revisionism. The new paleontologists were not taking for granted the assumptions and assertions of the past.

A TRANSITIONAL FIGURE in these times was Edwin H. Colbert. He started in paleontology under the tutelage of Osborn, becoming his research assistant in 1930, and went on to serve as curator of vertebrate paleontology at the American Museum. He wrote several technical and popular books on dinosaurs, most recently, in 1983, *Dinosaurs: An Illustrated History.* Colbert's approach to dinosaurs was, by and large, old-school. He spent most of his career with the museum digging in the field, assembling skeletons for display, and placing them on the appropriate twig of the dinosaurian family tree. To his credit are thousands of fossil finds (not all dinosaurs) that included more than fifty new species and ten new genera. In 1947, *Time* called Colbert "the Dick Tracy of the Mesozoic Age."

One of his most spectacular discoveries was made in the summer of 1947 at Ghost Ranch, near Abiquiu, New Mexico. George Whitaker, Colbert's assistant, came upon some bones embedded in the slope of a gulch. Of special significance in the first sampling was a little piece of claw, which Colbert identified immediately as belonging to *Coelophysis.* Among the earliest known dinosaurs, which lived more than 213 million years ago, *Coelophysis* had been first described by Cope in 1887, but until now its remains had been few and fragmentary. At Ghost Ranch that summer Colbert picked up the bones of a dozen complete skeletons. These were not large animals, less than three meters in length, and their bones told of the active, bipedal, carnivorous lives they must have lived in the late Triassic. The hind limbs were elongated and birdlike, made for speed, and the hands had three clawed fingers, made for capturing prey. Within the body cavity of at least one of the specimens were the bones of a young *Coelophysis.* As Colbert puzzled over this, he came to doubt that he was seeing an embryo and thus the first evidence that some dinosaurs might have given live birth to their young. The opening in the pelvis, he noted, seemed too small, affording passage for eggs, not baby dinosaurs. This left one alternative explanation. Colbert wrote: "The inescapable conclusion is that *Coelophysis* was cannibalistic, eating its own young on occasion, just as do some modern reptiles. Not a pretty picture, but a realistic one."

This was good old-fashioned fieldwork, but three years earlier Colbert had showed that he qualified as a transitional figure who, though a conservative among paleontologists, anticipated some of the concerns of the new paleontologists and did something about them. He took the temperatures of some Florida alligators. It was no easy task, tying gators to a stake and suffering their displeasure at having thermometers stuck up their rectums, but the results of the experiment stand as one indisputable given in the speculative hypotheses of dinosaur physiology that would come to stir so much revisionist emotion.

Since there was no way to conduct physiological experiments on the long-dead dinosaurs, Colbert decided to do the next best thing and investigate their closest living reptilian relatives, crocodiles and alligators. With Raymond B. Cowles, a zoologist at the University of California, and Charles M. Bogert, a zoologist at the American Museum, Colbert captured thirteen alligators ranging in size up to two meters and placed them out in the blazing Florida sun. They took their temperatures every ten minutes or less. As the alligators approached temperatures at which they might succumb, they were brought out of the sun and cooled off in the shade. The scientists took their temperatures over and over again. Some of the gators were even tied to wooden frames and tilted upright in erect dinosaurian poses. All this was too much for two of the subjects, which keeled over dead. From the experiment, however, Colbert and his colleagues established that the rate of temperature increase and decrease was directly related to the mass of each animal. The small alligators heated up rapidly in the sun, and cooled down rapidly in the shade. The large ones experienced slow temperature increases and equally slow decreases, in and out of sunlight. Colbert came away from the experiment bruised by his tussles with the gators, but with the impression that he had found a possible clue to the dinosaurs' success. Though presumably cold-blooded like other reptiles, they had the means, their large body mass, to retain body heat for long periods, giving them the advantage of constant body temperature that mammals and other warm-blooded creatures achieve through high metabolism. Dinosaurs could be active like mammals without being warm-blooded. Colbert's alligator experiments would be introduced as vital evidence in the dinosaur blood debates—were they warm-blooded animals unlike modern reptiles?—that broke out in the 1970s.

Colbert had a hand in another discovery that provided decisive evidence in behalf of a new scientific concept that not only accounted for the ubiquity of Mesozoic animals like the dinosaurs but illuminated the dynamic history of the entire earth. It would not be the last time that attempts to resolve a dinosaur enigma led to a stunning insight concerning earth history. On an expedition to Antarctica in 1969, Colbert, with Jim Jensen, found the bones and skull of *Lystrosaurus.* This was not a dinosaur, but one of the earlier lines of reptiles that lost out to dinosaurs in nature's continuing war of survival. It was one of the therapsids, the mammal-like reptiles that Robert Broom in Africa had brought to scientific prominence in the late nineteenth century. Colbert had spent time in southern Africa studying therapsids, including *Lystrosaurus,* a squat, four-legged animal the size of a large dog, and so knew what he was looking for in Antarctica. If African fossils from the Triassic were uncovered in Antarctica, there could be no more solid proof that Gondwanaland, the supercontinent of the south, had existed and, responding to the forces of plate tectonics, had broken apart toward the end of the Mesozoic. Scientists hailed the Colbert-Jensen discovery of *Lystrosaurus* on another continent as incontrovertible evidence pointing to the connection of Antarctica with Africa, thus establishing more firmly the fact of continental drift. The interconnectedness of the continents during much of the Mesozoic made it easier to understand why dinosaurs, including many closely related species, existed throughout the world. Only in Antarctica have their fossils not been found so far, but scientists would not be surprised to dig up dinosaurs there, too, along with *Lystrosaurus.*

Colbert retired from the American Museum in 1970. Some of his findings foreshadowed the research of the new era, and some of his students moved to the forefront of the revival in dinosaur studies. The new generation of paleontologists would not only expand on past accomplishments, like finding complete skeletons of *Coelophysis,* or revise them, like recapitating *Brontosaurus,* but they would move into the more complex and controversial areas of dinosaur evolution, the reasons for their success and failure.

IT NOW SEEMED more important than ever, and more possible, to understand therapsids. They had dominated terrestrial life for millions of years before the rise of dinosaurs. They lost out to dinosaurs and vanished, but not before a few of them made the fateful transition from reptiles to the first mammals. They were the ancestors of every bat and cat, whale and primate, every human being.

Less spectacular in appearance than most dinosaurs, therapsids never captured the human imagination the way dinosaurs have. They were neglected by scientists as well as the public. Not until 1981 did they rate a major conference devoted to their evolution. But the fossil record of these mammal-like reptiles and their ancestors is more complete than that of any other group of terrestrial vertebrates, with the exception of Tertiary mammals. They were highly diverse and successful.

The ancestors of the therapsids were the first group to depart from the basic reptilian style, more than 300 million years ago in the Carboniferous period. Reptiles had just evolved from amphibians. One line progressed in what may be called the more conventional reptilian direction, toward becoming crocodiles and dinosaurs, snakes and lizards. Another line, the subclass Synapsida of the class Reptilia, became the mammal-like reptiles. The first of these were the pelycosaurs, the best known of which was the fin-backed *Dimetrodon;* cartoonists love to portray this creature with the sail-like superstructure running along its spine and usually miscast it as a relative and contemporary of dinosaurs. Therapsids arrived about 265 million years ago, in the early Permian, and lived throughout the world in many sizes and species. They ranged from the size of a rat to that of a rhinoceros and came in some ludicrous shapes. Some of their bodies, as one scientist said, "looked like long alligator-covered coffee tables." John C. McLoughlin, in his book *Synapsida: A New Look into the Origin of Mammals,* said: "Most of them would look to us as if the forces of evolutionary selection had experienced a severe case of the jimjams during the therapsid heyday." Some were herbivores, some carnivores, and some omnivores. They showed signs of mammalian tendencies early on. They progressed from a sprawling, crawling, lizardlike posture to a somewhat more erect walk with all four limbs swinging under the body. The name "reptile," from the Latin *reptilis,* "crawling," was already becoming too restrictive, if taken literally, as a description of the extinct members in this broad class of animals.

Although it was assumed for a century that mammals arose from therapsids, only in recent years have scientists become certain of the link. From new fossil finds and new interpretations of earlier discoveries, scientists traced the important steps in the transition and determined that the decisive step must have occurred in the late Triassic, about 215 million years ago. Well-preserved skulls of mammals from that time, found in southern China and on the Navajo reservation in Arizona, proved revealing when compared with therapsid skulls. In his 1982 book *Mammal-like Reptiles and the Origin of Mammals,* Thomas S. Kemp of Oxford University wrote: "This is one example known where the evolution of one class of vertebrates from another class is well documented by the fossil record."

It was in the skull, particularly the jaw, that scientists identified some of the more striking evidences that therapsids were mammals in the making. They could be seen evolving the equipment for improved sight and hearing, as well as more efficient methods of chewing food. A. W. Crompton, of Harvard's Museum of Comparative Zoology, has made a study of the teeth-bearing bone, the dentary, of the therapsids and found telling clues to the evolutionary trend that would be the destiny of these reptiles. The reptilian lower jaw is a composite of a small dentary and other bones toward the rear of the jaw at the point where it is attached to the skull. The mammalian jaw is a single large dentary. The bones forming the jaw joint in reptiles, the articular and the quadrate, have long been recognized as comparable to a couple of bones in the mammalian middle ear. The reptilian middle ear has only one bone, the stapes.

Therapsid fossils found in South Africa, South America, and Britain, in particular, show the change taking place. Over time, the dentary grew larger, crowding out the smaller jaw bones. Finally, in the first known mammals, the bones of the reptilian jaw joint are incorporated into the middle ear as the malleus and incus. (A vestige of this reptilian heritage can be seen in mammal embryos. In the early fetal stages, the malleus is part of the lower jaw, moving into the middle ear only at a more advanced stage of development.) These bones, along with the stapes, give mammals a more acute sense of hearing over a far greater range of frequencies than other vertebrates. "We hear with bones that reptiles chew with," Crompton said. "Why this took place, we have no idea. But the impact of all this is incredible."

At the same time, according to studies of the fossils, the therapsids were evolving muscles for more complex chewing in which the lower jaw not only moves up and down but also forward and backward and from side to side. A gradual increase in the size of the nasal passages suggested that the therapsids were improving their sense of smell. But other characteristics that distinguish mammals from reptiles seemed to be missing in therapsids. They had yet to develop a large brain. Their teeth in infancy were for regular eating, indicating that they did not nurse their young. And, though the evidence is ambiguous, they apparently were not yet warm-blooded in the mammalian sense, but their metabolic rates may have been higher than those of ordinary reptiles. This became a point of contention.

According to recent findings, the therapsid that seems to be closest to the direct ancestor of mammals is a small carnivore known as *Probainognathus,* fossils of which are found in early Jurassic sediments. In their twilight years, only the small species of therapsid remained. The larger animals, it appears, did not survive the mass extinction at the end of the Permian period. From among the smaller survivors *Probainognathus* emerged, and it or its descendants evolved into at least three groups of early mammals—*Morganucodon, Kuehneotherid,* and *Amphilestid.* The latter, Crompton said, seemed to have "lived happily for a time and gone nowhere." Descendants of *Morganucodon,* however, evolved along lines leading to the platypus and other egg-laying mammals of today. *Kuehneotherid* is believed to be ancestral to almost every other type of mammal.

By the time of the therapsid transition to mammals, at the end of the Triassic or the beginning of the Jurassic, dinosaurs had established themselves as the immediate heirs to the therapsids in the sense that they now were clearly the dominant tetrapods, the scientific term for the earth's land-dwelling vertebrates or, literally, the "four-footed ones." Dinosaurs sprang from the other major reptilian line. They apparently owed their rise in part to the Permian mass extinction, and so, it appears, the time of the dinosaurs was bracketed by global catastrophes. Soon after the Permian extinction some swamp-dwelling reptiles, the thecodonts, began proliferating. They looked something like modern crocodiles and had an appetite for the remaining therapsids. In time thecodonts evolved themselves out of existence, being replaced in the Triassic by the archosaurs, the ruling reptiles that would reign through the Mesozoic. Branching out from the thecodont stem were the four main groupings of archosaurs—crocodilians and pterosaurians as well as the two lines of dinosaurs, the saurischians and ornithischians. Among the earliest of these ornithischians were the coelurosaurs, the lightly built, agile bipeds that represented quite a departure from the reptilian norm. One of these coelurosaurs was *Coelophysis,* whose bones were found in such abundance by Edwin Colbert. One of the earliest known saurischians was *Plateosaurus,* a much larger animal and a Triassic forerunner of *Brontosaurus* and *Diplodocus,* which was documented through excavations in the 1920s by Friedrich von Huene of the University of Tübingen. Many of the therapsids were probably no match for these swift and imposing predators; the ones that fed by day and rested at night were especially vulnerable to the rising dinosaurs. The therapsids that survived through the Triassic, until they could make the transition to mammals, must have found some relatively safe ecological niche. For example, those that evolved improved hearing and smell and could control their body temperatures in some way—all mammalian precursor traits—became nocturnal creatures. Those that could not adapt to the night life passed out of existence. Thus the more mammal-like of the therapsids survived and passed on their genes to descendants that became even more mammalian, and finally mammalian in fact. The legacy of their survival strategy endured through much of the Mesozoic. The little mammals living in the shadow of the mighty dinosaurs were generally nocturnal creatures.

IN COMPARING the therapsids and early mammals with the dinosaurs, Robert T. Bakker professed to divine the reasons for dinosaur "superiority" in the Mesozoic. He published his ideas in 1968, when he was only twenty-three years old and well on the way to being the enfant terrible of paleontology. He had graduated from Yale the year before and remained on campus to work at the Peabody Museum. Bakker would go on to earn a doctorate in geology and paleontology at Harvard in 1976, but in his first professional publication, "The Superiority of Dinosaurs," an article in the spring issue of *Discovery,* a Peabody journal, he served notice that his would be a mind and voice to be reckoned with. The article was less a scientific treatise than a manifesto calling for a new approach to dinosaur paleontology, its revival and revisionism.

Robert T. Bakker

Bakker defined the new approach, as contrasted to the old ways, in his opening paragraphs. He wrote:

> A new emphasis is permeating the science of paleontology. For more than a century paleontologists have been discovering fossils, describing them, and attempting to show how one ancient organism is related to another. Once a reasonable family tree had been sketched for a particular group, the classical student of ancient life usually considered his examination finished and went on to the family tree of some other group. In contrast, today it is the reconstruction of the details of the lives of extinct animals—what they ate, how they reproduced, how they defended themselves—that is capturing the interest of more and more paleontologists.
>
> Usually only the hard parts (bones and teeth) of vertebrate animals are preserved as fossils. However, muscles, tendons, nerves and blood vessels, and occasionally other soft organs and tissues, leave marks on the surfaces of bones. Detailed analyses of the anatomy of various living vertebrates reveal how these soft organs affect bone surfaces. From this it is possible to interpret the marks preserved on fossil bones. From these interpretations it is possible to infer something about the activity, physiology, and even the behavior of animals that are known only from fossilized bones.
>
> This new approach to studying fossil vertebrates is producing some evidence that challenges many of the theories about the habits and ecology of one of the most popular groups of extinct animals, the dinosaurs. These great beasts were reptiles whose closest living relatives are the modern croc-

> odiles. Generally, paleontologists have assumed that in the everyday details of life, dinosaurs were merely overgrown alligators or lizards. Crocodilians and lizards spend much of their time in inactivity, sunning themselves on a convenient rock or log, and, compared to modern mammals, most modern reptiles are slow and sluggish. Hence the usual reconstruction of a dinosaur such as *Brontosaurus* is a mountain of scaly flesh which moved around only slowly and infrequently.

This view of dinosaurs, Bakker pointed out, presented "a perplexing problem." How did these sluggish dinosaurs overwhelm the therapsids, which were presumably developing active mammal-like ways, and hold in submission the mammals throughout the Mesozoic? Bakker went on to note evidence from dinosaur postures and cardiovascular systems suggesting that these animals "were fast, agile, energetic creatures that lived at a high physiological level reached elsewhere among land vertebrates only by the later, advanced mammals." To illustrate his new vision of dinosaurs, Bakker drew for the journal cover a sketch of a couple of galloping horned dinosaurs, which he said were capable of speeds up to fifty kilometers an hour. There was more life in the dinosaurs, it seemed, than scientists had usually imagined.

In conclusion, Bakker wrote:

> We can now begin to answer the question posed at the beginning of this article: why did the mammal-like reptiles lose out in competition with the dinosaurs?
>
> Even the most advanced mammal-like reptiles, although usually pictured as erect or semi-erect creatures, are constructed along lizard-like, sprawling lines. Never did these animals even begin to develop dinosaur-like erect posture. Recently I had the opportunity to study the limb bones of the American Jurassic mammals, and these animals also had a sprawling build exactly like that of a lizard, or like that of the living Duck-billed Platypus. Apparently mammals did not acquire the more efficient, erect locomotion until late in the Cretaceous period, fully a hundred million years after the advanced thecodonts and early dinosaurs acquired it.
>
> Today we think of mammals as active, agile creatures, and reptiles as sluggish sprawlers. However, the dinosaurs and their kin achieved locomotory advancements long before the mammals, and this superiority in limbs undoubtedly was a chief factor in the success of the archosaurs and the extinction of the mammal-like reptiles.

The young Bakker, brash and provocative, had staked a position far to the front in the new dinosaur wars. These were not battles for possession of bones, as in the Marsh-Cope struggle. They were battles of interpretation: what could and could not be said about the lives and times of the dinosaurs? The warfare exploded into public view, to the chagrin of the more sober paleontologists. But this was inevitable. Dinosaurs, more than other fossils, are public property, creatures as much of the public imagination as of scientific resurrection. Science was taking a new look at them. The public was seeing, in the excitement of new discovery, the conflict of interpretation, the building and testing of hypothesis, the process of science at work.

11 *Hot Times over Warm Blood*

LATE ONE AFTERNOON in August 1964, John Ostrom and his assistant, Grant E. Meyer, walked a slope in south central Montana, near the town of Bridger. This was prairie, grasslands interrupted by eroded mounds and set among hills of pine and juniper. Ostrom and Meyer were winding up the third Yale University field expedition aimed at collecting fossil vertebrate remains from the early Cretaceous. Ostrom called this a "twilight zone" of Mesozoic life; because of the rarity of terrestrial deposits from that time, and thus a paucity of fossils to work with, paleontologists had long had trouble seeing patterns of evolutionary change that occurred in this 25-million-year interval. To rectify this, Ostrom had reconnoitered most of the early Cretaceous strata exposed along the flanks of mountain ranges in northern Wyoming and southern Montana. He and his teams of scientists and students had traversed and inspected some 1,500 kilometers of outcrops, digging here and there and finding the skeletons of several hitherto unknown species of animals, some of which were dinosaurs. Ostrom and Meyer had just examined one possible site for next year's excavations and were moving along the slope of an eroded mound to another site several hundred meters away when they came upon the claws reaching out.

"We both nearly rolled down the slope in our rush to the spot," Ostrom recalled. "In front of us, clearly recognizable, was a good portion of a large-clawed hand protruding from the surface. My crew had missed it. I saw their footprints just a few feet away."

The bones had lain there, unrecognized, for years and years. Ostrom could tell this by their weathered condition. He could also tell that the hand was something unusual. "I knew from the fragments there on the surface," he said, "that this was the most important thing we'd found so far."

Ostrom and Meyer fell to their hands and knees and brushed away the soil from around the fossils. Not expecting to do any digging that day, they had left their picks, chisels, and shovels back at the truck, but in their excitement, they dug the best they could with jackknives. They knew what it must feel like to discover a lost treasure. Within minutes they uncovered other parts of the hand. The several finger bones were somewhat larger than those of an adult human. The claws were large and sharp. Ostrom and Meyer had found a powerful, three-fingered grasping hand. They also came across some teeth, the sharp, serrated teeth of what had been a carnivore.

Returning the next day, equipped this time with tools more substantial than jackknives, the two paleontologists resumed digging and made an even more breathtaking discovery, the perfectly preserved bones of a foot. They looked at the foot in amazement. In all other carnivorous dinosaurs the foot is rather birdlike, with three main toes and one smaller toe at the inner side or at the back of the foot. The three principal toes are usually alike, with the middle toe the longest and the other two of equal length and diverging from the middle one. All in all, birdlike. But the foot of the creature they had found differed from this basic plan. The outside and middle toes were equal in length, and the innermost of the principal toes stuck out, Ostrom said, "like a sore thumb." And quite a "thumb" it was. This inner toe was longer than the others. Instead of having a short, pointed, triangular claw like the other toes, it bore a long, thin claw in the sharply curved shape of a sickle. Ostrom had never seen anything to compare with this terrible claw, but he could well imagine the uses to which it had been put and how this instrument surely marked the character and vitality of its owner. To this creature that had lived more than 125 million years ago Ostrom would give the name *Deinonychus,* meaning "terrible claw."

Deinonychus is one of the most remarkable dinosaurs ever discovered. Nearly everything about the animal, its arms and legs, its terrible claws and stiff tail, was soon to be introduced as Exhibit A in the case for the swift, agile, dynamic Bakkerian dinosaurs. The evidence, as seen by many paleontologists, seemed compelling, but the ensuing debate polarized dinosaur paleontology. Were dinosaurs as a group warm-blooded the way birds and mammals are? Was their metabolism more like that of mammals than that of other reptiles, giving them the capacity to lead more active lives? Ostrom, in his initial examination of *Deinonychus,* began to suspect that this might be the case. But the very idea contradicted the traditional view of dinosaurs as sluggish creatures in the reptilian mode. Traditional scientists held that dinosaurs, which were classified as reptiles on the basis of their skeletal anatomy, must have been cold-blooded. Modern reptiles are cold-blooded, dinosaurs were reptiles, and, therefore, dinosaurs must have been cold-blooded. This logic had not been seriously disputed until the new generation of paleontologists began taking a new look at dinosaurs and, in particular, at *Deinonychus.* For too long too many paleontologists, it seemed, had been blind to the apparent nonreptilian attributes of dinosaurs. Just because a fossil animal is assigned to a particular class, it does not follow that it possesses all the characteristics of the modern members of that class.

JOHN OSTROM, who was thirty-three years old at the time, made a brief announcement to newspapers in the fall of 1964, calling the fossils a "startling discovery" but refraining from further assessment. He had yet to name the animal or appraise its importance. Ostrom and his associates returned to the discovery site the next two summers. They dug deeper into the sides of the bald Montana hill, a sixty-meter-high mound resembling a scoop of ice cream melting a little at the base. Their intensive quarrying recovered more than a thousand bones representing at least three individual animals, each one a *Deinonychus.* There followed three more years of skeletal reconstruction and analysis back in Ostrom's laboratory at the Peabody Museum.

Site of Deinonychus *discovery in Montana*

As a graduate student at Columbia University in the 1950s, Ostrom had wondered about the physiology of dinosaurs. He remembered talking to his adviser, Edwin Colbert, about the possibility that the physiology of dinosaurs was not at all like that of living reptiles, but more like mammals. Perhaps no one today knows more about dinosaurs than Colbert, but his attitude toward novel ideas about the lives of these animals is generally conservative. In his fourscore years, he has read and heard many such ideas that came from out of the blue and usually ended back out there, too. Besides, it seemed improbable that fossils would ever yield strong clues to dinosaurian physiology. But *Deinonychus* began to change Ostrom's mind, if not Colbert's. Ostrom saw in this animal reasons to believe in his prescience as a graduate student.

Examining the skeletons, Ostrom concluded that *Deinonychus* was relatively small, as dinosaurs go, and lightly built. It stood approximately one and a half meters high and measured more than two and a half meters from the snout to the tip of its tail. Judging by the limb bones and vertebrae, the fully grown animal weighed no more than 80 kilograms, 175 pounds. Judging by the teeth, it was a carnivore and so classified with the saurischian dinosaurs in the same suborder as the tyrannosaurs. The structure of the fore limbs and hands clearly showed that the animal was an obligatory biped; it could not have walked on all fours even if it wanted to. Like most reptiles, *Deinonychus* had a rather long tail that accounted for about half its length, but the tail had a feature unlike anything Ostrom had seen. The entire length of the tail was encased in thin, parallel bony rods—ossified tendons, like those Dollo had noted in the Belgian iguanodonts. This mystified Ostrom at first, until he came to realize that a rigidized tail, presumably made possible by the bony rods, must have been important to *Deinonychus.* As Ostrom visualized it, the rigid tail could be moved up and down, sideway, and all-around-the-clock. The tail, he concluded, was used as a dynamic stabilizer, a counterbalance for an active, mobile bipedal animal. This and other skeletal evidence indicated to Ostrom that the posture of this biped was much like that of an ostrich, with the trunk held in a near-horizontal position, the neck curving upward, and the tail sticking straight out behind. "In my opinion," Ostrom wrote in 1969 in *Discovery,* "this is a much more natural-looking posture than the 'kangaroo' pose that is commonly illustrated for other carnivorous dinosaurs such as *Allosaurus* or *Tyrannosaurus.*" Indeed, he added, if the skeletons of these giants were as well preserved as those of *Deinonychus,* scientists would probably find that they, too, often held their tails out as rigid counterbalances rather than dragging them through the mud. Other paleontologists in interpreting other dinosaurs

forcefully in a paper he delivered that year in Chicago at the first North American Paleontological Convention. He was nervous beforehand, knowing that what he had to say would be controversial, which it was. Everyone agreed that Ostrom was the meeting's most provocative speaker. The title of his paper, "Terrestrial Vertebrates as Indicators of Mesozoic Climates," gave no hint of its radical message.

John H. Ostrom

It is well known, Ostrom noted, that modern fish, amphibians, and reptiles are so-called cold-blooded creatures. The term "cold-blooded," used by laymen more than scientists, has nothing to do with the temperature of the blood itself. Rather, it means that the animal's body temperature fluctuates with that of its surroundings. The cold-blooded animal lacks internal mechanisms to raise or lower body temperature much above or below environmental temperatures. Most reptiles are inactive in the cool of night and must bask in the sun to warm up for the day's hunt. Since their main source of heat is external, reptiles and other cold-blooded animals are, to be more scientific in the terminology, ectotherms. When ectotherms begin to get too hot, they must seek the shade; they are always having to do something about the weather. In contrast, warm-blooded animals, mammals and birds, have internal regulating mechanisms that maintain their body temperatures at approximately the same level, regardless of external conditions. They are known as endotherms. Humans, unless sick, maintain a temperature of 37.1 degrees Celsius, or 98.4 degrees Fahrenheit. Most other mammals operate at comparable temperatures, while birds generally have higher temperatures, averaging about 40 degrees Celsius. Many endotherms perspire and pant to help keep cool or have layers of hair or feathers to cut heat loss. But the primary mechanism of endothermy is a high basal metabolism: all living cells generate small amounts of heat as a by-product of the chemical processes occurring within them, and in mammals and birds these processes, known as metabolism, are at least four times as active as in ectotherms of comparable body size and temperature. Accordingly, endotherms can spring into action under almost any climatic conditions, whereas ectotherms are more severely influenced and restricted by the environment. It is this "climate dependency" of ectotherms, Ostrom said, that makes them useful for paleoclimatic interpretations. This was the point he was building up to.

If dinosaurs were ectotherms, according to the prevailing assumptions, then the millions of years during which they lived must have been a time of generally mild climate worldwide. Only in an equable environment could these reptiles have prospered in such number and over a range that seemed to run to the higher latitudes approaching the polar regions. They presumably could not have survived extreme seasonal changes. However, although pollen and invertebrate fossils tend to support the idea of a mild Mesozoic climate, Ostrom argued that paleontologists could not look to the dinosaurs as corroborating evidence. Dinosaurs, he said, were useless as thermal indicators because there was reason to question the assumption of their low reptilian metabolisms, their ectothermy. Throwing down the gauntlet, Ostrom declared: "There is considerable evidence, which is impressive, if not compelling, that many different kinds of ancient reptiles were characterized by mammalian or avian levels of metabolism."

Ostrom's analysis of *Deinonychus* had made him more conscious of the potential significance of dinosaurian posture. Dinosaurs were not sprawlers, as are the living reptiles—a distinction scientists had been aware of (but had made surprisingly little of) since the time of Huxley. *Deinonychus* and apparently most other dinosaurs, biped and quadruped alike, held themselves erect with their feet directly under their bodies. No living ectotherms have such postures. If they did, they would presumably be able to run faster and over greater distances than they do. At least some dinosaurs were apparently fleet of foot. The long limbs of *Deinonychus* and some other dinosaurs, as well as many fossil tracks, indicated that they could be swift runners. The evidence, Ostrom said, suggests that "erect posture and locomotion probably are not possible without high metabolism and high, uniform body temperature." He did not state flatly that dinosaurs were endotherms. They might have been homeothermic, which is to say that they maintained a constant body temperature by whatever means, internal or external. Whether homeothermic or possibly even endothermic,

Ostrom affirmed, dinosaurs were extremely active and extraordinary animals whose bioenergetic mechanisms seemingly set them apart from the usual run of reptiles.

Many paleontologists found the idea of warm-blooded dinosaurs unthinkable. Others thought it liberating, offering as it did a model of dinosaurian physiology that could explain their long success and perhaps even their extinction. Debate among scientists raged for years over the question of whether dinosaurs may have been ectothermic, endothermic, something in between, or something entirely different.

RECONSTRUCTING the thermal physiology of extinct animals is no simple matter. Nothing about the fossils affords a direct measure of how the dinosaurs regulated their body temperatures. There can be no thought of some brave scientist putting a thermometer under the tongue or up the rectum of a dinosaur. All the evidence introduced to support or challenge the endothermic hypothesis was of necessity derived from the inferences scientists extracted from the dinosaur bones. The results were bewildering. Different interpretations of the same bones produced conflicting hypotheses and guesses.

Microscopic examination of dinosaur bone produced evidence that lent support to Ostrom. As early as 1957, paleontologists had been puzzled when they found in dinosaur bone the characteristic pattern of an extensive Haversian system, a network of fine penetrating vessels for supplying the bone tissue with generous amounts of nutrient-rich blood. Haversian bone is capable of rapid growth and indicative of high metabolic rates. Beginning in 1968, Armand de Ricqlès, a University of Paris anatomist and paleontologist, reported the results of more detailed bone-tissue studies and concluded that the dense Haversian tissue "indicates rates of bone/body fluid exchange at least close to those of large, living mammals." It seemed at first to be the most direct evidence available to suggest, as Ricqlès said, "high levels of metabolism, and hence probable endothermy, among dinosaurs."

But more recent studies cast doubt on the reliability of this line of evidence. Haversian bone is not the exclusive property of endotherms; it is present in some turtles and crocodiles. Nor is it a uniformly endothermic characteristic; it is absent in many small mammals and birds. Such bone structure may be related to growth rate and body size rather than endothermy.

Ostrom continued to base his case on the fact that erect posture and gait occur only in endotherms, mammals and birds. But he acknowledged that his critics had a point when they argued that no cause-and-effect relationship between posture and physiology has ever been established. Still, he insisted, "the correlation between posture and endothermy or ectothermy is virtually absolute and surely is not merely coincidental." He also advanced another line of indirect evidence related to upright posture. Citing the research of Roger S. Seymour, a zoologist at the University of Adelaide in Australia, Ostrom noted that the greater the vertical distance between an animal's heart and brain, the greater the required blood pressure. A giraffe's blood pressure is double that of a human's. In the case of *Brachiosaurus,* to take an extreme dinosaurian example, the heart-brain distance was approximately six meters. To pump blood such distances, or even lesser distances, in an animal with upright posture, Ostrom said, would require an advanced four-chambered heart that is a hallmark of endotherms. Owen, in 1841, had wondered if dinosaurs had not had four-chambered hearts, but he never pursued such thinking. Crocodiles have imperfect versions of a four-chambered heart, indicating that such a feature was not out of the question among archosaurs. The heart-brain distance does not prove that dinosaurs were endothermic, as Seymour observed, but it helped make the case that many of them had need of and, therefore, must have possessed a heart and circulatory system capable of maintaining an endothermic physiology.

In contrast to Ostrom's cautious inferences and concessions to his critics, his former student Robert Bakker asserted flatly that the case for dinosaur endothermy was conclusive. To the usual arguments for endothermy he added a new and ingenious one: the relative abundance of dinosaurian prey with respect to dinosaurian predators.

Warm-blooded animals pay a high price for the metabolism that keeps them in an almost constant state of readiness. They must eat more, and this means spending extra time grazing or hunting. A lion consumes its weight in food every seven to ten days, whereas the Komodo dragon, a carnivorous lizard, eats its weight in food only every sixty days. This means that a given quantity of meat will not supply nearly as many endothermic carnivores as it would ectothermic ones. Bakker, therefore, decided to tote up the relative sizes of populations of prey and predators as revealed in fossils from the late Cretaceous. Surveying several collections of fossils, separating the predators from the prey by their teeth and jaws and calculating probable body weights, Bakker sought to determine the percentage of predators in the whole fossil population. A small percentage of predators would mean that they must have had hearty, endothermic appetites; in some African habitats today, predators constitute only 1 to 6 percent of the total animal population. For the dinosaurs in his fossil samples, Bakker found, the predators represented 1 to 3 percent of the total. The predator-prey ratios of pre-Mesozoic reptiles, which were unquestionably ectothermic, ranged from 35 to 60 percent.

These data became the keystone in Bakker's increasingly aggressive campaign for dinosaurian endothermy. By 1975 he had left Yale and was working on his Ph.D. at Harvard. He took his case to the public in an article in *Scientific American* entitled "Dinosaur Renaissance," in which he asserted: "Predator-prey ratios are powerful tools for paleophysiology because they are the direct result of predator metabolisms." In the same year, a Harvard colleague, Adrian J. Desmond, a historian of science, published *The Hot-Blooded Dinosaurs,* and to the dismay of the more conservative paleontologists, the general public joined the spirited debate and tended to side with Bakker's warm-blooded forces. People liked their dinosaurs lively, not languid. In drawings for Desmond's book and other publications, Bakker, who is a skilled artist as well as paleontological provocateur, portrayed dinosaurs that did not stand idly about, but were zippy, ferocious speedsters, chasing down little mammals for lunch or stalking one another and pouncing for the kill like lions. These were the "new and improved" dinosaurs.

Ostrom, meanwhile, had modified and qualified his position on endothermic dinosaurs. Though he had ignited the debate, he backed away from the conflagration that Bakker was doing so much to fuel. He and Bakker are as opposite in temperament as in the language they use in scientific discourse. Ostrom chooses his words with care, tempering the bold hypothesis with concessions that the evidence is less than conclusive; Bakker marshals pieces of evidence with skill and flair, rising to a crescendo that sometimes is less scientific than polemic. In this vein, he once declared: "We need endothermic dinosaurs; evolutionary theory demands them; the empirical data confirm that they existed." Bakker needed to establish dinosaur endothermy in order to reinforce his case explaining the ascendance of dinosaurs over mammals in the Mesozoic, suppressing their evolution for as long as they had to compete with dinosaurs. Only active endothermic animals, in Bakker's mind, could have maintained the dinosaurs' "superiority" in the Mesozoic. Most paleontologists opposed all or much of what Bakker believed and recoiled from his emotional rhetoric as the debate inflamed science through the 1970s.

Not that Ostrom had changed his mind about the agile *Deinonychus* or the vitality of many other dinosaurs; the claw, tail, and erect, bipedal locomotion still seemed indisputable evidence for high levels of activity. But he could not bring himself, on the basis of the evidence so far, to join Bakker in making sweeping generalizations about dinosaurian bioenergetics and superiority. "If Bakker had moved more cautiously, we'd have had less heat and a better reception," Ostrom said in 1983. "I was never able to convince him that understatement was more powerful than overstatement." Ostrom had personal reasons as well. "I was becoming concerned about my professional reputation," he said. "People knew Bakker had been a student of mine. They linked us together, saying Ostrom and Bakker were advocating endothermy. My position really was, We may be right but we haven't proved it."

ARGUMENTS FOR AND AGAINST endothermy were aired in 1978 at the annual meeting of the American Association for the Advancement of Science in Washington. The endothermists were headed by Bakker, and to a lesser degree by Ostrom and Ricqlès. Nicholas Hotton III of the Smithsonian Institution emerged as the leader of the opposition, though he had important allies in Dale Russell, Philip Regal of the University of Minnesota, and James Spotila of the State University of New York College at Buffalo. The proceedings of the symposium, published in 1980 as a book, *A Cold Look at the Warm-Blooded Dinosaurs,* stand as the definitive document in the controversy.

Telling shots were fired at Bakker's predator-prey argument. The opposition doubted the reliability of the fossil record he had used to calculate the ratios. How could Bakker or anyone know if the fossils gave an accurate indication of the proportion of predators among the living animals of the time? Because of the nature of their bones or the conditions of the habitat, some types of animals may have become fossilized more readily than others. The collectors may have had biases in the fossils they looked for and gathered up. Nor is there any way of knowing whether the herbivores in a given fossil community were all preyed upon by the carnivores there. Even if such interpretations of the fossil record were accepted as accurate reflections of predator-prey ratios, Pierre Beland and Dale Russell, both of the National Museum of Natural Sciences in Ottawa, questioned Bakker's calculations for the dinosaur community in Alberta. By their estimates, the ratio there was about four times greater than that calculated by Bakker, which, if true, weakened his argument that the predators must have been ravenous endotherms. Bakker insisted, however, that the corrected ratio still did not put the animals out of the endothermic range.

Another argument against Bakker revolved around the large size of most dinosaurs. Dinosaurs may have behaved like warm-blooded animals not because they were endotherms but because they were large. They may have owed their success to their sheer bulk.

If there is one thing beyond dispute about dinosaurs, it is their size. Hotton determined that 80 percent of living mammals are smaller than the smallest dinosaur, which weighed about ten kilograms, and that more than half of the dinosaurs weighed more than two tons, a size attained by only 2 percent of modern mammals. Large size, it would seem, was in some way critical to dinosaur survival and so the bigger individuals of a species would be more likely to reproduce, leading to the evolution of species of even larger animals—at least up to some point of diminishing advantage.

Several scientists, including Hotton, Beland, and Russell, presented data suggesting that ectotherms and endotherms become more similar with increasing size. Their metabolic requirements and hence predator-prey ratios may be very similar if both are large. Indeed, as Spotila contended, a large body mass results in a fairly constant body temperature. The dinosaurs could have been inertial homeotherms, animals that can maintain a constant body temperature by any means, including those dependent on the environment. Colbert and his colleagues, in their earlier experiments with Florida alligators, had shown that these animals, descendants of archosaurs, heat up more slowly when exposed to sunlight and cool off more slowly than do smaller animals. They thus can keep the temperature of their bodies fairly constant without endothermic mechanisms or any outside insulation like fur or feathers. The larger the alligator, Colbert found, the slower the rate of heat absorption and heat loss. In the warmer climate of the Mesozoic, moreover, the variations in the animal's body temperature would presumably be minimal. Dinosaurs, therefore, could have had most of the attributes of warm-bloodedness without endothermy.

Hotton summed up the implications of what he believed was the dinosaur's inertial homeothermy in this way: "Dinosaurs, like mammals, enlarged their capacity for continuous activity by reducing their dependence on the physical environment as a source of body heat. They did so, however, at low cost, by a system of heat conservation that shaped life-styles which were very different from those conditioned by the high-cost, heat-generating system of mammals. Locomotor mechanisms and size illustrate a fundamental difference: the activity of dinosaurs was more sedate than that of mammals. The basic strategy of dinosaurs in general was 'slow and steady,' and what it lacked in mammalian elan, it made up in economy."

One part of the strategy, Hotton further suggested, probably involved seasonal migrations over distances upward of 3,200 kilometers. In North America, dinosaur fossils have been found as far north as Yukon Territory, seventy degrees north latitude; even in the mild Mesozoic, the arctic was probably not a fit place for a dinosaur in the winter because of the chill and the darkness that suspended the growth of vegetation. The migrations may have begun with random drift in the course of everyday foraging. Large dinosaurs, herbivores and predators alike, would have had to be wanderers in order to gather enough food to keep themselves going, even at modest rates of ectothermic metabolism. Hotton offered two other reasons. The activity of migration would have provided a reliable source of internal heat. Second, the travels would have kept them exposed to approximately the same temperatures year-round, which was a vital consideration if, as ectotherms, the dinosaurs' tolerance of thermal fluctuation was restricted by a relatively narrow margin of heat output from resting metabolism. The concept that some dinosaurs, like many living birds, migrated north and south, season by season, is appealing and not implausible, but it was only speculation and probably not provable with direct evidence in the rocks and fossils.

Hotton also took issue with Bakker's contention that endothermy may have been a factor, along with their large size and naked skin, in the dinosaur extinction. Bakker had asserted: "In the face of sudden, prolonged cold stress, dinosaurs were too large to escape by hibernating in burrows or other micro-habitats available to small endotherms, and were unable to survive prolonged drops in their body temperature, unlike many turtles, lizards and other ectotherms. Exposure to prolonged severe cold would probably kill most of the living, naked tropical endotherms—rhinos, hippos, elephants, armadillos—and may well have eliminated the dinosaurs, the naked, tropical endotherms of the Mesozoic." On the contrary, said Hotton, "If dinosaurs had been endothermic, some of them should also have survived." If some of the small dinosaurs were insulated with feathers, which has been speculated but never established, they should have "survived in diversity comparable to that of surviving birds and mammals." Even the large, naked dinosaurs, if they could generate their own internal heat, should have had a few survivors for at least a short time, and yet no dinosaurs survived the mass extinction at the end of the Cretaceous. Hotton concluded: "The survival of ectotherms as well as endotherms across the Cretaceous-Tertiary transition further reinforces the view that there were great differences in thermal physiology between dinosaurs and living tetrapods."

Although the arguments favoring large size and inertial homeothermy as the controlling features of dinosaurian physiology seemed to satisfy many paleontologists, Bakker did not retreat. Such a thermoregulatory system, he pointed out, would not give rise to endothermic bone histology or the low predator-prey ratios or the success of many small dinosaur species with an adult weight of between five and fifty kilograms. The smaller dinosaurs were among the most agile and liveliest of the breed, more like endotherms.

In a spirited, uncompromising peroration at the symposium, Bakker insisted again on the importance of endothermy in the evolution and success of dinosaurs, and also their ultimate failure. Bare-faced endothermic chauvinism, sniffed his colleagues. Undaunted, Bakker declared:

> The first tetrapod group showing evidence of high heat production, the therapsids, quickly gave rise to dominant large land animals. Dinosaurs appear to represent a higher level of endothermy, and they replaced the therapsid-thecodont dynasties. The entire fossil history of large land vertebrates shows the progressive nature of evolution among large land tetrapods. Intense, direct biotic interactions have driven adaptive trends towards more complete optimization of performance of muscle, heart, lungs, and brains. Dinosaurs appear to have reached a level of performance in thermoregulation and locomotion comparable with that of many Late Cenozoic mammals. Some of the smaller predatory dinosaurs seem to have acquired brains of a size and complexity equal to those of modern ground birds of the same weights. . . . As reinterpreted, . . . the success of dinosaurs becomes part of an unreversed, coherent progression, leading from the first land tetrapods of the Devonian to the grand complex of modern mammals.

NO CLEAR WINNERS emerged from the debate. The question of dinosaur warm-bloodedness remains unanswered, perhaps unanswerable. In their introduction to the published proceedings of the symposium, the editors, Everett C. Olson and Roger D. K. Thomas, concluded: "No . . . resolution of the controversy over whether dinosaurs were scaled-up, cold-blooded reptiles or warm-blooded surrogate 'mammals' is reached here, although the weight of current opinion lies between the extremes."

The consensus seemed to be that there was no single thermoregulatory strategy for all dinosaurs. The largest dinosaurs, sauropods like the brontosaurs, were probably most nearly ectothermic. Their bones suggest that they were not swift or active, and it is difficult to imagine how sauropods could have found food to maintain a high metabolism. Most dinosaurs, because of their large size and the mild climate, probably maintained fairly constant body temperatures. They were inertial homeotherms. The smaller dinosaurs, with bones suggesting a capacity for speed and agility, may have been true endotherms. Indeed, the smallest ones, such as *Compsognathus,* which was a contemporary of *Archaeopteryx,* were probably too small to be inertial homeotherms.

John Ostrom now has doubts that all dinosaurs were endothermic. "If any of the dinosaurs were endotherms," he said, "the most probable candidates were the small carnivores." *Compsognathus,* for example, and *Deinonychus,* among others. He still feels, as he did in 1969, that *Deinonychus* must have led a vigorous warm-blooded kind of life as a fierce, swift, and agile predator. It was a most unreptilian dinosaur, and so perhaps were many others. Ostrom observed: "There is a lot of suspicion out there that some or most of these animals were physiologically very different from any living reptiles, perhaps more like mammals or birds. Unhappily, we'll never know."

The wonder of dinosaurs also is that they are an enigma seemingly beyond solution. Science has explained so much: the divisibility of atoms and the nature of subatomic particles; the decipherable code of heredity contained in DNA; the earth's restless crust; gravity, electromagnetism, and the age of the solar system. Science has identified hundreds of species of dinosaurs, assembling their bones and dating their time on earth, but so much about the lives of these strange and monstrous creatures defies explication. It is reassuringly human of scientists that, when it comes to dinosaurs, they can be just as stricken with puzzlement as the next person and find themselves with little more to work with than their imaginations. Yet they persist in their search for solutions to the riddle, knowing they will never fully succeed but believing they will learn something about the greater mysteries of life. This is the wonder of humans, their faith that there is much about dinosaurs worth knowing.

Scientists came away from the warm-blooded debates with, if nothing else, a new appreciation of the dinosaur enigma. Bakker, though he failed to prove that dinosaurs were endotherms, inspired a host of paleontologists to explore the ecology and community structure of these unusual reptiles and seek to understand their place in the evolution of life. Even Nicholas Hotton, Bakker's staunchest adversary in the debates, had to concede: "Alternative thermal strategies and life-styles available to dinosaurs may well have been as exotic as their body form, the like of which no man has ever seen."

12 *Living Descendants?*

IF JOHN OSTROM seemed to be putting distance between himself and Robert Bakker on the issue of dinosaur warm-bloodedness, he stood his ground on one important line of evidence advanced in support of the theory. Ostrom firmly believed that birds are direct descendants of dinosaurs. His study of *Deinonychus* had led him to an analysis of dozens of other dinosaurs, particularly the small running carnivores known as coelurosaurian theropods. His long fascination with the question of how animal flight originated had prompted him to examine anew pterosaurs and all the specimens of *Archaeopteryx,* the oldest known bird. The anatomical similarities between *Archaeopteryx* and the coelurosaurs, he found, were amazing. Except for the feathers, *Archaeopteryx* looked more like a small dinosaur than like any modern bird. There must be a close relationship between dinosaurs and birds, Ostrom concluded, closer perhaps than anyone had ever dared imagine.

Ostrom was reviving an old idea that had fallen on hard times. Thomas Henry Huxley's original proposal of a dinosaur-bird link won endorsements from the likes of Marsh and Williston. Other anatomists and paleontologists, however, had different notions, including lizard or pterosaur ancestry. According to another suggestion, flying birds arose from pterosaurs, and nonflying birds, such as ostriches and rheas, sprang from dinosaurs. On only one point could scientists achieve a consensus: birds had evolved from reptiles. But what reptiles?

For many years in the twentieth century, Huxley's idea was largely abandoned in favor of a compromise explanation, the common-ancestor hypothesis. Dinosaurs and birds were held to be only remotely related by virtue of having evolved from a distant common stock, usually identified as the primitive thecodonts. These were the early Triassic ancestors of all the archosaurs. Birds, thus, are no more related to dinosaurs than crocodiles are related to dinosaurs or pterosaurs. The many affinities between birds and some dinosaurs were, as George Gaylord Simpson asserted, "demonstrably parallelisms and convergences," which are modes of evolution that produce gross resemblances between unrelated creatures. In the case of parallel evolution, two organisms arise from a common ancestor, diverge into two distinct lineages, then develop structural similarities to achieve common capabilities, such as flying. Birds and pterosaurs stand out as examples of parallel evolution. In the case of convergent evolution, animals of two lineages independent of any common ancestor—dolphins and ichthyosaurs, for example, or bats and birds—develop similarities in adapting to the same kinds of ecological niches, such as the sea or air. Hermann von Meyer, it will be remembered, was the first to postulate this mode of evolution, as well as to identify the first known *Archaeopteryx*. Von Meyer's bird, it was now believed, should be viewed in the light of von Meyer's postulate. Since some of the small carnivorous dinosaurs and the protobirds shared similar ecological niches, running about after much the same food, they understandably evolved similar anatomies; but, according to this hypothesis, that should not be taken as a sign of close kinship.

The matter seemed to be laid to rest in the 1920s by Gerhard Heilmann, a Danish paleontologist. He, more than anyone else, was responsible for the widespread rejection of a direct dinosaur-bird link. In his definitive book *The Origin of Birds,* published in 1926, Heilmann acknowledged the "striking points of similarity" between coelurosaurs and birds. He remarked on the many birdlike features of the coelurosaurs: "Hollow bones of very light structure, exceedingly long hind limbs with strongly elongate metatarsals and a 'hind-toe,' a long narrow hand, a long tail and a long neck, large orbits and ventral ribs." But one distinctive avian feature was missing. The coelurosaurs, he noted, lacked any evidence of a wishbone or of the collar bones (clavicles) that are the presumed antecedents of the avian wishbone (furcula). If the coelurosaurs had no clavicles, how could their putative bird descendants have developed a furcula? *Archaeopteryx* had a wishbone, though it was not quite as distinct (being shaped more like a boomerang) as the familiar one in the chicken that children tug apart to make wishes come true. The absence of the clavicles in coelurosaurs, Heilmann decided, "would in itself be sufficient to prove that these saurians could not possibly be ancestors of birds." He suggested, instead, that the bird ancestors would probably be found among the pseudosuchians, a group of the early Triassic thecodonts. Earlier, in 1913, Robert Broom had found in South Africa a small, bipedal pseudosuchian 230 million years old,

Euparkeria, that appeared to possess all the necessary anatomical qualifications to be the ancestor of birds. Heilmann sided with Broom, not Huxley.

"That was the established belief," John Ostrom said, "until I stuck my foot into it."

First in 1973, then in 1975, Ostrom joined the debate with forceful arguments in behalf of a direct dinosaur-bird link. He was responding, in part, to yet another proposal for bird ancestry that denied a dinosaurian kinship. Alick D. Walker of Newcastle University proposed a variation of the Broom-Heilmann theory. He suggested that crocodiles and birds, including *Archaeopteryx,* derived from a common thecodont ancestor, but not the same one that led to dinosaurs. He based this idea on resemblances between the braincase and skull of modern crocodiles and birds, as well as some notable birdlike features of *Sphenosuchus,* a late-Triassic (220 million years ago) creature that is thought to be a primitive crocodile or a thecodont well on the way to being a crocodile. The inner ear of the extinct *Sphenosuchus,* Walker said, was more like that of a partridge than of a modern crocodile. Reading Walker's report in *Nature,* Ostrom decided the time had come to take his stand. He interrupted his studies of *Archaeopteryx* to write a rebuttal letter, declaring in no uncertain terms: "The skeletal anatomy of *Archaeopteryx* is almost entirely that of a coelurosaurian dinosaur—not thecodont, not crocodilian, and not avian."

Ostrom could be more assertive than Huxley had been because many more small bipedal dinosaurs had now been found and examined. Almost invariably their limbs, feet, and claws were quite like those of *Archaeopteryx.* A few of the newly discovered coelurosaurs appeared to possess the missing ingredient that had mattered so much to Heilmann; they apparently had clavicles. The Polish-Mongolian expedition had just returned with evidence that the *Velociraptor,* found in the Gobi, appeared to have a pair of collar bones. So did *Segisaurus,* an American fossil studied by Ostrom. Even the apparent absence of collar bones in other fossils, Ostrom argued, should not be considered definitive; this was "negative evidence only and thus inconclusive." In a jumble of bones the clavicles could be misidentified as rib fragments. Moreover, because these bones were membranous, they might have been present in many other small dinosaurs but, being unossified, would have been very poor candidates for fossilization.

Engaging in some paleo-orthopedics, as it were, Ostrom arrived at another bit of evidence to back up his argument. One apparently avian aspect of *Archaeopteryx,* in contrast to the coelurosaurs, was the backward orientation of the pubis as preserved in the Berlin specimen. In modern birds, the pubis runs backward below the other two pelvic bones. Closer examination of other *Archaeopteryx* specimens, however, persuaded Ostrom that the pubic bone in the Berlin specimen had been displaced and was not oriented in its natural position. He corrected it in his interpretative drawings to point straight downward or possibly forward, which is the orientation in all coelurosaurian theropods. The less *Archaeopteryx* looked like a bird and the more it looked like a theropod, the stronger was Ostrom's case for the dinosaurian ancestry of birds. Walker objected to this surgery, calling Ostrom's interpretation nothing but speculation.

Even so, summarizing the evidence for the dinosaur ancestry of birds, Ostrom wrote in 1975: "Is it more probable that *Archaeopteryx* acquired the large number of derived 'theropod' characters by convergence or in parallel at the same time that these same features were being acquired by some coelurosaurian theropods—presumably from a common ancestor? Or is it more likely that these many derived characters are common to some small theropods and *Archaeopteryx* because *Archaeopteryx* evolved directly from such a theropod? There is absolutely no question in my mind that the last explanation is far more probable."

Not all scientists could bring themselves to agree with Ostrom. K. N. Whetstone and Larry D. Martin of the University of Kansas reported new evidence of similarities in the inner-ear structure of birds and crocodiles that they said strongly supported Walker's view that both originated from a shared pseudosuchian ancestor long before the advent of dinosaurs. Max Hecht and Samuel Tarsitano of Queens College in New York argued that several anatomical features of *Archaeopteryx,* especially the wrist, pelvis, and shoulder, weakened the case for a dinosaur-bird link. In *The Age of Birds,* Alan Feduccia concluded: "On the evidence available so far, it is difficult to choose between the dinosaurian and pseudosuchian theories of avian ancestry." But Ostrom came away from an international conference on *Archaeopteryx,* held at Eichstätt in August 1984, feeling reassured that most scientists now sided with him and the dinosaurian origin of birds.

OSTROM'S REASSESSMENT of *Archaeopteryx* provoked a new round of debate on another question that has long divided scientists. It concerns one of the greatest mysteries of evolution: the origin of powered flight by animals.

As an adaptation, flight ranks in a class with the emergence of fish from

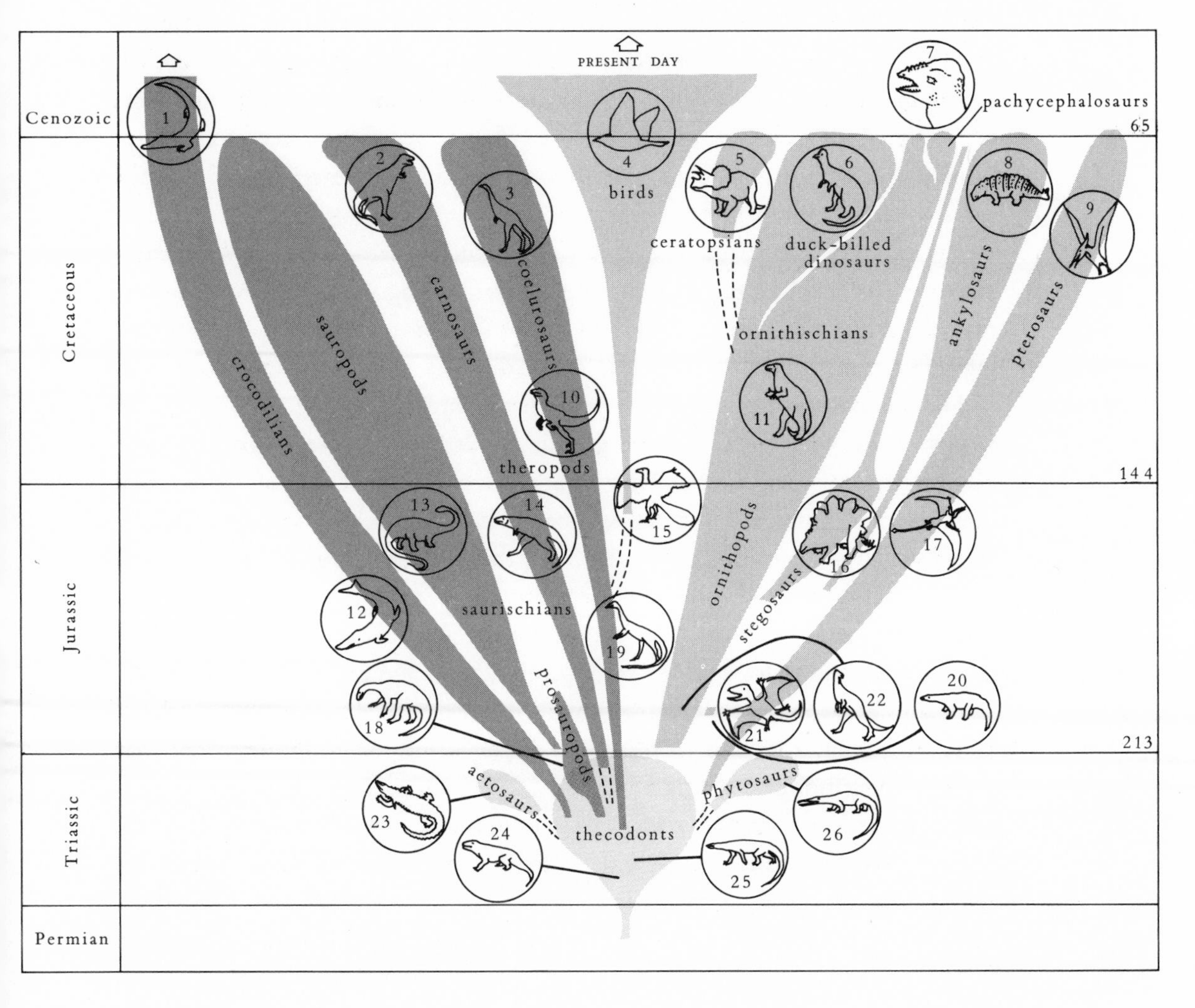

THE FAMILY TREE OF THE ARCHOSAURS

1 modern crocodile
2 Tyrannosaurus
3 Ornithomimus
4 modern bird
5 Triceratops
6 Corythosaurus
7 Pachycephalosaurus
8 Euoplocephalus
9 Pteranodon
10 Deinonychus
11 Iguanodon
12 Metriorhynchus
13 Diplodocus
14 Megalosaurus
15 Archaeopteryx
16 Stegosaurus
17 Rhamphorhynchus
18 Plateosaurus
19 Coelophysis
20 Scelidosaurus
21 dimorphodon
22 Lesothosaurus
23 Desmatosuchus
24 Erythrosuchus
25 Mandasuchus
26 Rutiodon

the sea more than 350 million years ago to become the first land vertebrates. The fossil record shows that true powered flight (separate from the parachuting of flying squirrels and some flying frogs or from the gliding of the colugo and flying lizards) evolved independently on several occasions. The first fliers were the winged insects, which appeared about 350 million years ago. Next were the pterosaurs, which probably were capable of powered flight. Then came the flying birds, perhaps as early as *Archaeopteryx* but certainly not long afterward in the Mesozoic. The only other known self-propelled flying animals, the bats, took to the air some 50 million years ago. But those who puzzle over the origin of flight have focused their attention on birds, the most appealing and accomplished of the aerial creatures.

The discovery of *Archaeopteryx* provided scientists with the most celebrated example of a creature at or near the transition between these two modes of life, flightlessness and flight. This inspired two broad schools of thought on how flight originated. For at least a century scientists have argued whether, to put it simply, bird flight evolved from the trees down or from the ground up.

Marsh, in 1880, was the first to propose the arboreal theory. He suggested that certain reptiles took to the trees to nest, feed, and escape from predators. These primitive ancestors of birds must have had a need to leap from branch to branch, then from tree to tree. And so any slight anatomical variant that enhanced this mobility would be passed down through succeeding generations by natural selection. In this way, presumably, the reptiles evolved rudimentary feathers on their forearms to slow their descent in jumping among the branches and in parachuting to the ground. Marsh, in making his point, cited the example of modern gliding animals, such as flying squirrels. (This example, Ostrom has said, was not apposite because these gliders are quadrupeds with flight membranes stretched between the fore and hind limbs.) Much later, according to Marsh's hypothesis, these reptilian protobirds could have adapted these wings and their muscles to achieve powered flight.

Support for the arboreal theory came from other scientists who noted that the opposed toes of *Archaeopteryx* seemed to indicate an ability to grasp tree limbs. Likewise, the clawed fingers were admirably adapted for climbing trees. But Marsh and others were unable to produce fossil evidence or otherwise explain how a glider might evolve into an active flier, which must have much different structural and aerodynamic characteristics. The theory, nonetheless, gained a wide following.

The other explanation, the cursorial theory (from the Latin *cursus,* "running"), was offered a year earlier by Samuel Williston. His purpose was to refute arguments against a dinosaurian origin of birds. "It is not difficult," Williston wrote in 1879, "to understand how the fore legs of a dinosaur might have changed to wings. During the great extent of time in the Triassic, for which we have scanty records, there may have been a gradual lengthening of the outer fingers and greater development of the scales, thus aiding the animal in running. The further change to feathers would have been easy. The wings must first have been used in running, next in leaping and descending from heights, and finally, in soaring."

Williston's cursorial theory was ignored until 1907, when Franz von Nopcsa came forward with an even stronger proposal along the same lines. He was a brilliant eccentric, something of a dilettante, whose ideas on paleontology could be provocative. There has never been anyone quite like him in the exploration of the dinosaurian past. Nopcsa was, if the expression can ever be applied, sui generis.

A Transylvanian nobleman who led many lives, Nopcsa (pronounced NOP-sha) owned and oversaw large feudal estates, wrote prolifically on paleontology, served as a spy for the Austro-Hungarian Empire in World War I, directed the Hungarian Geological Survey after the war, and through it all was obsessed with Albania. This was the strangest thing about this strange man. He studied the language and dialects, the geography and culture of Albania. He traveled there several times, often at great risk in the rough and restive countryside. At the end of the Balkan War in 1913, when Albania's situation was uncertain, Nopcsa asked Vienna to supply him with 500 soldiers, some artillery, and two fast steamships so he could invade Albania and set himself up as king. His plan was to marry the daughter of an American millionaire, who presumably would be so eager to have a royal connection that he would bankroll the country's economic development. Nopcsa was merely proposing to do as a filibuster what the Great Powers sought to do, which was to seize a piece of the disintegrating Balkans. Ignoring Nopcsa's scheme, Vienna installed its own puppet ruler, who after six months on the throne had to flee for his life.

Nopcsa lost most of his land at the end of the world war and sometimes seemed on the verge of losing his mind as well. A fracas with rioting peasants left him with a fractured skull, an injury from which he apparently never fully recovered. Nopcsa spent his remaining money on an extensive motorcycle trip through Europe with his Albanian secretary, who was also his homosexual lover. In 1933, his mind finally snapped. He gave his secretary tea heavily laced with a sleeping powder and shot him in the head. Then he shot himself. The "Almost King of Albania," as an obituary writer called him, was dead.

Almost to the end, though, Nopcsa published his ideas about dinosaurs. As a first-year student at the University of Vienna in 1899, he had written his first scientific paper, a description of a new genus of Cretaceous dinosaur found on his Transylvanian land. The paper was well received by European paleontologists, as were the dozens of others he produced over the years. In the course of studying dinosaur evolution, Nopcsa developed his own ideas of the cursorial origins of bird flight. Like Huxley and Williston, he argued that birds originated from bipedal dinosaurlike creatures that ran on the ground. He believed that to increase their running speed these protobirds spread out their feathered arms and swept them back and forth like oars. This skill eventually enabled the animals not only to run faster but provided the force to lift off and glide short distances. Nopcsa imagined this to be the beginnings of bird flight. But it was aerodynamically impossible, as critics have pointed out. For as soon as the animal left the ground, its legs could no longer propel it forward, and it would fall immediately back down.

Although Nopcsa's concept drew new interest in *Archaeopteryx* as a runner, not a tree climber, and to the dinosaur as its possible ancestor, the elemental flaw in his thinking set back the cursorial theory. Besides, scientists simply felt more comfortable with the arboreal theory. They could more easily imagine animals using gravity to descend from branches than struggling against gravity to take off from the ground. It must be significant, they also reasoned, that nearly all present-day vertebrate fliers are arboreal. Few, therefore, took the cursorial theory seriously until Ostrom reopened the debate in the 1970s.

In his studies of *Archaeopteryx,* Ostrom went beyond making a case for its direct kinship with dinosaurs to addressing the question of bird flight. Since *Archaeopteryx* lacked a sternum, the breastbone that anchors flight muscles, he raised doubts about this early bird's capabilities for powered flight. He believed it was "fleet of foot and probably a ground dweller." Its claws, for example, resembled those of modern ground birds such as pheasant, partridge, quail, and roadrunners. All this gave Ostrom an idea. He speculated that *Archaeopteryx* and other protobirds were predators that hunted by flushing out prey, mostly insects, and running it down. Their feathered forearms, he proposed, were used to beat insects out of the air. As the wing surfaces evolved to larger sizes, they conferred some power of lift during predatory lunges and, in time, might have enabled the creatures to take to the air in powered flight. Ostrom's insect-net idea provoked controversy, but also a reexamination of the cursorial theory.

Walter J. Bock, an ornithologist and professor of evolutionary biology at Columbia, supported the arboreal school. "If a flyswatter was required, a fine-meshed surface of overlapping feathers would not work," he asserted. "A flyswatter must have spaces for air to flow through as the swatter is swung."

Even Ostrom's cursorial allies saw problems in the hypothesis. Kevin Padian, a paleontologist at the University of California at Berkeley, wrote: "If wings really did develop first as insect-catchers, as Ostrom suggests, then one would think that natural selection would have acted strictly to improve them as flyswatters, not transfer their function to flying."

A scientist at Northern Arizona University read a description of Ostrom's insect-net idea in 1979 and decided on a study applying aerodynamic principles to the origin of bird flight. Gerald Caple, a chemist, enlisted the help of two faculty colleagues—Russell P. Balda, a biologist and ornithologist, and William R. Willis, a physicist and former fighter pilot. They developed and tested numerous models of protobirds based on different inferences drawn from *Archaeopteryx.* Their conclusions, reported in 1983, lent strong support to the cursorial theory.

Although Caple's team found it unlikely that the insect net could have developed the lift, thrust, and drag capacities for powered flight, they showed how bipedal runners could have developed the necessary flight stroke. They said that such animals, running and lunging after prey, could have used their fore limbs for balance, as humans do when making a broad jump. Such controlling motions resemble a rudimentary flight stroke, which is rather like a lazy figure-eight. If such a stroke were made with an aerodynamically suitable airfoil, such as feathered fore limbs, air would rush over and under the wing at different rates, thereby creating lift and prolonging the jump. They predicted that the rate of such evolution to powered flight was rapid. According to their hypothesis, moreover, there was no need for the animal to develop new and different muscles to perform powered flight, in contrast to the requirements for an arboreal glider to make the transition.

Ostrom was pleased to concede the defeat of his insect-net notion. "It did its job," he said. It might have been discredited, but it inspired Caple and his coworkers to produce evidence that bolstered Ostrom's case for swift-running bipedal dinosaurs being the precursors of birds. This was the idea that meant the most to him.

As for the arboreal and cursorial theories, both may turn out to be correct, to a degree, if it is ever possible to resolve the conflict and thus smooth all the ruffled scientific feathers. Bock, the arboreal proponent, has called "this sort of either-or thinking" simplistic. "It is quite possible—indeed probable—that proto-birds spent time both in trees and on the ground," he said, citing as examples such modern birds as the guans, chachalacas, and curassows of Central and South America. "They use their power of flight mostly to get up into trees and back down to the ground again."

But Bock, writing in 1983, argued that two interrelated features of proto-birds, feathers and warm-bloodedness, tended to favor the arboreal explanation of flight. Initially, he said, protobirds could have developed feathers as insulation, making possible their evolution toward warm-bloodedness. This would have been an advantage if the avian ancestors climbed trees, where temperatures are slightly cooler than on the ground. Bock reasoned: "Because there are fewer predators in the trees than on the ground, proto-birds might have stayed there longer and longer, in conditions that favored the development of an efficient surface layer of insulation and, eventually, a complete body covering of feathers. Moreover, if proto-birds used trees for nesting, then it would have been advantageous for adults to warm the eggs instead of relying completely on heat from the sun. Thus, selection forces in the trees would favor the evolution of endothermy and insulating feathers."

This scenario, though probably unprovable, could explain another puzzling aspect of dinosaurs and birds: if one is the ancestor of the other, does that mean that dinosaurs—at least those directly related to birds—were necessarily warm-blooded? Or, to put it another way, can the warm-bloodedness of birds be entered as evidence for the warm-bloodedness of their putative ancestors, the dinosaurs? Bock seemed to suggest that the reptiles in line to become birds evolved their warm-bloodedness only in the final stages of their avian transition. Robert Bakker, of course, had already become convinced that endothermy was not only common among dinosaurs, probably well before the bird transition, but was compelling evidence for a close dinosaur-bird relationship and, conversely, that the warm-bloodedness of birds was evidence of the warm-bloodedness of dinosaurs.

SO CONVINCED WAS BAKKER that, in characteristic fashion, he took a position well beyond the ranks of his allies. He proposed a drastic revision of the classification of animals, one in which dinosaurs would be separated from other reptiles and elevated to a status equal to mammals, reptiles, amphibians, and fish. This meant toppling birds from a class of their own and placing them in the same new class with dinosaurs. Bakker thought such a change was only appropriate, for it reflected what he said was the growing evidence that birds are the living descendants of dinosaurs.

In a letter to *Nature* in 1974, Bakker and Peter M. Galton of the University of Bridgeport reviewed the familiar evidence from bone histology, locomotor dynamics, and predator-prey ratios that, they said, strongly suggested that "dinosaurs were endotherms with high aerobic exercise metabolisms, physiologically much more like birds and cursorial mammals than any living reptiles." They also cited with approval Ostrom's recent work indicating that birds were direct descendants of dinosaurs and inherited their active metabolisms from dinosaurs. Therefore, they proposed the new class, called Dinosauria, and subdivided it into three subclasses: Saurischia and Ornithischia (for the two distinct groups of dinosaurs) and Aves.

Assigning dinosaurs a higher status was for Bakker only logical and fair. He had burst into paleontology with his proclamation of the "superiority" of dinosaurs, and now he sought to define their specialness in scientific terms. Like mammals, he argued, dinosaurs had made a transcending evolutionary break with their ancestors; mammals evolved from reptiles, progressing from ectothermy to endothermy, and so did the dinosaurs. "This new classification," Bakker and Galton wrote, "reflects more faithfully the major evolutionary steps. Ectotherms and forms transitional to endotherms are retained in the Reptilia and the two highly successful endothermic groups, mammals and dinosaurs, are given separate class status."

They further argued, in this regard, that it made no more sense to separate birds from dinosaurs than it would to separate bats from mammals. "The avian radiation is an aerial exploitation of basic dinosaur physiology and structure, much as the bat radiation is an aerial exploitation of basic, primitive mammal physiology," they contended. "Bats are not separated into an independent class merely because they fly."

Bold it was, this proposal by Bakker and Galton. And rash, according to most biologists and paleontologists. The venerable Simpson called it "utter nonsense." Theories may come and go, which is the dynamic of science, but the system of zoological classification should not be bent and warped in response to this and that theory; the system should be like a constitution—subject to amendment only after the most rigorous and ponderous deliberation. There were strong reasons to be cautious. Much of the case for a new classification assumed that dinosaurs were endothermic. But no such assumption is yet justified, though some of the arguments made by Bakker and others raise the definite possibility that at least some dinosaurs may well have been warm-blooded creatures and that many others must have had unreptilian physiologies. The matter may never be resolved to everyone's satisfaction.

The case for a new classification also assumed that birds descended from dinosaurs, an assumption based on seemingly stronger evidence. Still, scientists have yet to reach a consensus on the ancestry of *Archaeopteryx,* hence of birds. Ostrom, however, has won many adherents—to the point that the direct dinosaur ancestry of birds is becoming the prevailing theory.

It is an appealing theory. It means, as Ostrom once wrote, that dinosaurs "did not become extinct without descendants." And the feathers that some dinosaurs grew not only led to flight but, as thermal insulators, could be the primary reason for the success of these dinosaurian descendants. It is an appealing theory also because it means that one can never again look at a robin hopping on the lawn or a red-tailed hawk riding the thermals without thinking: so that's what probably became of the dinosaurs.

13 *Social Life of Dinosaurs*

THE SUMMER OF 1978 was much like the preceding ten for Jack Horner and Bob Makela. They had hunted dinosaur bones together since their college days at the University of Montana in Missoula. "We'd just pack up a bag of plaster of paris and a case of beer and go," Horner said of those days. They did it as a lark, the way some people spend a week or two out fishing or backpacking. In paleontology, pastimes tend to evolve into professions, and so it was with Horner. Though his disdain for required nonscience courses kept him from getting a college degree, Horner had gone east to work at Princeton University's Museum of Natural History; he was a technician who prepared fossils for the paleontologists fully invested with doctorates. Makela remained in Montana as a high-school science teacher in the little town of Rudyard. But each summer they joined forces and, stocked with digging tools and cases of beer, searched the Montana countryside for dinosaur bones. They often dug in the region of western Montana where Horner, when he was only seven years old, had found his first dinosaur fossil on his family's ranch. In 1978, the two friends were exploring and collecting bones along the Canadian border north of Rudyard, with only modest luck.

At the end of July, they were asked by another paleontologist to drop by a rock shop in Bynum, Montana, for a look at some dinosaur specimens the owners of the shop wanted to sell as souvenirs. The proprietors, Marion Brandvold and David and Laurie Trexler, had picked up the bones in the spring while walking over a ranch near Choteau. At the shop one evening, the dinosaur hunters identified the bones, which were of no special scientific interest. Then, as an afterthought, Brandvold pulled out a coffee can full of tiny fossil bones. She handed them two pieces, each less than a centimeter long. One was the distal end of a femur, the part of the bone most distant from the center of the body. A few moments later, Horner turned to Makela and said, "You're not going to believe this, but I think these are pieces of a baby duck-billed dinosaur."

Makela was skeptical at first, and rightly so, as Horner remarked some time later. Neither of them had seen a baby dinosaur in their decade of collecting. Few paleontologists had; the Argentine José Bonaparte had recently found a newly hatched dinosaur that was so small it could be held cupped in two hands, but this was a rarity. After Makela examined the bones more carefully, his skepticism evaporated. The two paleontologists explained to the shop owners the potential importance of these bones, whereupon Brandvold disclosed the discovery site.

John R. Horner and Robert Makela spent the rest of that summer and many summers thereafter at the site, living in tepees that made it look more like an Indian encampment than a scientific expedition. The site was on the James and John Peebles Ranch outside Choteau, a community west of Great Falls on the highway to Glacier National Park. To the west, beyond the Teton River, loom the Rocky Mountains. To the east lie the Great Plains. In between is a vast stretch of hummocky grassland, where wind and water have eroded away the last 80 million years of earth's sediments. There the two paleontologists dug into the gray-brown mudstone of the Two Medicine Formation. In a few days, working in the hot sun and lashing wind, they excavated the remains of a mud nest that contained fifteen fossilized baby dinosaurs. The nest was a hollowed-out bowl about two meters across and one meter deep at the center. Each nestling was about one meter long. These were the first baby dinosaurs ever found in a nest, and their clearly worn teeth indicated that they had been eating for some time.

This marked the beginning of one of the most illuminating dinosaur discoveries of the twentieth century. Horner and Makela eventually found more than 300 whole or partial dinosaur eggs in nests. Some of the eggs held the skeletal remains of the embryos. The two fossil hunters also dug up more than sixty whole or partial skeletons, including those of nestlings and juveniles and their parents. Nothing ever unearthed had afforded scientists such a revealing glimpse of the social behavior of dinosaurs. It was the first evidence that dinosaurs were apparently caring parents, a most unreptilian trait.

Later in the summer of the first digging season, Laurie Trexler, who was helping out, came upon the skull of an adult dinosaur at the site. "If I had only one part of an animal," Horner said, "I'd rather have a skull than anything else." But this skull puzzled him. It appeared to be unlike any known dinosaur. For months Horner would examine the reassembled specimen much as Hamlet contemplated the skull of poor Yorick. It was, he decided, a member of the archosaur subfamily known as Hadrosauridae, the duck-billed animals first described by Joseph Leidy. They were among the most abundant and diverse of the dinosaurs in the Cretaceous. Most other hadrosaurs, however, had a large naries (the opening for the nose) that crowded the orbits (the eye openings). This one had a small naries, with a large bone between it and the orbits. In that respect, the animal resembled an iguanodont. But the iguanodont had small, simple teeth and few of them. Horner's skull had a battery of hundreds of large interlocking teeth suitable for a more thorough grinding and chewing of coarse vegetation. This feature and others suggested a hadrosaurian relationship. From the size of the skull, moreover, Horner estimated that the animal had been eight to ten meters long. He finally concluded that this was a hadrosaur of a new genus and species, which he named *Maiasaura peeblesorum*. *Maiasaura* meant "good mother lizard," which from the early evidence seemed appropriate. The species name honored the ranch owners who let Horner dig to his heart's content.

Horner and Makela kept looking and digging in succeeding years. Wherever they saw tiny bones in the topsoil, they would sweep the area and screen the collected soil for more bones. If they sensed a rich lode, they would dig in earnest with picks, shovels, and jackhammer. Or they would rake the area, loosening the ground to encourage deeper erosion, "weathering," over the winter, and return to it the next summer with hopes of a full harvest. In this manner, they soon made enough discoveries to realize that they had found not an isolated nest or two but a colony.

Two more nests with baby hadrosaurs were excavated. In one the nestlings were even younger than those found earlier. They measured less than one-half meter. Others were older, grown to nearly two meters in length, and this gave Horner further reason to believe that the young were cared for by their parents for several months after hatching. Like a robin bringing worms back to its young, the maiasaur, the "good mother lizard," must have foraged for its young, returning to the mud nest frequently with berries, seeds, and green leaves.

Horner's team also found the weathered remnants of nine unoccupied nests, each containing an abundance of fossilized eggshell fragments. These hadrosaur eggs, when reconstructed, were twenty centimeters long with the shape of lopsided ellipsoids, approximately the size and shape of the protoceratopsian eggs found years before in the Gobi. The shells were slightly thicker than a chicken egg, more like an ostrich egg. The shell surfaces were ridged. The nests were at least seven meters apart, which Horner noted with keen interest because the distance was approximately equivalent to the length of an average adult hadrosaur. The nests all occurred in the same stratum, or what appeared to be a single "time horizon." This, indeed, must have been a nesting ground not unlike the breeding colonies of some modern birds.

In 1979, while digging in the side of a nearby knoll, Horner uncovered another likely nesting colony. The knoll was thereupon given the unofficial name of Egg Mountain. The ten nests there held the remains of as many as twenty-four eggs each. These eggs, with smooth outer surfaces, were slightly smaller and even more ellipsoidal than those previously excavated. They had been arranged in a circular pattern with their pointed ends buried in the nest's mud bottom. On hatching, the young emerged through the top portion of the egg, leaving the lower portion intact within the sediment. From the eggs and some bones Horner concluded that this site had been occupied by another kind of dinosaur, probably a species of the somewhat smaller hypsilophodonts.

Horner was able to draw two inferences about the nesting colony at Egg Mountain. The nests occurred at three slightly different levels in the ground. He took this to suggest that the adults had used the site year after year; it was the place they returned to each breeding season. Noting the absence of any juvenile remains in these nests, as well as the fact that the lower portions of the eggs were preserved rather than crushed by trampling of the young, Horner also inferred that the young of this species did not remain in the nests long after hatching. There were signs of parental care, nonetheless. Remains of fifteen to twenty small skeletons, varying in length from one-half to one and a half meters, were found nearby. If the young simply hatched and left the area, a couple of them might by chance have died there, but a toll of fifteen to twenty seemed improbable. This circumstance reminded Horner of the nurseries, or creches, in the nesting grounds of some birds. As he reported in *Nature,* these young dinosaurs "either remained in the colony or returned to the site frequently, either of which may have been a result of parental care."

Analysis of the bone development of the baby dinosaurs led Horner to further speculation. He saw evidence of rapid growth. The metabolism of these animals seemed to have been set to the faster tempo of warm-blooded creatures rather than that of the usual cold-blooded reptiles. "I used to argue with Bakker all the time," Horner said of the apostle of dinosaur warm-bloodedness. "And I still argue with him on some points, but it's hard to explain what I'm seeing any other way."

His reasoning was as follows: the nests of the hadrosaurs, in particular, held hatchlings not even one-half meter long, as well as one-meter juveniles and fragments of others that may have been nearly two meters long. They were either growing very fast or staying in the nest very long. The young crocodile, which is cold-blooded and a fellow archosaur, grows about one-third of a meter a year. Even the fastest-growing cold-blooded species would take a year to reach the size of the juvenile hadrosaurs Horner dug up. It seemed improbable that the young dinosaurs would have stayed in their nest three years or even one year, no matter how nurturing their parents might have been. It was more likely that the dinosaurs grew at a rate comparable to that of the ostrich, say, which is slow-growing for a warm-blooded creature; an ostrich achieves a length of about one meter in six to eight months. For some reason, the young of the good-mother lizards of Montana seemed able to grow this fast or faster, and so it could be that they were warm-blooded.

Scientists might disagree with this interpretation, and with some of the others, though the objections so far have been few and mild, but they were as one in viewing the discovery of the nestling dinosaurs as a wonderful surprise. Eggs had been found with great fanfare by the Andrews expedition in Mongolia and by others subsequently; a scattering of juvenile dinosaur bones had come to light over the years; but never any babies in the nest. Several ideas had been advanced by way of explaining this void in the fossil record.

Some paleontologists believed that dinosaurs laid eggs in places more subject to erosion than to deposition, and consequently their nests were erased from the record. Or perhaps, others said, dinosaurs lived so long that fewer juveniles were needed to sustain the adult populations, and the bones of those few, being fragile, seldom survived to become fossilized. Horner, however, figured that people had been looking in the wrong places. Charles W. Gilmore, a paleontologist for the Smithsonian Institution, might have solved the problem if he had appreciated the significance of one of his discoveries early in the century. As Horner recalled, Gilmore's field notes in 1928 mentioned the abundance of dinosaur eggshell fragments found in the Two Medicine Formation. Many of the small dinosaurs he collected, which he described as new species, were actually juveniles of known species. They were in sediments deposited by streams running out of the western Montana uplands, where Horner eventually did find the nesting colonies.

When Horner said people had been looking in the wrong places, he meant that most paleontologists had been locked into the idea of dinosaurs being creatures of the low river valleys, coastal plains, and swamps, and so that was where they looked when they sought anything dinosaurian. Nearly all of their bone discoveries have been made in such sediments. But this may have been a case of self-fulfilling prophecy: if these were the only places they looked, they would be the only places where they would find fossils. Horner, however, found his nests built on what had been higher, more arid ground. The site near Choteau, judging by some clam fossils in the flats, may have been a peninsula jutting out into a large lake. According to Horner's hypothesis, his dinosaurs migrated from the lowlands some 100 kilometers away to lay their eggs and care for their infants away from the carnivorous dinosaurs that preyed on them.

These were the kinds of insights into dinosaurian behavior that made the discoveries of Horner and Makela so appealing. Paleontologists might learn the sizes, shapes, and postures of these creatures from bones preserved after death, but so little had hitherto been known of them as living, flesh-and-blood animals—and almost nothing of their family lives.

THE FIRST ASPECTS of the dinosaurian way of life to be deduced with any degree of certainty, as we have seen, related to locomotion and sustenance.

If the animal's fore limbs were considerably shorter than its hind limbs, it was generally assumed to be bipedal. This was certainly true if the front limbs ended in pointed claws for grasping. But some dinosaurs had horny, hooflike growths on the digits of the shorter front limbs and must therefore have been quadrupedal for at least some of the time. The largest sauropods, with four strong, pillarlike limbs and elephantlike feet, were undoubtedly quadrupedal. Trackways of their fossilized footprints provided confirmation. The shape of the limb bones and configuration of the hips and shoulders, moreover, showed that dinosaurs stood more upright than other reptiles, which are sprawlers.

Similarly, the teeth provided clues to diet. If the animals had simple peg teeth, they probably lived on soft vegetation. If the teeth were larger and arranged on jaws to work like a pair of shears, the animals must have eaten coarse vegetation that required much cutting and grinding. A few dinosaurs had no teeth at all, which left them to survive probably on insects, eggs, and soft fruit. Those with the most menacing teeth, long and sharp or serrated, were the meat eaters, which preyed on the grazing herbivores like lions on wildebeests. Bones also betrayed the dinosaur's general taste in food. Denser, laminated bones belonged to carnivores.

In a few cases, scientists have found direct evidence of a dinosaur's diet.

A mummified anatosaur, for instance, had died on a full stomach, the contents of which included conifer needles, twigs, fruit, and seeds. This dry-land fare was discovered in 1922 but ignored by scientists because it contradicted the conventional image of hadrosaurs as aquatic animals. If it has a bill like a duck, the thinking went, it must eat like a duck—that is, feed primarily on aquatic plants. John Ostrom resurrected the anatosaur report in 1964 to correct this misimpression about the eating habits of this and probably other hadrosaurs.

Some dinosaurs may have swallowed rocks, as many birds ingest fine gravel, to aid in their digestion of food. Dinosaur hunters have often found extremely smooth stones associated with sauropod skeletons. They are called gastroliths, "stomach stones." But some dubious scientists call them gastromyths. More likely the stones were worn and polished by water from a long-ago stream, not by dinosaur gastric juices.

Scientists over the years have also sought to extract some idea of dinosaur physiology and behavior from the size and shape of their brains. They start by making casts of the brain cavity. Their brains, as people never tire of saying with an air of superiority, were extremely small in relation to their bodies and so their intelligence could not have been impressive. But some of their senses may have compensated somewhat for this mental deficiency. A careful examination of the brain structure has revealed fairly well-developed olfactory bulbs and optic lobes, indicating keen sense of smell and vision. The inner bone structure of their ears suggests excellent hearing. They must have been able to hear extremely high notes, perhaps the squeaky voices of their young—an ability important for maintaining family cohesion, if such existed. And all dinosaurs had orbits for very large eyes. What color? No one knows, but the eyes of modern reptiles usually run to red or yellow.

Nor is there any proof that dinosaurs could give voice to whatever thoughts crossed their small brains. But there are assumptions. Some bones in their skulls suggest that they had a good voice. W. E. Swinton, the British paleontologist, has written: "In this they may well have equalled the crocodiles, all of which have a short and loud croak or bark by means of which they identify one another in the dark or which they use when they are angry." Horner speculated that his Montana maiasaurs might have made a noise by blowing air through their nasal passages. This could have produced a deep tuba sound. Or a sound more like a French horn, according to Philip Currie of the Tyrrell Museum of Paleontology in Alberta, who observed that one duck-billed species had resonating chambers inside the crest at the top of their heads that resembled the chambers of that musical instrument. Perhaps, Currie said, the calls of the dinosaurs could be reproduced with computer simulations based on the size and shape of their skulls.

The dinosaurs, like all animals, must have had their means of attacking, fending off attack, or fleeing from attackers. The grazers may have relied on their sight and hearing to detect predators in time to flee, perhaps croaking or barking or sounding their tubas to alert others of imminent peril. Others had their claws, sharp talons, clublike tails, and spiky horns for attack and defense. The triceratops may have engaged in combat like belligerent rams, thrusting and parrying with their powerful horns. Their skeletons sometimes bear deep wounds in the bony frill that projected backwards like a shield over their neck and shoulders.

In 1971, the Polish-Mongolian expedition found in the Gobi the remains of two dinosaurs that quite possibly had killed each other. The predator, a small, swift *Velociraptor,* was locked around its prey, an armored *Protoceratops.* The *Velociraptor* had a sicklelike talon on each hind foot, which resembled the talons on Ostrom's *Deinonychus.* One of the predator's talons was embedded in the region that must have been the prey's belly. It was not clear how the *Protoceratops* had exacted its last-gasp retribution. Much, however, was made of this discovery as further support for the new view of dinosaurs as more agile and active animals than ordinary reptiles.

Even more has been made of the tracks left by dinosaurs. Footprints, as Richard Swann Lull of Yale once said, "are fossils of living beings, while all the other relics are those of the dead." From the trackways of footprints scientists have gauged the speed of running dinosaurs, witnessed predators in hot pursuit of sauropods, and drawn their first understanding of dinosaur behavior in groups. Dinosaurs, it seemed, often traveled in herds. They could be gregarious creatures.

One of the first major discoveries stemming from footprints rescued the brontosaurs from the water, in a sense, and deposited them firmly on land. Some picture books still show them up to their nostrils in swampy water, lethargic if not immobile, munching on soft aquatic plants. Paleontologists used to think this must have been the brontosaurs' lot in life. Their legs were not stout enough to support their massive bodies, the scientists reasoned, and so they needed the water's buoyancy to hold them up. And there was the nasal opening up on top of the head, which presumably enabled the animal to breathe while almost completely submerged; hence the lasting image of the brontosaur as the hippopotamus of the dinosaurs, only more sluggish. The image began to change—in the minds of scientists, if not always in the picture books—after Roland T. Bird of the American Museum of Natural History examined some dinosaur tracks in Texas in the 1940s.

Bird happened on the tracks in much the same manner as Horner came to find the baby dinosaurs. He had seen some track-bearing slabs of rock for sale at an Indian trading post. Following directions given him at the store, he arrived in the town of Glen Rose, southwest of Fort Worth, and could tell by the courthouse that his trip would surely not be in vain. A stone in the courthouse bore the imprint of a carnivore's three-toed foot, about one-half meter long. Sure, the townspeople said, they knew all about those "man tracks." Bird was told to look for them outside town in the bed of the Palaxy River.

Dinosaur footprints in Texas

There he found some four-toed prints, the first known tracks of a brontosaur. Each print was huge, a meter long. The prints were deeply impressed in what could only have been a mud flat either partly or completely exposed to the air. The prints, all two meters apart, were definitely those of an efficient terrestrial walker. The brontosaur could walk on its own four legs. It might have foraged in swampy waters, but not because their buoyancy was the only thing that enabled the animal to manage its heavy body. At another Texas site, Bird saw a continuous groove in the rock with the brontosaur footprints. The animal was dragging its long tail in the mud flat, another sign of walking, not floating. From this evidence, paleontologists realized that they should have known all along that the brontosaurs were not prisoners of water. Their fossils, it turned out, were not found in swampy sediments but in the same floodplain sediments that bore the remains of other dinosaurs of established terrestrial habits.

As Roland Bird followed the brontosaur's tracks in a subsequent digging season, he realized he was seeing a prehistoric drama unfold. Another dinosaur seemed to be chasing the brontosaur. The rock bore the prints of a three-toed carnivore, possibly an allosaur. The brontosaur swung left. The allosaur followed. Seeing this, Bird said, the digging crews could hardly wait to expose more of the rock. But they were never to know the outcome of the chase, for the rock bearing the prints eventually ran under a wall of limestone.*

The study of fossil tracks is a branch of paleontology known as "ichnology," from the Greek word for "track." The first dinosaur tracks to draw much attention were those birdlike impressions uncovered in the Connecticut River Val-

*The Glen Rose tracks have been cited by creationists as evidence that man existed at the time of the dinosaurs and that, therefore, the earth can be no more than 10,000 years old, a latter-day revision of Ussher's date. Creationist excavation teams claim to have discovered dozens of "man tracks" next to the dinosaur tracks. After examining these tracks, Steven Schafersman of the Texas Council for Science Education questioned the creationists' interpretation. In a letter to *Geotimes* (October 1983) he wrote: "Some [of the tracks] are poorly preserved dinosaur tracks, some are the rear-heel slide mark of single dinosaur footprints, some are dinosaur tracks made in extremely fluid mud in which the mud flowed back after the dinosaur extracted its foot, some are random depressions on the limestone surface with trace-fossil burrow casts misinterpreted as ridges between 'toes,' and some are artfully improved 'human footprints' showing superficial 'toes' carved in the softer lower limestone bed. . . . The molds of casts and photographs which the creationists have shown me are of decades-old, obviously carved footprints."

James Gorman reported in *Discover* (October 1981) that seventeen scientific creationists visited Horner's dig site in 1981. They were college students led by a "professor of genesis." Horner, wrote Gorman, "decided not to argue the merits of evolution, and just showed them the dig. In return, they helped find a nest."

ley of Massachusetts in 1802, when dinosaurs were still unknown. Hundreds of other trackways have since been found, in New England, Texas, Brazil, Australia, and more recently in the Peace River Canyon of British Columbia. Indeed, dinosaur tracks are more plentiful than dinosaur bones.

Two geologists who delve into ichnology, David J. Mossman of Mount Allison University in New Brunswick and William A. S. Sarjeant of the University of Saskatchewan, wrote in the January 1983 issue of *Scientific American* of their profession's analytical techniques:

> Ideally a trackway suitable for analysis should consist of a sequence of at least three footprints or casts. Among quadrupeds locomotion is initiated with the hind foot on one side, followed by the forefoot on the same side and then by the hind foot and the forefoot on the other side. In fast locomotion two or three feet touch the ground simultaneously; in slower locomotion three feet or all four do so. In jumping locomotion all four footprints are set close together; they do not overlap. Jumping tracks are extremely rare in the fossil record. . . . The tracks of bipeds normally show the left and right feet alternating; the footprints are rarely side by side.
>
> The analyst's first job is to make four basic measurements of a trackway. The first is a measurement of stride, or forward movement; it is made from a fixed point on one footprint to the same point on the next print of the same foot. The second is a measurement of pace; it is the distance between the right forefoot and the left forefoot and between the right hind foot and the left hind foot. The length of the stride is usually identical for the forefeet and the hind feet, but the length of the pace may differ greatly. The third is a measurement of pace angulation, or step angle; it is the angle formed by joining the midpoint of three successive hind-foot prints or three successive forefoot prints. The fourth is a measurement of trackway breadth. . . . the mark of an inefficient walker is a broad trackway and a short stride. Conversely, a narrow trackway and a long stride are evidence of an efficient walker moving fast. A trackway moderate in both width and stride, however, can be evidence of either a not too efficient walker or an efficient walker moving at a relatively low speed.

Through such analysis of the Peace River tracks scientists, using a formula devised by R. McNeill Alexander of the University of Leeds, determined that some dinosaurs were capable of moving quite briskly. Some medium-size carnivores were traveling 16.5 kilometers per hour, close to the highest running speed of a human being. Some of the slower carnivores were doing between 6 and 8.5 kilometers per hour. The herbivores were even slower, with top speeds of 6 kilometers per hour. In similar calculations, James O. Farlow, a former student of Ostrom and an independent dinosaur specialist from Michigan, reported in 1981 that some carnivores that left tracks in Texas attained running speeds of up to 42 kilometers per hour, much faster than humans but no match for greyhounds and thoroughbred horses. Some other estimates indicated that the tyrannosaur, when necessary, could exceed 45 or 50 kilometers per hour.

Tyrannosaurs, it appeared from the tracks, traveled alone or sometimes in pairs. But the pack or herd instinct must have been strong in other species. At Peace River, six trackways of medium-size carnivores are all headed in the same general direction as if they were in a hunting pack. At Connecticut's Dinosaur State Park, many of the prints run closely parallel, as if the dinosaurs were in a herd. Similar evidence of sauropod herds is prominent in Roland Bird's Texas trackways. Robert Bakker, in a recent reexamination of these tracks, believed that he recognized signs of a "structured" herd, with the young in the center surrounded and protected by the adults.

Jack Horner found evidence in Montana that his hadrosaurs not only had nesting colonies but remained in groups throughout most if not all of their lives. At several sites he uncovered the remains of three-meter-long juveniles in the company of six- and seven-meter adults. There were twenty-two juveniles together with ten adults in one place.

It may not seem like much to know that some dinosaurs traveled in packs or herds and others were caring parents, but such behavior clearly set these animals apart from other reptiles. Most reptiles, as well as fish and amphibians, abandon their eggs as soon as they are laid. Some fish and reptiles, including crocodiles, will guard their eggs until or shortly after hatching, and then the little ones must fend for themselves. No modern reptiles live in social aggregations like packs or herds. Dinosaurs were different. Some of them had a family life of sorts and a sense of community.

HORNER LEFT PRINCETON in 1982 and moved back to Montana, where he could be nearer to Egg Mountain. He became curator of paleontology at the Museum of the Rockies on the campus of Montana State University in Bozeman. By then, too, he had enough eggs, nests, and skeletons of young and adult dinosaurs to feel a theory coming on. He is bolder than many paleontologists in proposing theories and creating scenarios of dinosaurian life. "Too many scientists' idea of success is not wanting to be contradicted until after they're dead," he said, leaving no doubt that this was not his style. Armed with facts and much conjecture, Horner ventured into a thicket dense with snarling scientific predators, the area of sociobiology.

Horner felt that the professional risks were worth taking because social behavior inferred from the tracks and nests could have a bearing on the dinosaurs' tremendous success over 160 million years. Sociobiologists believe that certain basic behaviors are passed from one generation to the next through the genes. One such trait, the altruism of food sharing, is observed primarily in birds and mammals. If the maiasaur parents were bringing food to their young in the nests, as Horner had surmised, then perhaps they and some other dinosaurs carried such altruism in their genes. Without it, without some instinct for society in which food was shared, some dinosaurs might never have prospered in a world full of predators.

Hadrosaurs, for instance, were bipedal herbivores with no obvious means of effective defense—no horns or spikes or armor. Nor were they capable of running fast; they were slow waddlers. They must have been quite vulnerable to predation, particularly when alone or young. Therefore, as the new evidence indicated, they found it necessary to stay in herds and care for their infants for several months after hatching, keeping them in relatively well-protected colonies. They must have been doing something right, for despite their vulnerabilities, hadrosaurs were among the most abundant dinosaurs that ever lived.

Enough juvenile hadrosaurs were obviously surviving to replenish the population. As Horner concluded in 1983, this was probably because they employed a "survival strategy" comparable to one most common among birds, the building of nests in colonies. They laid many fewer eggs than other reptiles, protected the nest through incubation, and then took up the task of bringing food to the young. (The heavy adults did not sit on the eggs during incubation, which would have had a crushing effect on the breed, but probably covered them with vegetation and let fermentation generate the heat.) Colonial nesting and egg guarding are practiced by crocodiles, but not food sharing. For hadrosaurs, Horner argued, both food sharing and extended parental supervision were a necessity. Otherwise, he said, the probabilities of one or two of these small, nonaggressive individuals surviving out of a nest of twenty to twenty-five would be slim indeed. The fact that there were at least two juveniles for every adult in a presumed herd suggested an average 8 percent survival rate for the young. The fact that so many infants were found still in the nests suggested that the parents brought them their food. For the baby dinosaurs to go out foraging with their parents at that stage would be to run the risk of being eaten by predators or trampled to death in the herd.

Like many birds, the young hadrosaurs remained nestbound by instinct. How long they stayed is not known, but it must have been for several months, until they had grown to at least one and a half meters in length. Those fifteen hatchlings that Horner discovered first had stayed in their nest while the parents went foraging. When the parents, having met with some disaster, never returned, the babies remained in the nest by instinct and starved to death. "Ground nesting birds will do that—just stay there and starve," said Makela.

The hypsilophodonts on Egg Mountain were somewhat different, Horner said. They apparently remained in the nesting area for several months, but may have gone out foraging with their parents. These were lighter, faster, and more agile creatures, which must have improved their chances of survival while grazing. Whether their parents also brought food back to them is less clear than in the case of the hadrosaurs.

Such behavior as parental care and food sharing may have been restricted to only a few species, Horner concluded, but it could also reflect a broad "sociobiologic divergence" between the two main branches of dinosaurs, the ornithischians and the saurischians. The other species known to have arranged its eggs in circular nests with obvious care, as seen by Roy Chapman Andrews, was the *Protoceratops,* also ornithischian. Less is known about saurischian eggs, though some found in France could be an important clue. The round eggs of a brontosaurlike dinosaur, perhaps *Hypselosaurus,* were laid out in long linear rows, which is not the best arrangement if they had in mind nest feeding. It could be, as Horner said, that ornithischians laid eggs in circular clutches and saurischians laid eggs in rows.

The somewhat more sophisticated social behavior of some dinosaurs may have been an evolutionary adaptation tied in to herbivory. Though a few carnivores may have hunted in packs, the dinosaurs that are known to have traveled in herds, a more coherent form of group organization, were plant-eating sauropods. "Even if these were just aggregations and not strictly speaking herds, that's a behavior we don't see in any other reptiles," Horner said. "We see that only in birds and mammals." Moreover, the ornithischians, as Horner pointed out, were "the first large group of herbivores to inhabit the earth, and in order for them to have survived, competed, and particularly to have achieved such a triumphant success, a strong social order would have been a necessity."

Jack Horner conceded that his ideas on the social life of dinosaurs relied heavily on conjecture and in many instances were not testable by any known scientific observations. Most scientists, for these reasons, have so far reserved judgment. Hotton, for one, has some doubts about Horner's interpretations but no doubts about Horner, describing him as "a whiz—very intelligent, very capable, and with a streak of luck you wouldn't believe." Luck was with Horner and Makela in finding the dinosaur nesting grounds and nurseries in western Montana, and this discovery could not be ignored by those who were refining and revising the image of dinosaurs. It raised anew the debate over dinosaurian warm-bloodedness. The parallels between the assumed parental care of the maiasaurs and the nesting behavior of many birds aroused even more interest. The wonder of dinosaurs is that they were most peculiar animals, a world apart from living reptiles. The wonder also is that, after evolving, adapting, and enduring in ways that may forever defy scientific explication, their world came apart with such apparent suddenness.

14 *The Great Dying*

SOMETHING HAPPENED 65 million years ago, at the end of the Cretaceous, something so devastating that it altered the course of life on earth. With seeming abruptness, as geologic time goes, almost half of the genera living throughout the world disappeared, animal life and vegetable, marine and terrestrial, large and small. Gone in the great dying were all the ammonites, those flat spiral shellfish related to the chambered nautilus and squid. Gone were many bivalves, reef-building animals, sponges, and all but a few species of the single-celled marine plankton so critical to the food chain; one-fourth of all marine families perished. Gone, too, were the pterosaurs, most of the little marsupials, and all the large tetrapods. No species living exclusively on land and weighing more than twenty-five kilograms seem to have survived, and the most conspicuous of the nonsurvivors were the dinosaurs. Although the fossils of a variety of dinosaurs are found in the uppermost Cretaceous rocks, none has ever been unearthed in the Tertiary layer just above. The dinosaurs had vanished, never to be seen again. Extinctions at the close of the Cretaceous rang down the curtain on the Age of Reptiles.

Many dinosaurs had already expired. The armored stegosaurs departed before the Cretaceous began. The giants, *Diplodocus, Brachiosaurus,* and *Brontosaurus,* became extinct in the Cretaceous long before the great dying. All or nearly all such sauropods had disappeared. Most of the iguanodonts were already extinct. But dinosaurs still existed toward the end of the Cretaceous—ankylosaurs, ceratopsians, coelurosaurs, hadrosaurs, hypsilophodonts, and the great tyrannosaurs—though the number and range of these last dinosaurs are matters of much dispute. Among the other archosaurs, the marine crocodiles and many ichthyosaurs had probably already vanished, but the plesiosaurs, pterosaurs, and mosasaurs seem to have been flourishing at the end of the Cretaceous—and then were gone. Only some crocodilians, of all the archosaurs, managed to struggle across that eventful boundary of time from the Cretaceous into the Tertiary period and then survive to the present day.

The something that happened 65 million years ago is one of the most intriguing and perplexing mysteries of science. Scientists of all stripes, and just about anyone with a little imagination, have taken a stab at solving the puzzle, or at least speculating about it. The mystery may never be solved, though recent discoveries have reopened the case and rekindled a debate that once before incited geology and paleontology. Finding the culprit in the case of the vanished dinosaurs is considered important because the deed was so decisive for subsequent evolution—and a recurrence could yet again send global life off on an entirely different course.

THE DINOSAURS, of course, could not live forever. No creatures, no plants, no tiny bacteria are forever, not even *Homo sapiens.* As Georges Cuvier began to recognize long ago, and as all scientists now hold to be true, extinction is the fate of all species. As Cuvier did not recognize, because in defending extinction he denied evolution, extinction is the inevitable outcome of evolution and a critical agent in determining evolution's course. At least 99 percent of all species that ever lived are now extinct. Their allotted time may have been short or long; single species and groups of species, Darwin observed, "last for very unequal periods." And as large groups of creatures go, the dinosaurs had a long and prosperous run on earth before they went.

Extinction, moreover, sometimes occurs on an epidemic scale. Cuvier had noted this, too, in formulating his catastrophist model of geologic history. Darwin, while believing extinctions were usually part of a gradual process, acknowledged that in some instances they did appear to occur rapidly and virtually simultaneously. After studying the disappearance of many large mammals from South America, Darwin wrote: "Certainly no fact in the world is so startling as the wide and repeated exterminations of its inhabitants." These "wide and repeated exterminations" are now called mass extinctions.

Scientists argued about mass extinctions for years. Some said they may only seem to have been sudden and global because of the imperfect fossil record, which might not afford an understanding of trends leading up to the extinction. Fossils reveal so much of the past, but only so much. The resolution of time represented by a particular stratum is often no better than a few million years.

How, then, can the simultaneity of extinctions be established? But most scientists, including former disbelievers, now agree that the earth has suffered at least five great mass extinctions and several lesser ones.

Although as many as 70 percent of algal forms died out 650 million years ago, in the earliest known mass extinction, the list usually begins with the even more pervasive dying toward the end of Cambrian time, some half a billion years ago.* More than half of all animal species vanished then, including numerous species of trilobites. Another 30 percent of animal life, including many primitive fish, became extinct at the end of the Devonian, 360 million years ago. The most catastrophic extinction occurred 248 million years ago at the close of the Permian, when half of all animal families disappeared. Some 75 percent of the amphibians and all the surviving trilobites were wiped out. The toll was especially high among reptiles—an 80 percent loss—and this apparently cleared the field for the rise of the early dinosaurs. The dinosaurs somehow survived the next mass extinction, when most other reptiles died off 213 million years ago at the end of the Triassic. Then came the Cretaceous calamity, the most recent of the really great extinctions.

Identifying mass extinctions is one thing; explaining them is quite another matter. They have seemed to be random events, though a recent analysis suggests otherwise. Their occurrence near the ends of geologic periods simply reflects the fact that the stratigraphers who established the geologic time-scale chose major breaks in the fossil record as boundaries for most of these principal subdivisions; the fossil disruptions define the boundaries, not vice versa. Certain fossils are there in one layer of rock, then absent from the layer above, but the rocks are apparently bereft of any clue as to what caused the abrupt change. At least this seemed to be the situation until a surprising discovery was made in recent years.

But scientists have not let a scarcity of information discourage them from offering theories to explain mass extinctions, particularly the one that eliminated the dinosaurs. This is the ultimate wonder of dinosaurs, their apparently sudden extinction. Scientists seem to have as morbid a curiosity on this matter as schoolchildren. Some of the theories have seemed plausible, but are unsupportable by any known evidence. They are speculation and nothing more; true as speculation may in some cases be, there is no way of proving the truth.

*The five mass extinctions are based on N. D. Newell's estimates of the percentage of families that disappeared. D. M. Raup and J. J. Sepkoski, examining the fossil record for marine life, do not include the Cambrian extinction on their list. It is replaced with an episode at the end of the Ordovician, 438 million years ago.

Some theories have reflected human condescension toward the dinosaurs as the supposed dim-witted failures of evolution. Some have been outright flights of fancy, stopping just short of the notion expressed in 1941 by Will Cuppy, the humorist. "The Age of Reptiles," he wrote, "ended because it had gone on long enough and it was all a mistake in the first place." Dinosaurs were ugly, Cuppy said, and deserved extinction.

An enumeration of the many theories, from the serious to the facetious, was made in 1964 by Glenn L. Jepson, a Princeton scientist. He wrote:

> Authors with varying competence have suggested that dinosaurs disappeared because the climate deteriorated (became suddenly or slowly too hot or cold or dry or wet), or that the diet did (with too much food or not enough of such substances as fern oil; from poisons in water or plants or ingested minerals; by bankruptcy of calcium or other necessary elements). Other writers have put the blame on disease, parasites, wars, anatomical or metabolic disorders (slipped vertebral discs, malfunction or imbalance of hormone and endocrine systems, dwindling brain and consequent stupidity, heat sterilization, effects of being warm-blooded in the Mesozoic world), racial old age, evolutionary drift into senescent overspecialization, changes in the pressure or composition of the atmosphere, poison gases, volcanic dust, excessive oxygen from plants, meteorites, comets, gene pool drainage by little mammalian egg-eaters, overkill capacity by predators, fluctuation of gravitational constants, development of psychotic suicidal factors, entropy, cosmic radiation, shift of Earth's rotational poles, floods, continental drift, extraction of the moon from the Pacific Basin, drainage of swamp and lake environments, sunspots, God's will, mountain building, raids by little green hunters in flying saucers, lack of even standing room in Noah's Ark, and paleoweltschmerz.

ONE OF THE HOARIEST "explanations" for the dinosaurs' undoing sprang from the concept of racial senescence. Earlier generations of scientists believed that a race of animals, like the life of an individual, goes through stages of growth and decline. It has its youth, its period of adaptation and maturation, its more settled middle age, and, finally, its period of senility. And so, toward the end of the Cretaceous, senility must have come to the dinosaurs. Evidence for this senility was said to be manifest in the apparent overossification of the dinosaurs' skulls—the bony frills of *Triceratops,* the nasal plume of some hadrosaurs, and the solid-bone dome of *Pachycephalosaurus.* These were assumed to be abnormal and useless features, the result perhaps of a hypothetical malfunction of the pituitary gland. Subsequent research, however, revealed that these features probably had their functions in supporting jaw muscles and sensory organs. They were evidence not of senility but of continuing adaptability. Scientists no longer subscribe to ideas of racial senescence.

Nor is there now much support for the notion that dinosaurs were victims of their inferior brainpower. Humans, who probably have more brain capacity than necessary, are forever putting down other creatures in this fashion. Louis Dollo, the Belgian paleontologist, was among the first to call attention to the small and rather primitive brains of dinosaurs as a likely factor in their demise. Limited intelligence presumably made it hard for them to adapt to changing external conditions. Times changed; the dinosaurs could not. But some of the dinosaurs' contemporaries with apparently no greater intelligence, turtles and crocodiles, survived the mass extinction. Some dinosaurs, such as the tyrannosaurs and the stenonychosaurs, had evolved relatively larger brains, but this did not save them.

The scourge of disease has also been raised as an explanation, and generally disposed of. Rarely is a species wiped out by disease; natural selection acts to favor disease-causing organisms that do not rapidly or fully exterminate their host plants or animals. Even more rarely, if ever, have many related species along with unrelated life been destroyed almost simultaneously by disease.

Scientists thus turned increasingly to theories of a more widely catastrophic nature. They looked for various climatologic, geologic, and other physical forces that might account for a mass extinction. Once again, in the absence of certainty they let their imaginations run free—so free that David M. Raup, chairman of geophysical sciences at the University of Chicago, likens most of these theories to Rudyard Kipling's *Just So Stories.* "They are impossible to document, except by wishful thinking," Raup said.

Nevertheless, the Cretaceous Just So Stories illustrate the range of possibilities that have been considered in recent years. The following are some of the more interesting ones:

• Destruction of the earth's ozone layer. Since the late Cretaceous was a time of widespread volcanic activity, M. L. Keith, professor emeritus of geochemistry at Pennsylvania State University, suggested that chlorine from the hydrochloric acid in volcanic gases could have depleted the upper atmosphere's protective ozone layer. This region acts as a shield against the most damaging ultraviolet radiations from the sun. Bare-skinned creatures such as dinosaurs would have been particularly vulnerable. The furry mammals, feathered birds, and bottom-dwelling sea creatures must have had enough protection to account for their survival.

• Carbon dioxide and the "greenhouse effect." Volcanism sets the stage for the supposed conditions recommending this theory, too. Dewey McLean, a geologist at the Virginia Polytechnic Institute, proposed that a massive volcanic eruption could have so saturated the atmosphere with carbon dioxide that it caused a sharp rise in temperatures worldwide. Deep-sea cores drilled by the *Glomar Challenger,* an oceanographic ship, indicate that ocean waters, and thus presumably the atmosphere, grew warmer 65 million years ago. According to McLean, the excessive carbon dioxide would have permitted solar energy to enter the atmosphere but would have blocked the radiation of most surface heat back out into space, thereby creating a "greenhouse effect" not unlike that which exists on the hellishly hot planet of Venus. Rising temperatures could have killed off or reduced the activity of plankton, disrupting food chains and also compounding the climatic disaster because of plankton's normal role in converting carbon dioxide to oxygen through photosynthesis. A rise of only a few degrees can also affect adversely the fertility of large animals by diminishing their ability to generate viable sperm.* This had been suggested by Raymond Cowles in speculations arising from his and Colbert's experiments in the 1940s with alligator temperatures. Such infertility, McLean concluded, might have been what happened to the mastodon, giant ground sloth, and saber-toothed tiger at the end of the most recent ice age. It could also have killed off the dinosaurs. But this hypothesis, which has been around for several decades in various forms, is untestable. Testicles do not fossilize, and even if they did, there would be no way to infer their temperature tolerances.

• Arctic Ocean spillover. This theory assumes that, for a brief time at least, the surface waters of the ocean became cooler, not warmer. As the continents drifted apart during the Mesozoic, the Arctic Ocean could conceivably have become isolated. Its waters might then have become brackish or even fresh. Then, if the dam broke, say, between Greenland and Norway, the colder, lighter Arctic water would have poured into the warmer Atlantic, forming a layer of frigid water on top of the heavier, salty seawater. This could have

*Stephen Jay Gould recalls another sex-related hypothesis. "Someone once proposed in all seriousness," he writes, "that male dinosaurs became too heavy to mount their partners for sexual intercourse, although I could never figure out why little *Velociraptor* became extinct along with its giant cousins (not to mention what the giant brontosaurs were doing during the 100 million years or so of their success)."

caused a drop in the world ocean temperatures of as much as ten degrees Celsius. If this happened, according to Stefan Gartner and James P. McGuirk of Texas A & M University and John Kearney of Phillips Petroleum Company, a devastating chill and drought would have spread over much of the world. The hypothesis suffers one flaw: there is no evidence that the Arctic Ocean was ever fresh or brackish.

• Stress and thin eggshells. The dinosaurs may have suffered from too much of a good thing, or so it seemed to Heinrich K. Erben of Bonn University in West Germany. He got to thinking about this when he discovered that the eggshells of one dinosaur species grew progressively thinner with time. He went on to reason that a warm climate and luxurious swamps led to "biological prosperity," which, in turn, produced overpopulation, overcrowding, and all the attendant stresses. Stress in birds is known to result in an imbalance of the hormonal system. Stress could have increased the estrogen levels in the dinosaur females, causing them to lay eggs with shells too thin to assure the next generation of a start in life. But did this happen to all dinosaurs or only the one species?

• Magnetic reversals. From time to time, with no apparent regularity and for no known reason, the earth's magnetic field changes polarity. North becomes south, magnetically speaking, and vice versa. The last time this occurred, 700,000 years ago, the magnetic north pole was in Antarctica; a compass needle would have pointed in that direction. Then, over a relatively brief interval of time, the pole shifted to where it is now, to the north. Since magnetic minerals in rocks, when they form, align themselves with the magnetic field, whichever way it is pointing, scientists have learned how to read the history of magnetic reversals. These have occurred many times in the past, perhaps several times in the late Cretaceous. No one is sure, but this might have had a bearing on the extinctions. The magnetic field, like the ozone layer, acts as a shield against lethal outside forces. During a reversal, according to this hypothesis, the magnetic field became weak to nonexistent, which left the earth without one of its defenses against bombardment by deadly cosmic particles.

• Constipation and poison. Sounding a more frankly whimsical note, Anthony Hallam, a British paleontologist, proposed a few years ago that a change in plant life during the Cretaceous made all the difference. In view of the change in the plants dinosaurs ate and its possible gastrointestinal effect, Hallam said, "One is led ineluctably to the conclusion that the poor dinosaurs died of constipation." A related but more serious proposal is that the emergence of flowering plants could have poisoned them. These plants contained toxic alkaloids. Smaller animals with less voracious appetites could have survived the doses, but perhaps the dinosaurs could not. Ronald K. Siegel, a psychiatrist at the University of California at Los Angeles, suggested that most mammals are "smart" enough to avoid these poisons, being put off by their bitter taste. But the dinosaurs might not have had the sense or the livers. These beasts, he speculated, could neither taste the bitterness nor detoxify the ingested substances. This hypothesis is virtually useless to science. There is no way of knowing what dinosaurs tasted and what their livers could detoxify. Moreover, the flowering plants appeared more than 40 million years before the end of the Cretaceous. The dinosaurs, if so poisoned, must have suffered lingering species deaths of unrivaled duration.

The more serious attempts to solve the mystery focused on general conditions. It was not the dinosaurs themselves that had failed, but something greater. Species of animals that have survived for millions of years must be well adapted to their environment; otherwise, they would not be surviving. The dinosaurs generally were successful creatures. They would have continued to survive so long as the conditions of their existence did not change. If the conditions changed slowly, the organisms might have had time to adapt through ordinary evolutionary processes. Extinction occurs because of change, sudden change, the kind of change whose effects cannot be adapted to by individual organisms in a matter of a few generations. This is what overtook the passenger pigeon, the classic case of twentieth-century extinction; the clearing of the forest for agriculture robbed these pigeons of their food sources and the predation of man carried them over the brink before they had time to adjust to their straitened circumstances.

Some environmental crisis presumably spelled disaster for the dinosaurs. It had to be so sweeping that it affected countless other life forms, not only dinosaurs. Sometimes, as the terrestrial theories kept falling short, it seemed that there had to be a more exotic force at work, something extraterrestrial.

One favorite hypothesis of the extraterrestrial genre envisages the explosion of a dying star, a supernova, in our neighborhood of the universe. The beautiful Crab Nebula represents debris from such an explosion observed in the year 1054. Neither the Crab nor any other recorded supernova was close enough, however, to have any deleterious effect on the earth. But a proximate stellar explosion could have occurred some time in the course of earth's long history. If so, the explosion might have produced a huge magnetic shock wave that disrupted the earth's magnetic field, possibly reversing it, with dire effect, and also might have overwhelmed life on earth with a burst of radiation. Dale

Russell, the Canadian paleontologist, among others, proposed this cosmic catastrophe to account for what he believes was the sudden extinction of the dinosaurs. But why did the little mammals survive, or the crocodiles and birds?

Another scenario for disaster begins with a comet colliding with the earth. Harold C. Urey, the Nobel Prize–winning geochemist, raised the possibility in 1975, and many others joined in support. The impact of a comet the size of Halley's would have raised global temperatures and could have set off a chain of nuclear reactions. Because comets had recently been found to contain significant amounts of hydrogen cyanide and methyl cyanide, Kenneth J. Hsü of the Geological Institute of Zurich speculated that cometary cyanide poisoning had eliminated the marine plankton. The dinosaurs, he added, had died of heart failure from the shock of this invasion from outer space.

Hsü offered this hypothesis at a symposium on the Cretaceous extinction that was held in October 1979 at Copenhagen. "Nobody except the editor of *Nature* took me seriously," he remembered. Indeed, the scientists at the meeting seemed to have grown a little weary of all the untestable speculation, with so few facts in hand and no hypotheses that stood up to rigorous examination. "It seemed pointless," Hsü said, "to beat a dead horse"—or dead dinosaur.

These scientists seemed oblivious to the potential significance of what a California geologist had just discovered during his summers working in the mountains of Italy. He had dug up new evidence of what might well have happened to the dinosaurs. It was the kind of evidence that could pertain to the destruction not only of the dinosaurs but all the plants and animals that became extinct at the end of the Cretaceous. All of a sudden scientists had a hot clue and a new hypothesis that was testable. Science works with testable hypotheses.

15 *Out with a Bang?*

WHEN WALTER ALVAREZ found the clue, he was looking for something else. It was one of those serendipitous discoveries that sprinkle the annals of science.

Beginning in 1973, Alvarez and some colleagues had been going each summer to the Umbrian Apennines of north central Italy to study the dramatic exposures of limestone. The rock there formed out of deep-sea sediments laid down over a period of 155 million years, from the Jurassic to the Oligocene 30 million years ago. The sea gave way to dry land, and a few million years ago the rock from the former sea floor was raised in an upheaval of mountain building and exposed through eons of erosion. Nature was showing off one of its more beautiful creations, deep beds of pink limestone. They afforded esthetic pleasure long before scientific revelation. For centuries this pink limestone known as *scaglia rossa* has been a favorite of architects and stonemasons, who used it in many important buildings, including the Basilica of Saint Francis at Assisi. In the Bottaccione Gorge, near the medieval town of Gubbio, the limestone is particularly prominent and accessible, and it was here that Alvarez applied his skill as a geologist to a question of earth history. Dinosaurs were far from his mind.

His interests were paleomagnetic. Alvarez and his colleagues were looking for evidence in the rock marking reversals in the earth's magnetic field. They wanted to match the reversals found at Gubbio with the evidence of reversals being detected in the oceanic crust by ship-towed magnetometers. From this they hoped to develop, on land as well as in the sea, a more accurate and complete calendar of the earth's fluctuating magnetic history. In the course of their investigations, the geologists also sought to relate the reversals to the evolution and extinction of organisms found in the fossil record. The Gubbio limestone is rich in foraminifera, tiny (usually microscopic) creatures whose shells of calcium carbonate are the raw material of much of the world's limestone. With a hand lens, the geologists could see the forams in profusion all the way up through the beds of limestone to a point where all of them, save for a single species, disappeared abruptly. This point of foram disappearance marks the Cretaceous-Tertiary boundary, the time of the mass extinction.

Cretaceous-Tertiary boundary in the rocks at Gubbio, Italy

No magnetic reversal, it turned out, coincided with the devastation at the Cretaceous-Tertiary boundary. But where the forams disappeared, the limestone ended as well and was capped by a layer of reddish-gray clay one or two centimeters thick. The clay was almost completely barren of fossils. Above it the limestone resumed, full of fossils. Alvarez became intrigued with the story those clays might tell about the terminal Cretaceous extinction.

Alvarez, an associate professor of geology at the University of California at Berkeley, brought samples of the clay home with him in 1977 and described to his father what he had found. His father, Luis W. Alvarez, was a physicist at the Lawrence Berkeley Laboratory whose many honors included a Nobel Prize. The two scientists, father and son, wondered how many years were represented by the clay boundary, how many lean years for life on earth. With that knowledge might come an understanding of the Cretaceous-Tertiary extinctions.

The elder Alvarez, in particular, could not put the clay out of his mind. Luis Alvarez was like that. Though he specialized in cosmic rays and nuclear physics, he seemed to be one of those rare scientists who readily embraces new ideas and eagerly takes on challenges in new areas of inquiry. His interests extend, for example, over a wide range of topics in archeology and history. To him the accounts of Captain James Cook exploring the Pacific and of Sir Richard Burton disguised as a Moslem risking his life to see the Kaaba at Mecca are a source of endless excitement and inspiration. If Alvarez had been born in an earlier time, a colleague said, he would have been searching for new continents. As it is, he became a scientist and joined the search for the great unknowns of the twentieth century. "To be an explorer today," said Richard A. Muller, a physicist on the Berkeley faculty, speaking of Alvarez, "is to be a scientist."

More to the point, though, Luis Alvarez is said to have a "killer instinct" for unsolved problems worthy of attack. Though not a geologist, he plunged into the problem of the Gubbio clay; it was his kind of investigation. He describes himself as a "bump hunter," a particle physicist who looks for "resonances" or peaks that stick out above a distribution of background points. Hunting bumps was how he detected and identified cosmic rays, his primary interest. This was how he once tried to locate chambers of hidden treasure in an Egyptian pyramid. Cosmic rays are extremely high-energy particles raining on earth from all directions, and when they penetrate rock they are absorbed in proportion to the amount of rock they traverse; if there were a hollow in the rock, a hidden chamber, a higher concentration of the rays would pass through. By "X-raying" the pyramid, Alvarez hoped to find treasures as rich as those in Tukankhamen's tomb, the discovery of which was a sensation in his boyhood. But his search proved unrewarding. The Great Pyramid had no hidden chambers.

The Gubbio clay presented Alvarez with a new challenge. Typically, he met it by developing new methods of scientific investigation. He conceived of an idea for measuring how fast sediment collected on the sea floor to form the clay layer. Since cosmic dust and micrometeoritic material fall on the planet at a more or less constant rate, he reminded his son Walter, this should leave a chemical marker by which to estimate the time span at the Cretaceous boundary. Extraterrestrial material is chemically different from earth-surface material. The rare element iridium, for example, is several thousand times as plentiful in meteorites as it is in the crust of the earth. Having an affinity for iron, like other members of the platinum group of elements, most of the original iridium presumably settled to the planet's core along with the molten iron there. So Alvarez decided to take a measure of the iridium in the clay. He enlisted the assistance of Frank Asaro and Helen V. Michel, two nuclear chemists at Lawrence Berkeley Laboratory.

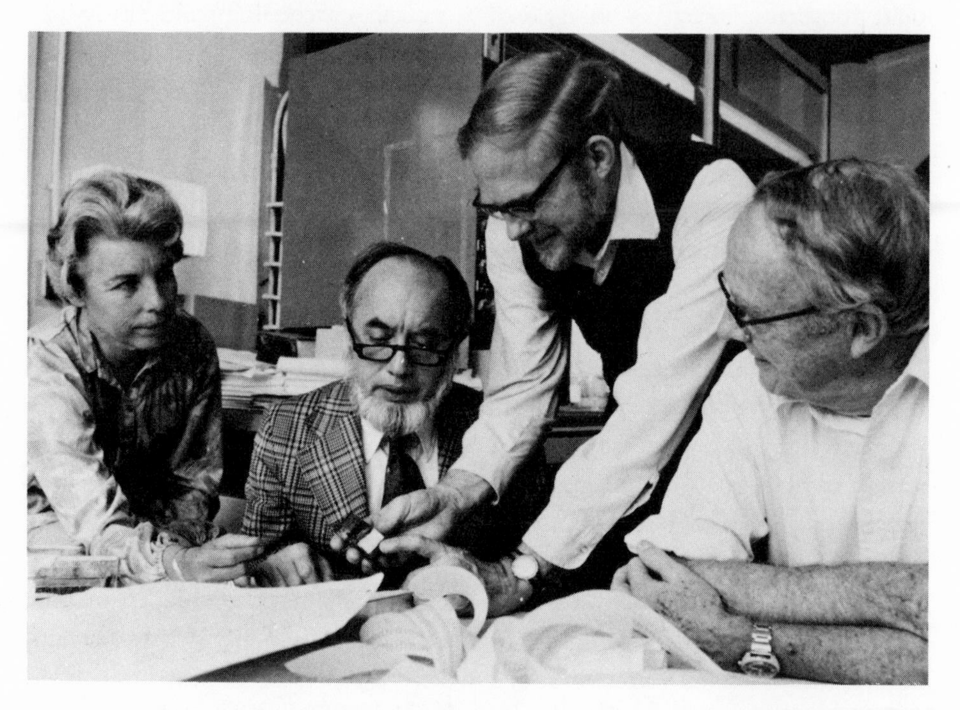

The team behind the asteroid-impact hypothesis: (From left to right) Helen V. Michel, Frank Asaro, Walter Alvarez, Luis W. Alvarez

In the geochemical study of the Gubbio clay, the Alvarez team was looking for amounts of iridium and any other telltale extraterrestrial matter so negligible in the sample that they might measure no more than one part per billion. But when Alvarez saw his first iridium "spike," he realized that the intended time-span experiment had failed, for he found more iridium in the clay than he had any right to expect on the basis of cosmic-dust fallout or normal earth processes. Thus the test was of no use as a time measurement.

In 1978, Walter Alvarez went back to Gubbio for a more complete set of rock samples running 350 meters below the boundary. The iridium concentration in them was found to be slight and fairly constant up to the boundary, where it increased sharply. The clay was thirty times richer in iridium than the sediments directly below or above it.

Asaro and Michel had supplied this astonishing information. They had measured the iridium by a technique known as neutron activation analysis. In this process, samples of the clay were irradiated in a small research reactor. Gamma rays emitted by the samples provided distinctive signatures, the bumps Alvarez looked for, that identified the kinds and amounts of elements in the material. To check themselves, when they saw the iridium anomaly, Asaro and Michel analyzed twenty-seven other elements in the boundary layer. There was nothing anomalous about their concentrations.

When the two Alvarezes saw this, they began pondering its meaning. They could not imagine that it was a coincidence for the iridium anomaly to be right there at the Cretaceous-Tertiary boundary, the time of the mass extinction. They could conceive of no "normal" depositional processes to account for what they saw. The iridium in the Gubbio clay, they felt sure, must be a significant punctuation mark in earth's history.

WALTER ALVAREZ made the first announcement of the Gubbio findings at a 1979 meeting of the American Geophysical Union in Washington. He said that the iridium evidence supported theories that it was an extraterrestrial event that triggered changes on the earth leading to the mass extinction. At first, he and his father thought the material might have come from a supernova.

Back at Berkeley, however, the four scientists did some more thinking and testing. They found reasons to reject the supernova idea. For an exploding star to have been responsible for that much iridium, they calculated, it would have had to be a mere one-tenth of a light year away. There was only a one-in-a-billion probability of that having happened in the last 500 million years. The supernova idea also failed two laboratory tests. A supernova would have produced a high concentration of plutonium-244, which would have showed up in the boundary layer. It did not. In addition, Asaro and Michel, in their neutron activation analysis, found that the clay elements were too similar to solar-system material to be from a supernova. The ratio of two common isotopes of iridium in the sample, iridium-191 and iridium-193, was almost identical to the ratio found in the solar system. It seemed too much to expect that iridium formed in other stars would exhibit the same isotopic ratios. And so the Alvarez team abandoned the supernova.

Whatever the source was, if it was extraterrestrial, the iridium enhancement would likely be seen worldwide, and in fact it was. The Alvarez team examined samples from Denmark and as far away as New Zealand and determined that the unusually high iridium concentrations in the same boundary layer seemed to be a global phenomenon.

The Alvarezes finally decided that the impact of a meteorite, a huge asteroid at least 10 kilometers in diameter, "provided a scenario that explains most or all of the biological and physical evidence" associated with the boundary layer and the mass extinctions. The asteroid, hurtling in through the atmosphere at 100,000 kilometers an hour, would have blasted out a crater 200 kilometers wide and hurled into the stratosphere a blizzard of dust, which would have spread rapidly to envelop the globe in darkness. This happened on a much lesser scale in 1883 after the eruption of the island volcano Krakatoa between Java and Sumatra. Dust from the volcano darkened skies everywhere. The haze lasted at least two years. Earlier, in 1815, the even greater eruption of Mount Tambora, also in the Dutch East Indies, cast a pall over the world, causing in 1816 what became known as "the year without a summer." Snow fell in New York State in June. Farmers lost their crops to sleet and frost as far south as Virginia. Bengal suffered famine and epidemic. A disaster of far greater magnitude would have followed the impact of the asteroid envisaged by the Alvarez group. The impact would undoubtedly have triggered violent earthquakes and monumental tidal waves. It might also have thrown up a volume of debris sixty times the asteroid's own mass. Dust from this ejecta could have turned day into night for several years. Without sunlight, photosynthesis would cease, killing plants and disrupting the food chain from the bottom up. It would have been an unmitigated disaster. Extinction would surely have been the lot of many species on the earth at the time the asteroid struck.

Recent astronomical research lent credibility to an asteroid hypothesis. Most asteroids travel in orbits safely distant from the earth, out between Mars and Jupiter, but some swing in and cross the earth's orbit. These are called Apollo objects, after the Apollo asteroid, which in 1933 was the first of these earth-crossing bodies to be discovered. From subsequent observations Eugene

M. Shoemaker, an astrogeologist with the United States Geological Survey, estimated that there must be at least 700 Apollo-class asteroids with diameters greater than one kilometer. He further calculated that on average one of these objects ten kilometers wide would collide with the earth once every 100 million years. This seemed just right for the purposes of the Alvarez team.

And so was born one of the more stunning hypotheses of modern science. The Alvarez team published their first full report, entitled "Extraterrestrial Cause for the Cretaceous-Tertiary Extinction," in the June 6, 1980, issue of the journal *Science.* The authors emphasized that the iridium anomalies were "direct physical evidence for an unusual event at exactly the time of the extinctions in the planktonic realm." They went on to declare: "None of the current hypotheses adequately accounts for this evidence, but we have developed a hypothesis that appears to offer a satisfactory explanation for nearly all the available paleontological and physical evidence."

The report then elaborated the scenario of the impacting asteroid, the enveloping dust cloud, and the lethal aftermath. Reaction to the report was swift. The popular press, which had treated Walter Alvarez's preliminary announcement with skepticism a year earlier, heralded the new report as possibly the definitive solution to the dinosaur-extinction mystery. There was appeal in the notions of a single-source cause and a devastating visitation from outer space. Gradualism may be fine in growing children and rising prices, but something there is about dinosaurs that cries out for a sudden, extraordinary end to their long, extraordinary existence.

Scientists in general found the report exciting to contemplate. Here, at last, they had before them an extinction hypothesis that not only was plausible but could be tested. A testable hypothesis can be examined and proved wrong. It can be examined and, with confirming evidence, be accepted as a working explanation of reality; however, it can never be proved correct beyond all doubt inasmuch as there is no way of knowing with absolute certainty that all factors have been considered. Still, unlike untestable speculation, testable hypotheses are a fruitful means toward understanding the nature of things, sometimes things only remotely related to the immediate question. Stephen Jay Gould wrote: "Many geologists, including myself, have long found themselves in the uncomfortable position of viewing extraterrestrial catastrophes as inherently plausible but rooting strongly against them because we knew no way of obtaining evidence for such catastrophes even if they had occurred. The asteroidal theory has changed all that."

As is the practice of science, others sought to corroborate or disprove the

Alvarez interpretation. Most of their immediate findings strengthened the case for an asteroid impact. Within two years, geologists found the same iridium-rich boundary layer at more than two dozen widely scattered sites around the world. The *Glomar Challenger* drilled into the sea floor off South Africa and brought up a core containing the clay layer with an abnormal amount of iridium. Charles J. Orth of Los Alamos National Laboratory reported that the clay layer in the Raton Basin of northeastern New Mexico also had the telltale iridium anomaly, which was the first to be recognized in sediments that did not originate on a sea floor. This was, it seemed clear, a global phenomenon. Another scientist, Ramachandran Ganapathy of the J. T. Baker Chemical Company, examined clay from Denmark and saw that eight other elements, besides iridium, occurred in proportions similar to those of a typical meteorite.

Then came another important piece of evidence. An impacting asteroid should have melted rock and flung droplets of the molten material, spherules, far and wide. Jan Smit of the Geological Institute at the University of Amsterdam was the first to find such spherules in the boundary clay, in samples from Spain. Similar discoveries were made elsewhere. The crystal arrangement of the spherules suggested formation while molten. Their composition and large size (too large for extensive atmospheric transport) suggested that they were presumably not volcanic. In most cases, interestingly, the spherules also contained high concentrations of iridium.

Some scientists who accepted the impact hypothesis were not yet prepared to believe an asteroid had been the perpetrator. They clung to notions of a cometary collision, but they could muster little support. Too little was known of the chemical composition of comets. Since comets are low-density objects, with a large component of ice, the impacting body would probably have had to be unrealistically large to have left such a distinct iridium calling card. Even so, the comet idea would live again.

There were skeptics, of course, and some of them wanted to know why the asteroid impact had left no known crater. Walter Alvarez said that he would like nothing in the world more than to find a crater to match his asteroid. But only three craters 100 kilometers or more in diameter are known. Two are Precambrian and thus too old; the other is too young. More than likely, with two-thirds of the earth covered with ocean, the asteroid would have plunged into the sea, in which case the crater may have escaped notice, or probably has been eroded beyond recognition, or may have slipped out of sight beneath the continents as a result of the dynamics of plate tectonics. In the last 65 million years, according to the estimated rate of sea-floor spreading, about half of the Cretaceous sea floor has probably disappeared back into the earth's mantle as new sea floor was created.

The asteroid hypothesis, to skeptics and supporters, added fresh yeast to the study of extinction and evolution. In October 1981, some 120 people from across the spectrum of science—astrogeologists, atmospheric physicists, geophysicists, oceanographers, climatologists, paleontologists, biostratigraphers, and biologists—met for four days at the resort of Snowbird, Utah, to discuss what they knew or thought, as well as what they did not know but thought they needed to know, concerning the iridium anomaly and the effects of huge impacts on life. Despite its title—"Conference on Large Body Impacts and Terrestrial Evolution: Geological, Climatological, and Biological Implications"—the meeting gravitated, as everyone knew it would, toward the question uppermost in all minds: how strong was the case for the Alvarez asteroid hypothesis?

Walter Alvarez held firm on the matter of iridium. It was indisputably there in the boundary clays. He reported that the number of sites containing the anomaly had now risen to thirty-six, though he had to withdraw "with some embarrassment" an additional sample that had been recently reported; the test results were not reproducible and thus could not be authenticated. The iridium in this instance was traced to contamination from the wedding ring of a technician who had handled the sample; jewelry platinum contains about 10 percent iridium.

Further investigation, Alvarez also reported, showed that the Gubbio layer and at least three others had been deposited within the same paleomagnetic period, a time of reversed polarity. (Alvarez, in this case, was getting back to the work that had taken him to Italy in the first place.) The other samples had either not been analyzed yet or were resisting analysis because they lay in sediments that did not yield a clear magnetic fingerprint. Establishing a common time zone for all the boundary clays would strengthen a major premise of the hypothesis, which was that the terminal Cretaceous extinctions had occurred simultaneously throughout the world and that the iridium-rich clays served to incriminate an earth-impacting asteroid. But even without a clear magnetic marker, Alvarez argued, the iridium anomaly, if the impact hypothesis was correct, would itself serve as a worldwide time marker of high precision. Others, however, were not ready to agree.

Alvarez encountered a serious challenge to the entire hypothesis on the first morning of the Snowbird meeting. Owen B. Toon of the National Aeronautics and Space Administration's Ames Research Center questioned whether dust from the asteroid impact would have remained in the stratosphere as long as the Alvarezes assumed. They had given an estimate of three years, based on reports after the Krakatoa eruption describing dramatic sunsets around the world for that length of time. Toon thought it more likely, based on new knowledge of the behavior of aerosols, that the Krakatoa dust fell out in about three months. It was not dust, but the volcano's sulfurous gases, that had created the more persistent haze that produced the striking sunsets long after the eruption. Even if the asteroid impact had flung greater volumes of dust into the sky, Toon continued, the longest the darkness could have lasted was three to six months. The tiniest particles, which alone might remain airborne for two years, would tend to coagulate into larger particles heavy enough to fall out at much faster rates.

Toon's argument exposed a potential weakness in the hypothesis. It now appeared that the impact dust could not have remained in the stratosphere long enough for winds to distribute it across the latitudes from one hemisphere to another. Experience with particles from hydrogen bomb tests in the 1950s showed that it takes approximately one year for suspended material to move from the Northern Hemisphere to the Southern Hemisphere. How, then, could the asteroid have caused a global darkness? Luis Alvarez recalled later: "We were in very serious trouble, except for one comforting fact—we had already seen the iridium layer worldwide, so we knew there had to be a transport mechanism."

Two groups of scientists, from Los Alamos and the California Institute of Technology, came to the Alvarezes' rescue the next day. They reported computer calculations, executed overnight, showing that the impact dust could have been spread not by stratospheric winds but by a much faster mechanism, ballistics. Perhaps the material actually went into ballistic orbits, like minuscule satellites or missiles, and was spread worldwide in a matter of hours. According to these calculations, the energy necessary to propel the particles into ballistic trajectories came from the convective winds generated by the fireball created by the impacting asteroid.

Not only did the Alvarez team then have a plausible mechanism for transporting the dust worldwide, but the downward revision of the duration of the hypothetical darkness, from three years to as little as three months, came as a relief to paleontologists at the conference. What bothered them, and still does to some degree, was that the fossil record does not give unambiguous support for a sudden, consuming catastrophe occurring simultaneously on land and sea. A three-year darkness should have wreaked greater havoc than the fossils testify to. Leo J. Hickey, director of Yale's Peabody Museum and a friend of Walter Alvarez from graduate school, had just published a highly critical report in *Nature* to the effect that "the geographically uneven and generally moderate levels of extinction and diversity change in the land flora" appeared to contradict sudden-catastrophe hypotheses. In particular, Hickey, a paleobotanist, argued that tropical plants, the ones least resistant to prolonged darkness and the resulting cold, came through the extinctions in better shape than the more northerly plants. When he heard Toon's revised estimate, Hickey conceded that tropical plants might have been able to survive a few months of darkness.

A three-month darkness also made it easier to explain the fact that the extinctions were apparently more sudden and extensive in the sea than on land or in freshwater bodies. David H. Milne of Evergreen State College in Washington State and Christopher P. McKay of the University of Colorado reported calculations that the microfauna of modern seas would consume their food reserves within 10 to 100 days of the beginning of a blackout, producing approximately the degree of extinction among oceanic plankton that is observed in the fossil record, whereas such a brief darkness would only slightly stress land plants and animals.

A brief darkness appealed to paleontologists because it "offered a means of decoupling the marine and terrestrial extinctions," reported Richard A. Kerr, a science journalist, in an article about the conference for *Science.* "The geochemists and planetary scientists could have their impact," he said, "and the paleontologists could have their gradual extinctions on land." But this deferred rather than settled the debate over whether the impact, if it did occur, caused the mass extinction.

At least one scientist, Michael R. Rampino of NASA's Goddard Institute for Space Studies, posited some less catastrophic causes to explain the iridium anomalies. Perhaps a change in seawater chemistry altered sedimentation rates or caused a hiatus in sedimentation of other elements, thus causing an abnormal concentration of iridium. Rampino noted, as an example, the significant iridium anomalies in manganese nodules found on the sea floor. But changes in seawater chemistry would not explain the iridium discovered by Orth in the terrestrial clays of New Mexico. Sounding a cautionary note, Karl K.

Turekian, a Yale geochemist, counseled against a premature acceptance of the iridium's extraterrestrial provenance. Nature, he noted, "has a way of concentrating elements in the most remarkable ways."

EVEN SO, the meeting at Snowbird ended with a consensus on the iridium. Many participants believed the Alvarez data on the anomaly to be well-nigh irrefutable. They felt that there probably was a large-body impact at the end of the Cretaceous. But they stopped short of declaring their support of the scenario of extinction that was part of the Alvarez hypothesis. The evidence on that point was not conclusive. Walter Alvarez seemed to recognize that the impact, even if established beyond doubt, might not answer all the questions about the great dying. In the conclusion to his report, published a year later in the Snowbird conference proceedings, Alvarez said: "[The] concordance of results supports the suggestion that darkness was probably at least a contributing factor in the Cretaceous-Tertiary mass extinctions." He was not saying it was *the* factor, but that it was a factor.

His father, however, was more fervent in the defense of their hypothesis. He seemed genuinely puzzled and hurt by those who continued to express doubt. In April 1982, in a lengthy and emotional presentation to the National Academy of Sciences in Washington, Luis Alvarez declared: "I think the first two points—that the asteroid hit, and that the impact triggered the extinction of much of the life in the sea—are no longer debatable points. Nearly everyone now believes them. But there are always dissenters. I understand that there is even one famous American geologist who does not yet believe in plate tectonics and continental drift." But he conceded that the third point, that the impact had something to do with the extinction of dinosaurs and the land flora, "is very much open to debate, although I believe that it very definitely did."

Luis Alvarez then reviewed four impact-induced "killing mechanisms" that could have contributed to the extinctions. There was, first, the global darkness of three to six months that halted photosynthesis. "I am confident," he said, "that it is the only one we need to explain the catastrophic extinctions in the oceans." A second "killing mechanism," he said, was the "greenhouse effect." As several scientists had suggested, an impact in the ocean could have introduced a vast amount of water vapor into the sky, which could have acted as a lid over the earth, holding in heat. Scientists estimated that the result in a few months could have been an increase of ten degrees in global temperatures, sufficient to kill many land animals. A third mechanism, suggested by Toon, would have produced dire effects because of a reverse phenomenon, a global cooling. In the period of darkness, global temperatures could drop eighteen degrees and remain at those levels for six to nine months, long enough to wipe out most animals that did not know how to hibernate. A fourth killing mechanism was based on the possibility that the fireball from the impact would have produced so much radiant energy that enormous amounts of nitrogen in the atmosphere would have been converted to nitrogen oxides. The result would have been a worldwide fall of deadly acid rain.

Luis Alvarez, in resting his case before the National Academy, said: "I think the chances are that all four of these scenarios had some part in the various extinctions, and it is going to be a life's work for some people to untangle all these things."

The paleontologists, inspired by the clues in the clay and the subsequent controversy, went back to the field to see to the untangling. They had a hypothesis to test, which is to say they could now approach the question of the mass extinction that killed off the dinosaurs with a reasonable hope that it might be answerable in a scientific way. The Alvarezes might be right, or at least partly right. But certain paleontologists were frankly skeptical, which disconcerted Luis Alvarez, who complained: "I simply do not understand why some paleontologists—who are really the people that told us all about the extinctions and without whose efforts we would never have seen any dinosaurs in the museums—now seem to deny that there ever was a catastrophic extinction. When we come along and say, 'Here is how we think the extinction took place,' some of them say, 'What extinction? We don't think there was any sudden extinction at all. The dinosaurs just died away for reasons unconnected with your asteroid.' "

But many paleontologists wanted another, closer look at the fossils in and near the boundary layer. They believed the fossils would tell them a somewhat different, more complex story about the fate of the dinosaurs.

16 *Out with a Whimper?*

THERE IS NOTHING like a bold new hypothesis to galvanize scientists into reaction and then action. Some of them responded to the asteroid hypothesis as if Georges Cuvier had returned to life, raising again the banner of catastrophism and threatening to overthrow the latter-day conventional wisdom of gradualism in all things geologic. Scientists, being human, have prejudices, and one of the more entrenched prejudices in geology and paleontology is a belief in gradualism. Rocks and fossils speak to geologists and paleontologists of change occurring slowly over immense periods of time, the legacy of Hutton and Lyell. The lenses of their minds resolve long-ago time in million-year quanta—hardly a time-scale into which to fit episodes of sudden change.

Many geologists today incline to working philosophies that allow for a mix of gradualism and catastrophism. They see the evidence for mass extinctions and the potential for global change wrought by the earth's shifting crust, the glaciations of the most recent ice age, and enormous landscape-transforming floods. Catastrophes, though not exactly of the kind Cuvier imagined, do happen. Even so, most paleontologists and many geologists were extremely reluctant to accept a theory that invoked such a singular event as a huge meteorite or comet crashing in from outer space. This was too simple, too neat.

There was, however, no denying the iridium data. It was there in the boundary layer at Gubbio and at dozens of other places around the world. Leo Hickey, who had been skeptical at first, came to accept the "physical reality" of the impact. "The geochemical evidence is now overwhelming," he said in 1983, noting in particular an independent test by two of his Yale colleagues that gave the hypothesis another boost. Jean-Marc Luck and Karl Turekian determined that the ratios of two isotopes of osmium found in the boundary layer, osmium-187 and osmium-186, were more similar to those in extraterrestrial material than to those from the earth's crust. They acknowledged that volcanic eruptions could have accounted for the unusual osmium ratios, but said that an eruption of the magnitude necessary to deposit the amounts of osmium they found "would be less likely than a large impact."

If scientists were going to shoot down this hypothesis, therefore, they would have to take aim with something more unerring than professional prejudice in favor of gradualism. They began to rethink their premises, reexamine what they knew or only thought they knew, and search for more evidence concerning the world at the time the dinosaurs perished. Many of them, like Hickey, while conceding that there might have been a devastating impact 65 million years ago, questioned whether that could have accounted for all or most of the biological consequences as revealed in the fossil record. The Alvarezes might have been right about the impact, but not about their scenarios of how it triggered the mass extinctions. A single-event cause presupposed a single, comprehensive wave of extinctions. The fossil record does not seem to support this presupposition.

First, there was the problem that had long baffled scientists. No obvious pattern emerges from the lists of those plants and animals that died off in the terminal Cretaceous extinction and of those that survived. Marine plankton species were devastated, but freshwater organisms were virtually unaffected. Land plants in North America suffered greatly, but not tropical plants. Pterosaurs perished, but not birds. Most of the marsupials disappeared, but few of their fellow mammals, the placentals and multituberculates. Ammonites were wiped out, but not their relatives, the squid. Dinosaurs vanished, but not their fellow archosaurs, the crocodiles. Size was not a reliable indicator, either. Small dinosaurs were gone, and yet their fellow reptiles of comparable size, the champsosaurs, maintained their presence. Small mammals—the only mammals then were small, in the size range of shrews to small dogs—were among the survivors, but they did not escape unscathed. The extinctions were certainly widespread among the animal kingdom, which would invalidate the many theories attributing the disappearance of dinosaurs to their own supposed deficiencies. But the extinctions were also highly selective, which cast doubt on any single-cause hypothesis.

Opponents of the impact scenarios pointed to another troubling aspect of the fossil record: many of the affected species were apparently on the wane or had already died off in great numbers before the hypothesized catastrophe. This called into question any concept of an abrupt, instantaneous extinction of the kind envisaged by the Alvarezes.

From his studies of marine organisms, for example, Erle G. Kauffman of the University of Colorado found that approximately 75 percent of the groups "were well on the evolutionary wane" in the late Cretaceous. He based this on the groups' longevity, abundance, or patterns of diversification. "Even at the end of the Cretaceous," Kauffman said, "only certain warm-water plankton species disappeared suddenly and completely. Most of the other victims had been declining in numbers and diversity for two to five million years before that, which makes me think that the extinctions were caused by a combination of gradual changes in sea level, current patterns, and climate. I don't rule out a meteorite or an ecological collapse as the final straw, but it wasn't the cause."

The dinosaurs appeared to have been among the dwindling races. Thomas J. M. Schopf of the University of Chicago cited evidence that by the late Cretaceous dinosaurs had already disappeared in South America, southern Europe, and perhaps northern Europe. They survived in any substantial number only in the western regions of North America, and there the signs of decline were ominous. At least thirty-six genera of dinosaurs were living in North America about 11 million years before the end of the Cretaceous. The number dropped to between fifteen and seventeen—including, most notably, *Tyrannosaurus* and *Triceratops*—in the final million years or so.

Dale Russell, however, believed that the evidence of decline was more apparent than real. The higher estimates for dinosaurs in the earlier phase of the Cretaceous, Russell said, were based on the recovery of many more specimens. If a comparable number of specimens were available for the late Cretaceous, he argued, the result would be a truer census and that would probably reveal no lessening in dinosaurian prosperity. Paleontologists, he implied, had not done a thorough job searching for late Cretaceous dinosaurs. Russell had a point, though most scientists were disinclined to accept it. They said that fieldwork in the uppermost Cretaceous sediments had been just as intensive as in the lower sediments, and yet had produced fewer specimens. And since they could see no reason to believe that dinosaurs were any less likely to be preserved in the latest Cretaceous than in other times, they assumed, as Schopf said, that the dearth of genera "may not be an unreasonable reflection of dinosaur generic diversity at that time."

For many scientists the implications were clear. Life toward the end of the Cretaceous was under great stress. There may have been some catastrophic event, particularly at the time of the mass marine extinctions. This event could have delivered the coup de grace for other species of diminishing strength. But something else must have been happening, gradually and cumulatively, over the tens or hundreds of thousands of years leading up to the Cretaceous-Tertiary boundary. The extinctions may have been widespread, but it seemed impossible to prove that they were contemporaneous.

If Walter Alvarez and his team looked to the clays of Gubbio to support their hypothesis, the skeptics looked with renewed interest to the sediments of eastern Montana. Most of what is known of life and death at the Cretaceous-Tertiary boundary has been based on marine fossils from rocks in northern Europe, much of which was then a sea floor. The only reasonably complete record of change in nonmarine life before, during, and after the boundary lies in the badlands of Montana, at Hell Creek, south of the Fort Peck Reservoir on the Missouri River.

EARTH'S MEMORIES of past time and vanished life lie exposed at Hell Creek in the eroded gullies and ravines and on the steep slopes of buttes. Down several hundred meters is the layer of gray mudstone known as the Bearpaw Shale, which contains invertebrate and vertebrate fossils deposited when this was the floor of the last of the great inland seas that once divided North America and favored the region with a semitropical climate. Above the Bearpaw is the Fox Hills Sandstone, sediments from the beaches, lagoons, and barrier islands in the time when this was the shore of the regressing sea. Farther above, in the exposure most accessible to the paleontologist's pick, is the dark gray Hell Creek Formation. This is a thick sediment laid down by rivers that used to flow eastward out of present-day Idaho and Nevada across a broad floodplain. During the latest Cretaceous time the terrain from Alberta down to New Mexico appears to have been an extensive stretch of floodplains bounded to the west by the slowly emerging Rocky Mountains and to the east by the shoreline of the regressing inland sea. The rivers flowed through the plains for the last 2 or 3 million years of the Cretaceous and still flowed there well into the Tertiary. In the sediments, now turned to siltstones and sandstones, lie the remains of small mammals, frogs, salamanders, lizards, fishes, sharks, birds, and dinosaurs. Barnum Brown dug the first tyrannosaur skeleton out of this formation, on the banks of Hell Creek. *Triceratops* bones are plentiful, up to a point. Scientists suspect that on these plains, or a little to the south, perhaps, after the departure of the epicontinental sea, the dinosaurs made their last stand on earth.

The Cretaceous-Tertiary boundary, or what had long been called the boundary here, is an unmistakable seam of low-grade coal running along the top of the Hell Creek Formation of the Cretaceous and at the base of the Tullock Formation of the Tertiary. Mining geologists call it the "lower Z" coal. In and above the coal no dinosaur bones have ever been found—if there were no dinosaurs, it was assumed, there was no Cretaceous. This crude measure of time seemed adequate for paleontologists and geologists until they had to confront the impact hypothesis and seek to confirm or disprove it.

William A. Clemens with Hell Creek badlands in background

William A. Clemens, who had worked the Hell Creek area many summers, returned there after the impact hypothesis had been widely publicized. He wanted to see if he could find the iridium enrichment. If it was there, he hoped to determine where it lay in relation to the last dinosaur bones. Clemens, as a professor of paleontology at the University of California at Berkeley, was a colleague of Walter Alvarez. But he had been skeptical of the Alvarez hypothesis from the outset. The argument between Alvarez and Clemens was essentially over what the geologists see and what the paleontologists do not see.

Clemens and his team, to be sure, found the iridium-enriched layer at four sites in the Hell Creek area. The layer, no more than a few centimeters thick, is always just below or in the lower Z coal. This made a good benchmark for further explorations. One line of investigation led to the discovery of a sharp break in fossil pollen at the Hell Creek boundary layer, indicating a fairly sudden alteration of plant life.

But it was not clear that whatever had happened had anything to do with the dinosaur extinction. Clemens found that the last dinosaur remains lay at least three meters below the boundary. The dinosaurs, it appeared from this evidence, had died off thousands of years before the assumed asteroid impact. This was true not only at Hell Creek but also in other areas of Montana, as far north as Alberta, and to the south in Wyoming. The last dinosaur bones consistently lay well below the zone of flora changes found in the Cretaceous-Tertiary boundary.

"This is where I'm up to my heels in it," said Clemens during his 1983 fieldwork. "You've got to have more than circumstantial evidence to prove the asteroid hypothesis. Right now, the major weakness with the hypothesis is that the physical effects of an asteroid impact don't seem to explain the biological change we're seeing, or not seeing. It was a time of extinctions no doubt, but we tend to magnify it because of our attachment for dinosaurs."

In his investigations, Clemens sought to catalogue all life at the end of the Cretaceous, not only dinosaurs, and to give more attention to those significant survivors of the mass extinction, the mammals. To this end the minuscule specimens of pollen, so resistant to decay and thus prime candidates for fossilization, and the tiny teeth and bones of mammals destined to inherit the earth were coveted more than another *Triceratops* femur. These new ways of the dinosaur hunters puzzled some of the people of Jordan, the rough-hewn little town near Hell Creek. They had seen their share of paleontologists come and go over the decades, had learned the difference between a small stone and a coprolite, and knew something about the big fossils they found on their ranches. At the Hell Creek Bar one night, Sonny Olson, speaking from under a cowboy hat, asked: "What are those people doing out there? I could take them out right now and find them all the dinosaurs they'd ever want, easy."

But Clemens felt that the new digging strategy was producing evidence of profound biological changes that did not necessarily correspond with the presumed effects of a sudden catastrophe. Explorations by J. David Archibald, a former graduate student of Clemens and now on the faculty at San Diego State University, uncovered fragments of thirty species of mammals in the Hell Creek Formation of eastern Montana. A tiny tooth or a scrap of delicate bone was usually the most telling clue, and looking for such fragments would have been an exercise in frustration if it were not for the paleontological equivalent of the proverbial fine-tooth comb—the practice of screen washing. Like a prospector panning for gold, a paleontologist takes a scoop of dirt from a quarrying site, puts it in boxes with fine-mesh screen stretched across the bottom, and dunks the boxes into a lake or stream. The water breaks down and washes away the clay and sand, leaving a residue of pebbles and fossils. Some of the fossils are so small that they can be identified only under a low-power microscope. Tedious work, and a far cry from the broad-ranging search of the usual dinosaur hunters, with their eyes out for big bones, but it had its rewards. The thirty species of mammals that Archibald identified largely in this way belonged to a now extinct order of rodentlike animals (the multituberculates), three families of opossumlike marsupials (the modern opossum foraging in the night comes from the most venerable of extant mammalian lineages), and several families of insectivorous creatures. This was about as far as mammals had progressed after their transition from the mammal-like reptiles, the therapsids. All were quite small and presumably representative of mammalian life throughout the western floodplains of that time.

More surprising were the results of similar searches in the upper levels of the Hell Creek Formation around Bug Creek, also in the area of the Fort Peck Reservoir. Robert E. Sloan of the University of Minnesota and Leigh A. Van Valen of the University of Chicago found there fossils of mammals that were not previously known to exist in the Cretaceous. They were assisted in their discoveries by the acquisitive ants, whose hills in the region rise, on an ant scale, to Himalayan heights. As John Bell Hatcher had noted a century earlier, the ants have a keen eye for tiny bones, which they collect and place on their hills. In tribute, one sequence of sediments Sloan and Van Valen worked is named the Bug Creek Anthills. Out of the thousands of teeth and jaw fragments they collected the scientists identified specimens more closely related to mammals of the Paleocene, the first epoch of the Tertiary, than of the Cretaceous. Some were multituberculates of a more advanced evolutionary stage than their Cretaceous cousins. Some also were tiny ancestors of the ungulates, the division of mammals that have hooves. These ancestors of the horse and cow and hog had yet to develop hooves, and so are given the name Protungulatum, but still it was a surprise to find them living along with dinosaurs. They had previously been thought to be strictly Paleocene animals.

The absence of dinosaur bones just below the boundary and the apparent proliferation of mammals in the same sediments gave the gradualists their strongest argument against the Alvarez hypothesis of sudden mass extinctions. A major ecological shift producing distinctive evolutionary changes, it seemed, was very much in progress before the end of the Cretaceous. As the dinosaurs were losing their place at the top of the food chain, the mammals were perhaps already rising above their lowly rank in the scheme of things. Further studies by Archibald revealed that, while the number of species of typical Cretaceous mammals was decreasing from nineteen to two, the species of Paleocene-like mammals were increasing from five to thirteen. Other discoveries suggested that a similar transition was occurring in the late Cretaceous in Saskatchewan. Paleobotanists were finding evidence of Paleocene-like plants taking root during the late Cretaceous. The world was changing, but not necessarily with deadly suddenness. This was the message at Hell Creek and Bug Creek.

Proponents of the Alvarez hypothesis, moreover, were handicapped by their inability to prove that the extinctions at the boundary occurred within a span of months or a few years. Did the forams at Gubbio die out instantly? Did they die at the same time as did the plants bearing the pollen at Hell Creek? The Alvarez supporters could not say for sure. For all they could prove, the mass extinction in question occurred over a period of thousands or hundreds of thousands of years. "Walter is looking for an event that took place in a matter of weeks, months, or a few years," Clemens said. "So there's a problem of time resolution. There's no place in the world where we can match up the record of marine and terrestrial extinctions with that kind of precision."

The precision in timing events that long ago is at best on the order of thousands of years, and probably not nearly that good. One method is radiometric dating, in which the age of a layer of rock is derived from the decay rates of radioactive elements like potassium or strontium in the rock. Another method is magnetostratigraphy, in which the magnetic orientation of rock can lead to a gross determination of the time it was formed. In neither case is the resolution much better than plus or minus 500,000 years, hardly sufficient for the Alvarez theory.

In a 1982 article in *American Scientist,* Archibald and Clemens noted that the major transition in life across the Cretaceous-Tertiary boundary in western North America probably took place during the same period of reversed polarity of the earth's magnetic field, one of those times when a compass needle would have pointed south. If so, Archibald and Clemens said, this affords "a very crude estimate of the time it took for the observed biotic changes to occur." For the twenty-five-meter-thick Bug Creek sequence, where Sloan and Van Valen found the rapid mammalian developments, they estimated a time of at least 200,000 years. For the gap of three to nine meters between the apparent dinosaur extinction and the marked floral changes, they estimated an interval of 20,000 to 80,000 years.

Geologists would call this a brief interval of time, but it was surely too long for those who sought to establish a direct link between an asteroid or comet impact and the Cretaceous-Tertiary mass extinction. To Archibald and Clemens, Sloan and Van Valen, Schopf and the many other gradualists, life toward the end of the Cretaceous was under stress and undergoing widespread change at a relatively rapid pace—but it was a *pace,* gradual and cumulative, and not a sudden tumble.

In reassessing the facts in the dinosaur mystery and probing the earth for new facts, mostly prompted by the Alvarez challenge, many gradualists came to believe, as Thomas Schopf said, that "a satisfactory explanation of the cause of the extinction of the dinosaurs has been known for some years." The explanation was, of course, the essence of gradualism: a multiplicity of forces over a long stretch of time, probably several million years, apparently conspired to doom the last of the dinosaurs.

The Alvarez team had discovered the iridium anomaly, surmised an asteroid impact, and, with some justification, conceived of repercussions to account for many, if not all, of the extinctions at the end of the Cretaceous. Perhaps there was an impact and global darkness. Gradualists were neither conceding nor denying the possibility. Perhaps the impact wiped out in one sudden catastrophe the marine plankton, many of the land plants, and some vertebrates. But Schopf saw no necessity to "invoke an unusual event to account for the demise of the dinosaurs." Many of the extinctions, which in hindsight seem to have been synchronous, may in fact have come earlier, the consequence of much more subtle forces. The dinosaurs may well have been dead and gone before the asteroid or comet, whatever it was that left the iridium, blasted the face of the earth.

SEVERAL GEOLOGISTS advanced arguments that the iridium concentrations were not necessarily of extraterrestrial origin. They could have come from deep beneath the earth's crust, in the region known as the mantle, which is a source of material disgorged by erupting volcanoes. Support for this thesis was derived from several observations. An examination of sediments as far apart as Texas and Denmark, as well as core samples from the sea floor, revealed an apparent "flux" of iridium deposits throughout the final 10,000 to 100,000 years of the Cretaceous. Since this hardly seemed the consequence of a single, instantaneous event, geologists considered the possibility of episodes of volcanism occurring worldwide over that period of time. On the Deccan Plateau of India, one of the largest continental lava fields in the world, is evidence of volcanic activity from 100 to 30 million years ago, the result of chaotic disruptions set in train by the movement of crustal plates that sent India crashing into the rest of Asia. Dating of the volcanic rock there indicated that the major episode occurred at the end of the Cretaceous. The iridium signatures, moreover, suggested that the volcanism there and probably elsewhere had global effects. A study of airborne particles from a recent eruption of Kilauea on Hawaii found relatively large amounts of iridium; hence the suspicion that the iridium anomalies in the Cretaceous-Tertiary boundary clay might be terrestrial in origin. And many samples of the Cretaceous-Tertiary clay were found to contain, in addition to iridium, more arsenic and antimony than would be expected for a meteoritic source; the abundances of these elements were more like those in the airborne particles from Kilauea.

Reviewing these findings, Charles B. Officer and Charles L. Drake, geologists at Dartmouth College, wrote in 1985: "We conclude that iridium and other associated elements were not deposited instantaneously at the [Cretaceous-Tertiary] transition, but rather that there was an intense and variable influx of these constituents during a relatively short geologic time interval on the order of 10,000 to 100,000 years. Further, we suggest that the available evidence favors a mantle origin rather than a meteoritic origin for these constituents."

Officer and Drake went on to offer an alternative scenario of the environmental catastrophe that swept the world at the end of the Cretaceous. It required no impact by an extraterrestrial object. It was not a sudden cataclysm, though it might seem so on the scale of geologic time. In this scenario, the steady breakup and drifting of the continents must have reached a critical phase, unsettling the earth everywhere. Volcanic eruptions throughout the world destroyed life and habitats, darkened the skies, and fouled the atmosphere. Many species, including the dinosaurs, were doomed.

Other forces of change besides extensive volcanism, according to the gradualists, probably included falling sea levels, rising continents, cooling climate—all of which had a potential for widespread environmental alterations. The largest retreat of the sea between the Permian and the Oligocene, an interval of 200 million years, reached its maximum at the Cretaceous-Tertiary boundary. The subtropical climate that had prevailed at the higher latitudes came to an end. Dinosaurs could not adapt fast enough to the cooler temperatures and changing vegetation. "When you see the late Cretaceous, you figure Murphy was an optimist," said Sloan, alluding to the facetious but apt Murphy's Law that anything that can go wrong will go wrong. "Everything went wrong at almost the same time."

The gradualists and the impact proponents settled into fixed lines, while other scientists stood off at a safe distance and reserved judgment. Someday, in retrospect, the reaction and action following the Alvarez hypothesis may be viewed as a classic example of the workings of science.

The Alvarez team and allies stood their ground on the fact of the iridium anomaly, offering more revealing samples from the Cretaceous-Tertiary boundary. The iridium and spherules at the boundary were their two strongest arguments for the impact. A discovery reported in October 1985 was interpreted as further evidence supporting the case for an impact and the ensuing global devastation. Geochemists at the University of Chicago found a "surprisingly large amount" of soot in the 65-million-year-old boundary clays. The soot appeared to be worldwide, was most likely produced in flames, and so represented, as the scientists surmised, fallout from fires that swept the world at the end of the Cretaceous.

The conflagration was presumably ignited by heat from the impact of a huge asteroid or comet. It must have destroyed much of the world's vegetation and poisoned the air with carbon monoxide. The dense smoke, even more than dust clouds, must have absorbed sunlight and brought a killing darkness and chill to the world.

Other scientists examined more carefully the evidence for a gradual decline in life prior to the Cretaceous extinction. Was the evidence real or an artifact in the fossil record? Was the mass extinction truly abrupt?

David Jablonski, a paleobiologist at the University of Arizona, noted that nearly all mass extinctions seemed to be preceded by a long period of falling sea level. This could well have been a causal factor in extinctions, and could also have skewed the fossil record. A regression of the sea would result in fewer sedimentary rocks being deposited and thus fewer rocks available for finding fossils. If so, what appears to be a decline in life may really be a decline in available fossils. To measure this possible artifact Jablonski looked in the fossil record for species and groups that disappear in times of falling sea level and then reappear with rising sea level. He refers to these reappearing life forms as "Lazarus taxa." Jablonski found that in some cases, such as the ammonites, the gradual decline seemed to be real, but for many groups it was only apparent, the result of a decreased volume of fossiliferous rock. He concluded that for many plants and animals extinction at the end of the Cretaceous was abrupt and somehow special. Mass extinctions, then, are not merely the cumulative effects of gradual dyings. Something unusual happened.

Jablonski divined another pattern of dying that seemed to set mass extinctions apart from ordinary times. Some forms of life contain many species, and these groups appear to prosper during the best of times but are more susceptible to extinction in the worst of times. By contrast, other forms that contain few species, the species-poor groups, fare better in mass extinctions. These groups, in order to survive in competition with the species-rich ones, usually develop broader geographic and ecologic range. They probably tolerate the extreme environmental conditions associated with mass extinctions. "More important in our context," Stephen Jay Gould wrote, this pattern "emphasizes the qualitative difference between normal times and catastrophic zaps."

In response to the gradualists, Walter Alvarez and his colleagues, now joined by Erle Kauffman and Finn Surlyk, brought forth new fossil evidence in 1984 to bolster their case for a sudden extinction of many life forms. A reexamination of the fossil record, they said, showed that there had been a gradual decline in the fortunes of four major invertebrate groups, the ammonites, cheilostomate bryozoans, brachiopods, and bivalves. The gradualists had, of course, made this argument in support of gradualism. But the Alvarez group contended this did not mean that these invertebrates were headed toward inevitable and virtually simultaneous extinction. The ammonites, for example, were indeed suffering a decline well before the end of the Cretaceous. But this had happened many times before, and the ammonites had recovered, for there appear to be both long-lived ammonite genera and families, which neither increase nor decrease dramatically through time, and short-lived groups, which account for most of the variation in abundance and diversity through time. "This suggests a subtle but significant change in the conclusion that should be drawn from the paleontological data," the Alvarez team pointed out. "Formerly the extinction of all short-ranging ammonites was taken to mean that a gradual extinction was nearing completion, with the final dying out of remaining long-ranging taxa a predictable denouement. In the view presented here, the extinction of those long-ranging taxa was the critical and unpredictable event—without it the ammonities probably would not have disappeared." The long-lived ammonites were thriving up to the end, and then they vanished suddenly. The message to the gradualists, therefore, was: you can have gradual decline, the evidence for which is strong and undeniable, and this deterioration can have a bearing on the extent of devastation at the time of a mass extinction. But you still have very rapid turnovers in life at the end of the Cretaceous, the result of a sudden insult to the environment like the impact of an extraterrestrial body. Accordingly, it is "counterproductive," the Alvarez group said, to view this scientific question as a conflict between gradualistic and catastrophic interpretations. The message was delivered in a report published in *Science* and coauthored by Kauffman, who initially had been skeptical of any implied direct connections between the impact and the mass extinctions.

Another rebuttal published in the same issue of *Science* (March 16, 1984) attacked what had been the gradualists' strongest position, the fossil record at Hell Creek and Bug Creek. Jan Smit and S. van der Kaars, both of the University of Amsterdam, contended that the fossils there had been misread because they had been all mixed up in the sediments. This was a floodplain, and the water coursing through it had apparently washed away the dinosaur bones, which would account for their absence at the boundary, and over time deposited more recent bones in the sediments that were assumed to be from the late Cretaceous. "Considering the large amount of Cretaceous sediments eroded by this meandering river," Smit and van der Kaars wrote, "the occurrence of outwashed dinosaur bone fragments and other Cretaceous fossils is not surprising." In their opinion, based on a study of the sediments, the Bug Creek animals of Paleocene form were mixed into the Cretaceous deposits through erosion. They were Paleocene, not Cretaceous. There had thus been no proliferation of more modern mammals during the late Cretaceous.

As the authors stated,

> In our interpretation a gradual faunal change is not justified. On the contrary, the evidence appears to underscore a catastrophic scenario as outlined in the marine record. Extinction and new radiation [evolution into a diversity of forms] are separated in time, in accord with the predictions of the catastrophic scenario. The Cretaceous Hell Creek dinosaur and mammal faunas disappear, overlain by an iridium-rich level associated with a sharp

> pollen break. After a certain time (it is difficult to determine how long because of the great range in sedimentation rates in the fluvial environment), the explosive radiation of new mammalian groups followed. In view of the close association of the iridium-enriched level and mass extinction both on land and in the sea, it seems logical to assume that both have been caused by the same event—a large impact. Moreover, it is easier to understand that the origin and early development of the new mammalian groups, including the "Paleocene aspect" mammals of the Bug Creek channels, took place in the early Paleocene, because the disappearance of their main predators and competitors, the dinosaurs, opened up to them the ecological opportunity to diversify and radiate.

If the Hell Creek sediments, with their absence of dinosaurs and presence of advanced mammals, were really jumbled beyond recognizable pattern by ancient river-channel erosion, then the gradualists' case would be seriously weakened. The gradualists, however, were not ready to concede. Van Valen explained that the Smit–van der Kaars argument was based in part on research at outcrops eighty kilometers west of the Bug Creek Anthills and that it was virtually impossible to correlate those two widely separated sediments. "I don't think any new work is going to change the conclusion that the Protungulatum community was present before the extinction of the dinosaur, which occurred before the boundary," Van Valen asserted. "The best evidence for each side does not impinge on that for the other, and neither side has a satisfactory explanation for the opposing evidence. It may be that not everything has been thought of even now."

The gradualists might concede the fact of the iridium anomaly, but they still resisted the single-cause hypothesis. The extinctions were more complex. To them the world of the dinosaurs and most other Cretaceous life ended not with a bang but a whimper. In a report in the summer 1981 issue of *Paleobiology,* Clemens, Archibald, and Hickey had concluded their case for gradualism and the dinosaurs with an admitted butchering of T. S. Eliot's famous lines, to wit:

> *This is the way Cretaceous life ended*
> *This is the way Cretaceous life ended*
> *This is the way Cretaceous life ended*
> *Not abruptly but extended.*

Gradualists have yet to agree on a "whimper" scenario for the decline and fall of the dinosaurs. But a broad outline, drawn from recent discoveries and reports by the gradualists, would read something like the following:

In the final few million years of the Cretaceous, the seas retreated from the land. The vast shallow seas that had transgressed most of the continents dried up. Ocean levels everywhere dropped 100 to 200 meters, adding more dry land at the continental margins and depriving shallow-water creatures of their habitats.

And the land heaved. Mountains rose from the plains, notably the nascent Rocky Mountains. Volcanoes erupted with relentless fury throughout the world, changing the landscape and sullying the skies and seas. In the upheaval, plateaus often replaced floodplains and swamps. The land was rising and spreading at the expense of the water.

A global cooling ensued. The higher continents altered the flow of air. With no epicontinental seas, there were no sea breezes warming the interior lands. Currents of the newly restricted oceans shifted, and the effect was felt everywhere. Global temperatures fell many degrees. In the high and middle latitudes seasons of changing weather appeared where there had been semitropical conditions year round.

With the change in the weather and the loss of moist lowlands, many of the remaining dinosaurs sought more favorable habitats. Some were successful, for a time. But many more found their pathways of migration in the earlier Mesozoic cut off by the higher elevations and most certainly by the new breaks in the continental connections. For the continents had mostly gone their separate ways. At the start of the Mesozoic, the world had one supercontinent, Pangaea. Dinosaurs could migrate just about anywhere and everywhere, which they apparently did. But the inexorable forces of continental drift, brought about by the shifting crust of the not-so-solid earth, had broken Pangaea asunder and by the end of the Cretaceous had brought the fragments closer to their present positions. Realigned continental masses contributed to falling sea level and no doubt affected oceanic and atmospheric circulation, all causes of climate change. The other effect was to sever the land bridges between the continents. The dinosaurs, extensive migrations thus denied them, had to make the best of what they had where they found themselves in the final few million years of the Cretaceous.

The small animals, with brief life spans, managed to adapt. Through evolution over many short generations they responded to climate and habitat change by adapting into creatures fit for the new times. Some of the more adaptable mammals, with fur coats to keep them warm, began to flourish and compete with unaccustomed boldness in a world that had been dominated by the dinosaurs. Dinosaurs, with life spans of 75 to 300 years,* were less malleable. They had changed before, in previous ecological crises, but this time the stresses were overwhelming. Not enough generations were left them to make the necessary evolutionary adjustments to new conditions. Not enough room was left for their grazing and hunting. As the density of buffalo decreases from twenty-five to one per square kilometer with the lowering in annual rainfall from 200 to 50 centimeters a year, the numbers of dinosaurs steadily dwindled with the coming of a cooler, drier climate and the consequent loss of food over their range. If they were warm-blooded, either endotherms or inertial homeotherms, but without fur or feathers for insulation, they found it more and more difficult to retain their body heat in the colder seasons. The dinosaurs spread out seeking warm weather, and then could spread no farther.

Dinosaurs vanished in Africa and South America, then in Europe and parts of Asia and North America. A few species may have clung to life in Mongolia almost to the end. When that stage was finally upon them, the dinosaurs were struggling for survival in western North America along the former shores of the great inland sea, which had since disappeared. Many of the plants the herbivores used to eat no longer existed, victims of climate change. The herbivores consequently scattered or perished, and this left the carnivores without prey and to their own starvation.

The last of these reptiles, which had prospered for 160 million years, through most of the Mesozoic, probably died somewhere in western North America. Perhaps around Hell Creek in Montana. Or farther south, in New Mexico. Exactly where, or precisely when, we will probably never know. If an asteroid or some other large object crashed into earth, as it seems to have done, this was of no concern to the dinosaurs. They were probably already extinct. If a few had survived to that fateful moment, the asteroid impact only hastened their inevitable end. This is the Cretaceous doomsday scenario of the gradualists.

The conflicting interpretations of the events leading up to the demise of the dinosaurs and causing the Cretaceous-Tertiary mass extinction are not likely to be settled any time soon, if ever. There could be no disagreement, however, over the consequences. A revolution swept the world toward the end of the Cretaceous, and it brought forth a new world. It was a world, going into the Tertiary, without dinosaurs.

*Such estimates are educated guesses. From an examination of the microstructure of dinosaur bones, scientists have inferred probable growth rates; since the animals appeared to have matured slowly, it is thought that they had proportionately long life spans. The larger dinosaurs in particular are believed to have had the longer life spans.

17 *Cycles of Extinction*

So it was known, on the authority of Cuvier and a succession of later scientists who study the rise and fall of life, that mass extinctions occur from time to time in the course of natural events. So it was known, on the basis of more than a century of paleontological exploration, that the dinosaurs were the most famous victims of a mass extinction. But these events seemed to be phenomena without pattern, without any apparent common cause, and so it was believed until a few years ago that the mystery of mass extinctions, whether of the dinosaurs or of other animals and plants, might be beyond solution.

Thinking changed after the announcement of the Alvarez impact hypothesis. A solid, testable theory that stimulates a rush of new research and new ideas inspires scientists to believe that solutions may be within their reach. As their optimism grows, they begin to see relationships where there had been only disparate data points. Their enthusiasms may take them too far in one direction or another, but some excess can be tolerated as the price for greater creativity. The Alvarez hypothesis revitalized the study of extinctions, heretofore something of a cottage industry in science, and raised new questions about the dynamics of extinctions and their importance in evolution.

The Alvarez hypothesis, in its original form, applied only to the mass extinction at the end of the Cretaceous. The telltale iridium enrichment was eventually found in sediments at the time of other extinctions, but not all of them—at least not yet. This frustrated scientists who hoped to find some common denominator for all mass extinctions, something to suggest a pattern to these catastrophes. But they were not to be disappointed for long.

For several years, beginning before the Alvarezes made known their findings, J. John Sepkoski, Jr., of the University of Chicago had been compiling an exhaustive set of data on extinctions, the most complete record ever developed. It was a daunting task, tedious in method and monumental in scope, a scientific tour de force. Drawing on the observations of thousands of scientists, Sepkoski prepared a listing of some 3,500 marine families—the unit of life just above genus—including 50,000 fossil genera and a quarter of a million species. Included for each family was the geologic time of its appearance and its disappearance. He confined the compilation to marine organisms because their fossil record is more complete and more precisely dated. "The reason is pretty simple," said Sepkoski. "The oceans are receptacles of sediment. They are areas of net sedimentation, whereas land is an area of net erosion, which means fewer rocks and fewer fossils."

The objective at first was a broad study of the distribution of marine life through geologic time. "We looked at the whole question of diversity, how the numbers and kinds of animals change through time," Sepkoski said. "That diversity increases during periods of great evolutionary radiation and decreases during periods of mass extinction."

Then Sepkoski and David Raup, a colleague at Chicago, decided to examine the data for any evidence of a pattern in the timing of the mass extinctions. They doubted that they would find them to be anything but random. But they recalled a report in 1977 by two Princeton geologists, Alfred G. Fischer and Michael Arthur, who had suggested that mass extinctions of marine life occurred in regular cycles, once every 32 million years. Scientists had paid little attention because the Fischer-Arthur data were not subjected to rigorous statistical analysis. Moreover, as Sepkoski said, "In 1977, people weren't thinking about mass extinctions that much, and they certainly weren't thinking in terms of extraterrestrial causes. So that paper was treated as a curiosity."

In their more careful reading of the fossil record, specifically that of 500 marine families over the last 250 million years, Sepkoski and Raup were surprised to discover that life has vanished in staggering numbers at regular intervals, roughly every 26 million years. They checked for errors and confirmed the pattern with various methods of statistical analysis. Still they saw the cycle—at 26.2 million years, to be more precise.

The first of the extinctions in this pattern was the greatest one, 248 million years ago at the end of the Permian, when some 90 percent of all species in the oceans perished. There followed nine other probable extinctions, one every 26 million years, give or take a couple of million; scientists find these discrepancies acceptable, considering the imprecision in telling geologic time that far back. "Where the dating is best in the geologic record, the mass extinctions are just bang-on," said Sepkoski. "Where the dating gets worse, they're still pretty close." After the Permian extinction came the devastation at the end of the Triassic, which apparently doomed the mammal-like reptiles and set the stage for the rapid proliferation of the dinosaurs. Then came three extinctions in the Jurassic, the middle one showing up only weakly in the Sepkoski-Raup plot, and three extinctions in the Cretaceous, the earliest one being something of a question mark. After the terminal Cretaceous event, the one associated with the iridium and the dinosaur demise, two other extinctions were true to the cyclical pattern. One was at the end of the Eocene. The most recent occurred 13 million to 11 million years ago. Which means, according to this cycle and assuming some restraint on human power and population, that the next mass extinction is not due for another 13 to 15 million years.

Sepkoski and Raup finally felt sure enough of their data to share them with other scientists at a conference on mass extinctions held in August 1983 at Northern Arizona University in Flagstaff. The landscape surrounding Flagstaff gave dramatic expression to the contrasting views of the gradualists and catastrophists alike. The Grand Canyon, to the northwest, spoke of slow, steady, Huttonian change, the present as the key to the past. Barringer Crater, to the east, bore the scars of a meteorite impact, a sudden catastrophe visited upon the earth.

But when Sepkoski broke his news, old arguments were set aside momentarily for an excited appraisal of this curious pattern to the mass extinctions. Many scientists were incredulous, much as they had been at the first word of the Alvarez hypothesis. They suspected that the cycles were a statistical artifact. They could not bring themselves to accept the regularity of mass extinctions, which they assumed to be the result of conditions too complex and apparently random to be predictable. Nonetheless, they listened respectfully to Sepkoski. He explained that the pattern had not been observed before because the least of these mass extinctions had not been clearly detectable against the background levels of ordinary extinctions; it had taken hard work to bring these events out of the statistical "noise." Other scientists, David Jablonski reported, were "intrigued but cautious" in their reaction to the Sepkoski-Raup report. "There is something very seductive about a periodic stress during all the major evolutionary patterns we see," Jablonski said. "So you try to be very careful not to be seduced."

What made the Sepkoski-Raup findings so seductive was the implication that there may indeed be some triggering mechanism common to all mass extinctions in the last 250 million years. But paleontologists were bothered by the fact that, though three of the events were of great magnitude, the other peaks in the data indicated much less significant extinction. Could the lesser and greater extinctions be caused by the same type of triggering mechanism? The variations in extinction intensity, it was argued, could perhaps be attributed to conditions preceding the catastrophe. On some occasions life on earth was already under great stress from other causes, such as the gradual environmental deterioration brought on by falling sea level and climate change, and so many plant and animal communities were set up for a fall. On other occasions, life generally was prospering, and so the effects of catastrophe, whatever its cause, were minimal.

The apparent periodicity of mass extinctions thus excited and bewildered scientists. After the Flagstaff meeting, Jablonski said: "The data are very convincing. The statistical tests are very convincing. So we've got ourselves a problem: we can't explain it."

Neither could Sepkoski and Raup explain the cycle. "I'm entirely stuck for a mechanism for causing such a period," Sepkoski said at the meeting. "We are aware of no documented process with a cycling time of approximately 26 million years. But with that long a cycle, we suspect that the forcing agent will not be terrestrial (either physical or biological) but rather solar or galactic."

There it was again, the extraterrestrial factor. Inspired and emboldened by the Alvarez hypothesis, scientists allowed themselves to contemplate extraterrestrial forces that periodically disrupt the "normal" course of life. Everything goes apace, slowly and gradually, for time on end, and then the world is turned topsy-turvy by the intervention of some unusual force or combination of forces. The result is catastrophic. Though some scientists still eschew the term, put off by its mystical and religious overtones, catastrophism in some form must account for the episodic course of natural history. Georges Cuvier had not been entirely wrong, after all. There were growing reasons to redefine geology's guiding tenet, the uniformitarianism of Hutton and Lyell, to take into account transforming catastrophes and to look beyond the planet for their source.

Scientists could not, however, conceive of an Alvarez-like asteroid striking earth so frequently and with such regularity. It was not likely to happen more than a couple of times over 250 million years and certainly not at regular intervals. The solution to the mysterious cycles, if their occurrence was corroborated by further research, seemed to lie in the stars. Jablonski remarked: "We're all running to our friendly neighborhood astrophysicists in search of possible solutions."

THE ASTROPHYSICISTS responded eagerly and inventively. It was as if they had been waiting for an excuse to turn away briefly from their cosmic concerns over black holes and the missing mass and exercise their talents on the earthly concerns of vanished dinosaurs and mass extinctions. Within days or weeks the ideas began flowing out of laboratories from Berkeley to New York.

Speculations, and there was nothing more than speculation at first, ran to thoughts that the sun somehow erupts every 26 million years or that the solar system perhaps encounters some periodic perturbation in its passage through the Milky Way galaxy, interacting with other stars or intergalactic dust. No evidence could be mustered to support the solar-eruption idea, and so it sank from sight. But the sun and its assemblage of planets do bob up and down through the galactic plane every 33 million years or so, and this seemed close enough to the apparent extinction cycle to warrant further study.

Two months after the Flagstaff meeting, Richard B. Stothers and Michael R. Rampino at NASA's Goddard Institute for Space Studies in New York City calculated that during a passage through the galaxy's central plane the solar system should encounter one of the massive interstellar clouds of dust and gas in that region. The gravitational force of such a cloud would be sufficient, they argued, to dislodge a swarm of comets from their normal orbits at the outer edge of the solar system. This happens to a lesser extent when a passing star shakes some comets loose, sending them falling into orbits closer to the sun, where they sometimes put on a spectacular show for people on earth. But an encounter with an interstellar dust cloud could send so many comets plunging through the solar system that the odds are great that at least one or two would crash into the earth during each bombardment. The effect would be much the same as that hypothesized by the Alvarezes for the asteroid impact.

The Stothers-Rampino theory had problems, the most serious of which was the lack of a close correlation between the assumed times of plane crossings and the mass extinctions. The solar system is now moving up to the galaxy's central plane, when it should be in position for bombardment, and yet nothing like that seems to have happened in recent geologic time.

Scientists, nonetheless, were attracted to the idea of cometary impacts as the likely triggering mechanism common to so many mass extinctions. It was an idea whose time had come and gone once before, in the days when scientists confined their speculations primarily to the dinosaur extinctions. Comets, of course, had long been viewed as portents of doom. The basis for fear, it is tempting to imagine, lay imprinted deep in genes passed on from mammalian and reptilian ancestors that suffered a time of cometary terror. Such notions are, of course, unscientific. But it was intriguing to think that comets and dinosaurs, two of nature's most spectacular and mysterious phenomena, may be so decisively linked.

Another hypothesis invoking bombardment by comets drew more interest and some support. It excited a new round of far-reaching investigation.

In the fall of 1983, Luis Alvarez received in the mail the report by Sepkoski and Raup and decided to talk to Richard A. Muller, a former student and a professor of physics at Berkeley. Alvarez had concluded that the Sepkoski-Raup findings were wrong and was planning to write them a letter of dissent. But first he wanted to talk it over with Muller. "He asked me to play devil's advocate, which we do all the time," Muller recalled.

In that moment, confronted with the question of what happened to the dinosaurs and the larger question of mass extinctions, Muller felt transported back to boyhood. Like so many children, he had passed through a phase of dinosaur love. He drew countless sketches of dinosaurs and made a pipe-cleaner model of a *Tyrannosaurus* fighting a *Triceratops.* It puzzled him to learn that the dinosaurs had vanished and no one knew why. "It was the first problem I ever heard about in science that was admittedly unsolved," Muller recalled. He thought of becoming a paleontologist, but all the digging for bones looked "terribly boring." Instead, leaving dinosaurs back in childhood, he became an astrophysicist, which was about as far from the study of dinosaurs as one could imagine—or so it seemed to him until the day he saw Alvarez about the Sepkoski-Raup paper.

Alvarez had been Muller's thesis adviser, and the two had maintained a symbiotic relationship in which they nourished each other's thinking. In his role as devil's advocate, Muller argued forcefully against Alvarez's criticisms of Sepkoski and Raup. Later, Muller said: "This was a case where, in playing devil's advocate, I convinced myself that Raup and Sepkoski were right. That led to an argument with Alvarez. I was trying to show him that his case against them was not right. In the process, Alvarez told me that if I wanted to stand on my case I would have to come up with a model that would account for this phenomenon."

Muller thus gave birth to a new hypothesis.

In the gestation period, however, Muller struggled with self-doubt. It was exciting to be thinking again of dinosaurs, believing that he might be the one to solve—or help solve—the mystery of their extinction. But when his arguments in favor of the periodic extinctions failed to win immediate converts, he had the uncomfortable feeling that he might be fooling himself and wasting his time. Of these feelings, Muller said: "It was very tempting to forget the whole thing, and go back to my usual astrophysics research. All of the pressures of normal academic life pushed me to abandon my work. All of the pressures except one: Alvarez. Although he thought I was wrong, he too recognized the situation. And he knew that when you have such a problem, and the arguments of others don't convince you that your analysis is wrong, then you must stick with it. So every day he asked me how my work was coming. Could I fit everything together? Did I have a theory that could explain the periodic extinctions?"

In the two months following his meeting with Alvarez, Muller weighed six different theories and found reasons to reject them all. He and Marc Davis, another physicist at Berkeley, also had an idea similar to the Stothers-Rampino hypothesis, but they dismissed it after a few days because of the lack of correlation between the extinctions and the solar system's likely encounters with an interstellar dust cloud.

It then occurred to Muller, instead, that a dim companion star orbiting the sun once every 26 million years could be responsible for the cycles of extinction. He reasoned that, since most stars come in pairs, one orbiting the other or both orbiting a common center of gravity, the sun could have an undiscovered companion, probably a faint dwarf star one-tenth its mass. At first, Muller thought that the companion star might swing close enough to the sun every 26 million years to disturb the orbits of asteroids in the region between Mars and Jupiter. He was thinking asteroids because of the Alvarez hypothesis. Then he realized the flaw in this mechanism. An orbit with a 26-million-year period that passed that close to the sun would be unstable. The sun's gravitational force would so alter the course of the companion that on its return it would pass too far from the asteroid belt to have any effect.

Scientific inquiry, like life, can turn on the fortuitous intersection of people. A few days before Christmas 1983 Davis telephoned Muller and said that Piet Hut happened to be visiting the Berkeley campus. Hut was then a physicist at the Institute for Advanced Study at Princeton and an expert in orbit dynamics, the very area where Davis and Muller were having their most difficulty. At a meeting the next day in Davis's office, Muller described to Hut all of his theories and explained why each one had failed. It was then that Hut offered a suggestion.

The companion-star hypothesis might be more plausible, Hut said, if the star, instead of passing close to the asteroid belt, was assumed to pass through the more distant comet belt. Out beyond the planet Pluto there is believed to be a cloud of interstellar debris from which comets originate. Jan H. Oort, an astronomer at the University of Leiden, had deduced the existence of this cloud of comets in 1950 and it bears his name. From time to time stars coming close to the solar system could dislodge comets from the Oort cloud and send them coursing in toward the inner planets. These encounters, however, were random events. But if the sun had a companion star, Hut suggested, its orbit could take it through the Oort cloud once every 26 million years. The required orbit would not be very eccentric and thus should be stable enough to fit the scenario of periodic extinctions.

The moment Hut made his suggestion, Muller remembered, "is the closest I ever came to the proverbial 'Eureka!' "

In an hour the three scientists made and checked their calculations. Everything about the numbers looked good. It took them a week to make sure that the theory violated no other established facts of physics, geology, and astronomy. They had to be sure, for example, that it was possible for a companion star of the sun to have eluded detection by astronomers. They were so assured.

The scientists were influenced in their thinking by a new study of the dynamics of comet showers. In 1981 Jack G. Hills, a theoretical astrophysicist at Los Alamos, had recalculated the population and distribution of the comet cloud. Hills concluded that the comets were far more numerous and closer than previously assumed. According to his calculations, the densest population of comets must dwell in the inner region of the Oort cloud about 1,000 to 10,000 astronomical units away; that is, 1,000 to 10,000 times as far from the sun as the earth is. The traditional view held that the cloud was 20,000 astronomical units away. At the closer distance, the cloud would presumably be immune to perturbations by the ordinary passing stars. But once every 500 million years, Hills estimated, a star might pass close enough to trigger a shower of one billion comets lasting 700,000 years—a fireworks display to end all fireworks displays, and perhaps to end much of the life on earth. In such an event, the earth could not escape being blasted by 10 to 200 of these comets during the 700,000 years, a rate of bombardment more than 1,000 times greater than normal. Sometimes more comets would hit the earth, sometimes fewer, and this might account for the variations in intensity of the mass extinctions. At the time, in 1981, with the Alvarez hypothesis in mind, Hills said that he found it "tempting to join the 'me-too' parade and suggest that this bombardment could have led to the extinction of the dinosaurs."

With the Hills calculations in mind, Muller, Davis, and Hut formally proposed their hypothesis of the sun's companion star—not a passing star—disrupting the inner Oort cloud every 26 million years and causing the lethal shower of comets. Their report, published in April 1984 in *Nature,* said: "If and when the companion is found, we suggest it be named Nemesis, after the Greek goddess who relentlessly persecutes the excessively rich, proud and powerful. We worry that if the companion is not found, this paper will be our nemesis."

The theoretical star also came to be known as the "death star." Was there some scientific basis for the word "disaster," which is derived from the Latin words for "evil star"?

In his *Natural History* column in August 1984, Stephen Jay Gould raised an objection to the name Nemesis. As the "personification of righteous anger," Gould argued, "She represents everything that our new view of mass extinction is struggling to replace—predictable, deterministic causes afflicting those who deserve it." It would also mean placing one more Western figure in the sky. Gould recommended instead that the companion star be named for Siva, the Hindu god of destruction, who, he noted, "forms an indissoluble triad with Brahma, the creator, and Vishnu, the preserver. All are enmeshed in one—a trinity of a different order—because all activity reflects their interaction." In Gould's opinion, Siva would reflect the knowledge that extinctions not only destroy life but are a source of creation as well. The dinosaurs rose after one extinction, and mammals came into their own after another one killed the dinosaurs.

Muller felt that Gould's criticism was somewhat unfair. In the original manuscript of the report, Muller said, a playful footnote was added to propose that, if it was found, the star should be given one of four possible names. Nemesis was placed at the head of the list. The other suggestions were: Kali, after the Hindu goddess who is the destroyer of men and animals and yet is infinitely generous and kind; Indra, the verdic god of storms and war who uses a thunderbolt (comet?) to slay a serpent (dinosaur?); or George, the Christian saint who slew the dragon. Only two of the four names were western. But the editors of *Nature,* Muller said, deleted all the names but Nemesis—and so the theory soon became known as the Nemesis hypothesis.

The companion star, by whatever name, was fascinating to contemplate. Working independently, another team of scientists, headed by Daniel P. Whitmire of the University of Southwestern Louisiana and Albert A. Jackson IV of Computer Sciences Corporation in Houston, came up with their own version of the death-star hypothesis. Their concept differed from that of Muller-Davis-Hut mainly in estimates of the star's mass, brightness, and orbit.

Soon after Muller, Davis, and Hut conceived their solar-companion hypothesis, Walter Alvarez suggested a test of both the Sepkoski-Raup cycle and the comet showers. These developments had undermined the original Alvarez asteroid theory, but not the basic premise of extraterrestrial causes and global disaster. The iridium signatures could have been left by comet impacts. Though little is known of the composition of comets, they are believed to be conglomerations of water, ammonia, and methane ices and some solid material—"dirty snowballs," in the astronomers' analogy. Some may have rocky cores, which, like other extraterrestrial bodies, could contain unearthly amounts of iridium. (Some of this ignorance may be dispelled through the intensive study of Halley's comet during its 1985–86 apparition.) If there had been cometary bombardments, they must have left their mark on the land, with traces lingering to this day. Alvarez, the geologist, and Muller, the astrophysicist, analyzed thirteen impact craters larger than ten kilometers across that have been accurately dated as being created between 5 million and 250 million years ago. They found what they had hoped to find. The craters had been gouged out at intervals of 28.4 million years, a statistically close fit with the cycle of extinction. The coincidence, while not proof, was encouraging.

The cratering analysis was met with some skepticism. If all the large craters are assumed to be the result of comet impacts, where are those formed by asteroids? Asteroids could not be so casually dismissed. Gene Shoemaker, the astrogeologist whose calculations of asteroids had lent early support to the Alvarez hypothesis, expressed doubt that the putative companion star could have maintained an orbit sufficiently stable over 250 million years to account for all the major extinctions. At a meeting in Berkeley in March 1984, Shoemaker and several other scientists noted that the companion star presumably had to have formed 4.6 billion years ago along with the sun and the planets. It probably was much closer to the sun then; otherwise the companion might have long since escaped the sun's gravitational grip. As it was, with each orbit the little star, in response to the sun's gravity, would have been flung farther and farther out. This point, the probable instability of the companion star's orbit, would be argued over and over again.

Shoemaker continued to emphasize the "severe difficulties" with the Nemesis hypothesis. "At the farthest point in its orbit," he pointed out in 1985, "this companion would be almost as far away as Proxima Centauri, our sun's nearest known stellar neighbor. It would be so weakly bound to the sun that small perturbations from passing objects could cause it to drift away. I have carried out calculations with my colleague Ruth Wolfe, and found that there is less than one chance in a thousand that the postulated companion star has a long enough lifetime and an orbit stable enough and eccentric enough to do what it is advertised to do."

Even if the death star did exist, scientists realized there was a good chance that it had been stripped from the solar system. Being so small and in such an elongated orbit, the star could have done its last damage 13 to 11 million years ago and then, out where its gravitational tie to the sun was weakest, been pulled away from the solar system by the tug of a passing star. But if the companion star remained in the sun's gravitational embrace, however weakly and distantly, perhaps it could be found.

The search began in the summer of 1984. The astronomers were looking for a reddish dwarf star about 2.5 light-years distant, about halfway to the nearest known star. It would be between 6th and 13th magnitude, or brightness. (A magnitude-6 star is the dimmest visible to the unaided eye; a 13 star is 300 times dimmer.) The fact that a star so near to the sun had gone undetected did not surprise or trouble Muller. The closest known star to the sun, Proxima Centauri, as Muller noted, would probably never have been observed if it had not been so near another star, Alpha Centauri, that attracted careful study. Some scientists believed that they had a 50 percent chance of discovering the companion star within three years of searching—if, that is, it exists. "This would be," Muller said, "the most fantastic star you can imagine and the first ever discovered on the basis of paleontology."

The whole of paleontology was charged with excitement over the cosmic turn of events. John Sepkoski stood by his data. "The result is clear and crisp," he said. He was delighted by the creative response from the astrophysicists. "It's rare that anyone pays much attention to what's going on in paleontology," he said.

The criticism of the extinction cycle and comet hypothesis was surprisingly mild, in the beginning. The star might indeed be found. A typical cautionary note was sounded by Steven M. Stanley, a paleontologist at Johns Hopkins. In the June 1984 issue of *Scientific American,* he wrote:

The alleged 26-million-year cycle itself needs further study. To begin with, the most recent extinction peak in the cycle, about 13 million years ago, is extremely weak and would probably go unnoticed if it were much older; further back in time there might be more such events that are obscured by the fossil record and do not fit the cycle. Moreover, the peaks older than 90 million years that Raup and Sepkoski did identify do not fit the cycle very well. It may be the peaks are not truly periodic but only somewhat closer to a 26-million-year cycle than they would be if they were distributed randomly over time. Such a condition requires no extraterrestrial explanation; it would have arisen if after each mass extinction there had to be a lag before another crisis could occur. The environmental change that precipitated the initial crisis might have persisted for several million years, preventing the biotic recovery that would have to precede the next pulse of extinction. Even if the environment did improve, the decimated biotas might have required millions of years to rediversify to the point where they included species that were particularly vulnerable to mass extinction.

So many great ideas in science do turn out to be wrong. Some critical point may have been overlooked, and its discovery could demolish the hypothesis. Or another theory, equally persuasive, could be advanced at any moment.

One such idea was introduced at the end of 1984. Daniel Whitmire, who had conceived of a companion-star hypothesis similar to Muller's, revived the notion that somewhere out beyond Pluto there is another large planet, known as Planet X, and that its orbital travels could produce the perturbations accounting for the periodic rain of destructive comets. Something like Planet X must be out there, astronomers suspect, to produce the gravitational disturbances responsible for the peculiar orbital behavior of Uranus and Neptune. According to Whitmire's new proposal, developed with John J. Matese, also of the University of Southwestern Louisiana, Planet X could be orbiting the sun once every 1,000 years in a region far beyond Pluto in the inner fringe of the Oort cloud. Being fairly close to the sun, it would have a stable orbit. Over time, of course, it would have cleared out a comet-free gap in the cloud. But just as Planet X presumably influences the motions of the outer planets, it would be tugged by the gravitational forces of those planets, causing its orbit to precess. That is, instead of retracing the same orbital path each time, Planet X could follow an ellipse that continuously changes. The planet, Whitmire and Matese proposed in *Nature,* could pass through the Oort cloud's regions of dense comet population twice every 52 million years and cause the destructive comet showers every 26 million years. This theory, however, found few early supporters.

But scientists continued to assess the validity of the companion-star hypothesis. Most criticism of it centered on the problem of the presumed instability of the orbit of a star so weakly bound to the sun and vulnerable to jolts from the gravitational pull of other bodies. In an October 1984 article in *Nature,* Michael Torbett of Murray State University in Kentucky and Roman Smoluchowski of the University of Texas at Austin concluded that even the most stable orbits conceived for such a star could not last the entire age of the solar system, 4.6 billion years. Most scientists estimated that the expected lifetime of the star in an orbit with a period of 26 million years was, at most, a billion years. (Muller's team acknowledged this limitation in its original report.) Either the star was captured by the solar system long after the sun formed, an event considered quite unlikely, or the companion star was more tightly bound when it and the sun were born and has been nudged out to its present orbit by the gravitational perturbations from passing stars or other bodies. Piet Hut favors the latter explanation. It would mean that the cosmic clock of periodic mass extinctions is not precisely tuned. Such notions will be hard to prove. The hypothesized periodicity of mass extinctions is based on an examination of the fossil record extending back only to 250 million years. Older data are too sketchy and imprecise to determine what was happening then. Without better geological data from the fossil record and cratering evidence, however, the nature and exact timing of the periodic mass extinctions will probably remain unresolved—unless, of course, the "death star" should be found.

All that Richard Muller could do now was to hope that he had not overlooked an insurmountable flaw in his theory and wait for the reports from the astronomers searching for a companion to the sun. Muller never became a paleontologist, but the boy who had a passion for dinosaurs was now, thirty years later, very much in the thick of the debate over their fate.

THERE SEEMS to be no end to the scientific creativity stimulated by the new hypotheses addressing the question of what happened to the dinosaurs. Many scientists believe that the Alvarezes have established the validity of their Cretaceous impact hypothesis. Further evidence may yet authenticate the findings of Sepkoski and Raup. The death star may be found, or perhaps some other force will be identified to account for the apparent periodicity of mass extinctions. One good hypothesis seems always to lead to another and then another good idea, until thinking in a wide range of sciences is jogged, then jolted, and ultimately transformed. Paleontology has not heard the last of the Alvarez hypothesis in all its many ramifications.

In one sense, the new mass-extinction ideas are expressions of a transformation in scientific thinking that reflects cultural changes. Science does not operate in a vacuum; it is a human enterprise as much as are the arts or commerce. In another time, for instance, Walter and Luis Alvarez might have seen the iridium in the Gubbio clay and dismissed it as just another inexplicable fact of nature. Or they might have taken it as a clue leading down some entirely different line of questioning. But they practiced science in a culture sensitive to catastrophe, a legacy of world wars and nuclear weapons as well as of Cuvier's recognition of extinctions and the newly appreciated instability of the earth's crust. They practiced science in an intellectual climate in which the earth is increasingly being viewed as an interacting system set in the cosmos, a space-age perspective. Their culture also encouraged, or at least tolerated, the seemingly irrelevant pursuit of knowledge about such matters as dinosaurs. So catastrophism and dinosaurs converged in the minds of the Alvarezes, and out flowed the dinosaur-extinction hypothesis. This cultural convergence prompted Ellen Goodman, the syndicated newspaper columnist who is a self-styled "dinosaur groupie," to remark: "I wonder whether every era gets the dinosaur story it deserves."

The new focus on extinctions, inspired in no small part by the Alvarez hypothesis, is producing a transformation in thinking about the nature of evolution. The traditional Darwinian view holds that competition among species drives the history of life, with changes in the physical environment being of subordinate importance. Organisms are in a constant struggle for advantage. Those that improve themselves through slow, evolutionary change gain over others that do not; this leads to new, improved species. There was, perhaps not coincidentally, a Victorian flavor to this Darwinian view. Those who managed empires liked to believe in the survival of the fittest. Those who lived in competitive economies found it natural that species rose and fell in competition with other species. Those with an abiding faith in progress, a tenet of Victorian liberalism, liked to believe in gradual change leading to new, improved life. The point is, the contemporary Zeitgeist might well have influenced Darwin in unconscious ways and must have contributed to the acceptance of Darwinism as the guiding doctrine of natural history.

This is not to diminish Darwin or doubt the theory of evolution by natural selection. Darwin glimpsed a great truth, though not the whole truth—which is why the theory of evolution itself is evolving.

A major challenge to orthodox Darwinism developed in the 1970s when Stephen Jay Gould and Niles Eldredge of the American Museum of Natural History proposed their theory of "punctuated equilibria." Their interpretation of the fossil record led them to assert that species do not change gradually throughout their existence. They usually remain in equilibrium for millions of years and then, for unknown reasons, a small, isolated population of the species begins to evolve rapidly, changing into a new species that settles into another long period of equilibrium.

The Gould-Eldredge theory met with criticism from stalwart Darwinists. The incomplete fossil record, they argued, was playing tricks on Gould and Eldredge. As the debate was subsiding, without reaching general agreement, the asteroid-impact hypothesis raised anew questions about just how gradual the processes of evolution are. Scientists began thinking that competition has less to do with major evolutionary change than does extinction.

In the newer view, evolution is seen as having a substantial opportunistic component. There may be long periods in which life evolves gradually through competition, but these periods are interrupted by episodes of extreme environmental change, and these upsets drive the history of life. The primary struggle is with climates, geologies, and perhaps extraterrestrial assaults. The losers become extinct, often in great waves of death. The survivors take over the vacated habitats and thrive in ways that had not been open to them before the mass extinction. All in all, it is a time of death and creation. Extinctions not only reset the clocks of evolutionary change but point life in entirely new directions. It may be that palentologists, aided and abetted by the Alvarezes and Raup and Sepkoski, as well as their neighborhood astrophysicists, will find that life's history is shaped in decisive ways by heavenly forces.

One thing is certain, though. The dinosaurs left humans with more than some fossilized bones to think about. They may be dead, these fascinating and mysterious creatures, but in life they surely shaped the course of evolution for some 160 million years and in death set its course over the last 65 million years.

18

The World Thereafter

ONCE, YIELDING to a fanciful urge, Dale Russell, the paleontologist who said he studies dinosaurs because he never outgrew a childhood enchantment, tried to imagine how things might have turned out if the dinosaurs had not become extinct. The more he thought about it, the more he thought himself and his fellow humans out of existence. Some dinosaurs, instead, might have evolved into the beings of commanding intelligence.

As the Mesozoic drew to a close, Russell knew from recent studies, a few small dinosaurs had achieved a ratio of brain weight to body weight, or encephalization quotient, that compared favorably to that of early mammals. One of these dinosaurs was *Stenonychosaurus inequalus,* a species he had unearthed in 1968 in Cretaceous beds near Dinosaur Provincial Park in Alberta. From the skull and assorted bones he determined that this had been a bipedal carnivore weighing forty kilograms and standing one meter tall and, with its tail outstretched, at least two meters long. The size of the brain cavity indicated that the stenonychosaur had an encephalization quotient of 0.3, probably enough to make it several times more intelligent than most other dinosaurs and probably as intelligent as the most advanced of the little mammals among its contemporaries. (In humans, the quotient is about 7.5.) Other features, as well, set this diminutive dinosaur apart. It seemed to have an opposable thumb, one digit opposing two other claws that might have given it considerable manipulative skills. It may also have had stereoscopic vision. "It looked," Russell said, "as if it had all the ingredients of success that we see later in the development of the apes."

With this idea in mind, Russell set about conceptualizing the kind of animal the stenonychosaur might have become by now if it and the other dinosaurs had not become extinct 65 million years ago. His concept took three-dimensional shape in the form of a fiberglass model, created with the help of Ron Sequin, a taxidermist, that stands on display in the National Museum of Natural Sciences in Ottawa. Russell calls the model a dinosauroid, the intelligent creature that might have been—the assumed twentieth-century culmination of uninterrupted dinosaurian evolution.

Dinosauroid, as conceived by Dale A. Russell, with reconstruction of Stenonychosaurus *in the background*

The dinosauroid model, according to Russell, is the product of guesswork and a "conservative" extrapolation of certain evolutionary trends. Assuming a trend toward bigger brains in the dinosaurs, which was manifest before they vanished, the dinosauroid should by now have evolved an encephalization quotient of 7.1, which is within the human range. To make room for the larger brain, the skull in his model was constructed somewhat larger than the stenonychosaur's and the face relatively smaller, as is seen in the evolution of the anthropoid apes. The eyes are large ovals, which is characteristic of dinosaurs. The posture is upright. The neck is shorter than usual for dinosaurs, for it would have been difficult for the dinosauroid to carry its larger skull at the end of a long horizontal neck. The tail, thus being unnecessary as a counterbalance to the neck, would have disappeared, and so the dinosauroid has no tail. Its skin is scaly and its hands have three fingers, both established dinosaurian features. Since Russell further assumed that the animal would have evolved away from egg laying to live births, the dinosauroid has a navel. But Russell surmised that the infants would have been fed regurgitated food, like baby birds, and so the dinosauroid has no nipples. The dinosauroid's lack of external sex organs is typical of reptiles.

Whatever the physiology and social behavior of dinosaurs in their time, Russell concluded, the dinosauroid by now would have been a vigorous warm-blooded creature probably living in a community of fellow hunters. These creatures might have had birdlike voices and perhaps even some kind of language, though no one knows at what level of encephalization language becomes possible or inevitable. In Russell's model, which is conservative, as he said, the dinosauroid has not quite attained levels of human intelligence. But he does not dismiss the possibility that the descendants of *Stenonychosaurus* or some other of the brainier dinosaurs might have evolved into a species wiser and wittier and more sophisticated than *Homo sapiens.*

But this, of course, was not to be. *Stenonychosaurus* never had a chance to realize its hypothetical potential. No dinosaurs survived the mass extinctions at the end of the Cretaceous. No fossils of these creatures have ever been found in any rocks younger than the Cretaceous. The occasional reports of dinosaurlike animals being sighted in Africa have never been confirmed. Though some monstrous animals of curious dinosaurian aspect may yet be found, it is highly unlikely that true dinosaurs would have survived the last 65 million years without leaving a scattering of fossils, which should have been discovered years ago.

Dinosaurs live today only in the minds of the species that in all likelihood owes its existence to the dinosaurs' demise. If the dinosaurs had not become extinct, if their kind had continued to dominate the land, mammals might still be small rodentlike creatures foraging by night and hiding by day from the mighty reptiles. Or if the dinosaurs had lived on beyond the Cretaceous to become extinct in more recent times, the Age of Mammals might only be in its infancy, with no humans or even protohumans yet in sight. We have every reason, therefore, to be fascinated with dinosaurs, especially their extinction.

MASS EXTINCTIONS, as scientists are coming to recognize, have been pivotal events in the course of life on earth. After the terminal Cretaceous extinction, there must have been desolation everywhere, a stillness where there had been robust life, and opportunity everywhere for those survivors adaptable enough to seize it. Birds had the sky to themselves; no more pterosaurs. Fish and clams and other creatures of the ocean did not have to contend with ammonites and mosasaurs. The little mammals emerged from their lowly existence; no more giant reptiles, save for the crocodiles, and they were unable to carry on the supremacy long held by their archosaurian relatives.

With stunning rapidity, in terms of evolution and geologic time, the mammals occupied the varied habitats of the extinct reptiles. Some were the multituberculates, the rodentlike animals that had been the most abundant mammals for more than 100 million years, but they would die out completely in another 25 million years. Some were the few marsupials that survived the catastrophe. Some were monotremes, egg-laying mammals that must have been remnants of an evolutionary experiment whose only survivors today are the platypus and echidna of Australia. Most were placentals, forerunners of nearly all modern mammals. Finding so many of their competitors and predators gone forever, most of the mammals abandoned their largely noctural, insect-eating habits and assumed a daylight existence. The little hoofed animals took to the unpopulated grasslands and grazed where the ceratopsians used to roam. Other mammals developed a taste for meat, initiating new predator-prey relationships in nature. Some took to the trees, and this led to monkeys. Some took to the sea, and this led to whales and porpoises. Some took to the air, and so there are bats today. All the decisive steps in the radiation and diversification of mammals seem to have occurred in 10 to 15 million years after the fall of the dinosaurs and other giant reptiles left so many ecological niches open.

In the Oligocene period, after the Eocene extinctions 38 million years ago, cooler, drier climates promoted an even greater surge in mammalian evolution. Hoofed animals grew to large sizes; the first true cats, dogs, and rhinoceroses appeared; pigs and bears came on the scene. A few million years later, monkeys and apes went their separate evolutionary ways, and in Africa a tailless ape called *Oryopithecine* emerged as the probable joint ancestor of the modern great apes and humans. In this creature are seen for the first time some characteristics of the human brain. About 5 million years ago, in the Pliocene, branches of the great apes became gorillas, chimpanzees, and ape-men. The ape-men began walking on their hind limbs and making tools out of stone. They were scavengers first, then hunters. They began to specialize, the males hunting and the females gathering fruits and nuts. The females thus had more time for prolonged nursing and maternal care. By this time, the ape-men were developing decidedly humanlike brains.

Modern man, *Homo sapiens,* appeared in archaic forms something like 500,000 years ago. Truly modern man, *Homo sapiens sapiens,* may be no more than 40,000 years old. The species had already developed language and its quintessential feature, consciousness. This was an intelligence of a transcendental kind, entirely novel in the course of life.

Alone among all the creatures, we humans possess consciousness, a profound awareness of self and of others, of the past and of the future. Other animals have knowledge and a sense of their surroundings, but, unlike humans, they do not know that they have this knowledge and sense; they cannot contemplate what the knowledge means or try to understand what others may be feeling and thinking. Only humans wonder about their origins. Only humans worry about the future and know that they eventually will die. Such self-awareness is the source of religion and justice, the arts and sciences—our humanity.

It did not have to be thus. Nothing in the evolution of life, as we understand it, preordained the development of consciousness by one species. By no reasonable extrapolation can it be said that Russell's stenonychosaur, no matter how much it progressed in skill and brainpower, would have necessarily developed consciousness. No one can look at fossils of the early mammals or even the early apes and find unambiguous signs of the exceptional future that was to be. In the opinion of most scientists, Gould has said, "consciousness is a quirky evolutionary accident, a product of one peculiar lineage that developed most components of intelligence for other evolutionary purposes."

By a succession of accidents, then, we gained the vision to look back and glimpse the progression of life that preceded us. This is one of the most illuminating accomplishments of the last two centuries. Looking back in time we are amazed that we are here, and not some brainy stenonychosaur. We have gained knowledge of life's variety, tenacity, and fragility. We have seen ample evidence of global catastrophes dooming the dinosaurs and countless other creatures. We have reason to suspect that it could happen again in another 11 to 13 million years. But in contemplating the fate of the dinosaurs, the very phenomenon that made our own evolution possible, we are drawn to dark thoughts of our own extinction. We realize that we are, as Niels Bohr once observed, both spectators of and participants in the phenomenon of nature.

The peril is not millions of years off. It could be imminent. Of all the species that ever lived, only we have attained the power to bring about our own extinction—and the consciousness to be aware that we have dooms of our own making to fear. We can look into the future, an immediate future, and contemplate our death as a species in circumstances not unlike those that befell the inhabitants of the late Cretaceous. The only difference is that the dinosaurs had the elements or the stars to blame; we would have only ourselves to blame.

Luis Alvarez was quick to recognize the parallels between the hypothesized catastrophe that doomed the dinosaurs and nuclear war. In 1982, he explicitly compared the impact of the putative asteroid with the destructive potential of nuclear weapons, a comparison that cast doubt on hopeful notions that nuclear war is survivable. This set other scientists to thinking. If the impact of a huge asteroid or comet nucleus could produce global dust clouds and falling temperatures, what would be the effect of nuclear war on the world's climate?

Paul J. Crutzen, director of the Max Planck Institute in Mainz, West Germany, and John W. Birks of the University of Colorado had already begun an examination of the ecological consequences of nuclear war. It occurred to them that, in all the concern over the poisoning of life by radioactive fallout, another dire effect of nuclear war had been overlooked. The Dutch-born Crutzen was an authority on the various chemical constituents of the atmosphere and had made a study of the distribution of smoke from burning forests in Brazil. Fires ignited by nuclear explosions, Crutzen and Birks said, could generate tremendous amounts of smoke and soot as well as dust, severely attenuating the sunlight reaching the ground. Dust merely scatters sunlight, but soot absorbs it. The result could be global darkness.

At the same time, another group of scientists at Cornell University and the Ames Research Center in California had been studying the effects of atmospheric dust on sunlight, based primarily on new knowledge of volcanic eruptions and the global dust storms on Mars. When these scientists pondered the

Alvarez scenario for the terminal Cretaceous extinction, they decided to direct their studies to the creation of computer models of the likely climatic effects of nuclear holocaust. They also took into account the Crutzen-Birks findings in assessing the effect of soot from burning cities and forests. In 1983, the scientists—Richard P. Turco, Owen B. Toon, Thomas P. Ackerman, James B. Pollack, and Carl Sagan—concluded that widespread nuclear war would probably generate the same kind of darkening that some thought had wiped out the dinosaurs. The blasts of bombs and the insidious radiation would be horrible enough, but the nightmarish darkness might be the ultimate undoing of life on earth. Though some critics dismiss such thinking as a "dangerous myth," many scientists say that they have confirmed the general outlines of what the Turco group calls the "nuclear winter." The world would be plunged into sooty darkness for weeks, cutting off sunlight for plant growth and producing a bitter chill everywhere. The result could be the extinction of the human species.

Dying dinosaurs and Martian dust storms, atmospheric physics and smoky fires in Brazil—important ideas can have the unlikeliest provenance. It is unwise to assume that any course of study or exploration is irrelevant.

At the 1983 meeting on extinctions, where Raup and Sepkoski startled scientists with their report on the apparent cycles of mass extinctions, the example of the dinosaurs was invoked again in weighing the prospects for life on earth. Dinosaurs, it seems, are no longer simply a synonym for obsolescence or the dead-and-gone; their doom is increasingly recalled as a cautionary metaphor for the fate that could befall mankind, if we are not careful. We may never know what really happened to the dinosaurs, but we already know enough to wonder if it could happen to us. If it was a sudden catastrophe that did in the dinosaurs, we think of nuclear war, and shudder. If their demise came more gradually, through an accumulation of environmental disruptions, then we think of the effects of overpopulation, deforestation, chemical poisons, and spreading pollution on the earth's habitability. Even if nuclear war is somehow avoided, scientists at the extinction conference were reminded, the world still faced the immediate prospect of extinctions that might rival or surpass those at the end of the Cretaceous. Two ecologists, Paul Ehrlich of Stanford University and Daniel Simberloff of Florida State University, warned that human populations are growing so explosively and are modifying the environment so drastically that other species are perishing at an alarming rate, which could reach mass-extinction proportions in the next 200 years. "For the first time in geologic history," Ehrlich said, "a major extinction episode will be entrained by a global overshoot of carrying capacity by a single species—*Homo sapiens.*"*

Consciousness imposes a profound responsibility on those possessing it. As wondrous as they were, the dinosaurs were limited. They were incapable of causing their own extinction, or of foreseeing and preventing it. Humans, more wondrous still, are endowed with these capacities. There may be nothing else like us in the universe. In our exploration of time, we have driven down a highway and searched under the junipers for some dinosaur bones and come face to face with ourselves.

*Some scientists suspect that the extinction of the mastodons, mammoths, and other large animals at the end of the Pleistocene, the most recent ice age, resulted from human hunting.

ACKNOWLEDGMENTS

IF I HAD any reservations about writing this book—Should a grown man spend several years contemplating dinosaurs? Was there anything really new to be said about dinosaurs?—they vanished at the sight of some ancient bones lying in a dry wash somewhere in southern Utah. History has always fascinated me, and here in my hands was a message from a past so long ago that it diminished conventional history to a tale of a few yesterdays. I committed myself then and there to write this book about the exploration of time by the many people who have found the lure of dinosaurs irresistible. It seemed fascinating and important to tell the story of the people who continue to find the mystery of the dinosaurs an infinite challenge and the inspiration of some of today's most interesting and fruitful scientific inquiries into the history of the earth.

My guide to the fossil beds of Utah was James A. Jensen, and my debt to him is great. We spent a delightful week in July 1981 bouncing about the raw countryside in his pickup truck, digging here and there, talking from morning to night about fossils and geology. Many times later, while perusing the accounts of earlier fossil hunters, I thought of Jim and the terrain we covered and the bones we found in the ground; the thought gave me a measure of empathy with the endeavors of Sternberg and Hatcher, Douglass and Brown, Cope and Andrews, among the many great dinosaur hunters. Jim is retired now, and I wish him well on his memoirs. I am also grateful to Jan Hemming for arranging my journey with Jim. When I first set to paper an account of Jensen and the dinosaurs for *The New York Times Magazine,* my editor was Holcomb Noble, who has been a sensitive collaborator in many of my writing efforts for the *Times.* Some material from that article is incorporated in the prologue, "Time in Utah," by permission of the *Times.* Richard Flaste, director of science news at the *Times,* has been understanding and encouraging when it counted.

Other visits were made to dig sites in Montana and Wyoming. William A. Clemens, John R. Horner, and Bob Makela took hours away from their work to attend to my education in the ways of paleontology, particularly regarding their important findings. Jeff Crane, one of the last of the real cowboys, gave me an enlightening tour of Como Bluff, much of which lies within the fences of the cattle ranch he runs with his brother, Frosty.

Many others submitted patiently to interviews and responded generously to endless requests for information and research documents. John H. Ostrom of Yale's Peabody Museum was especially helpful in this regard. Dennis R. Dean of the University of Wisconsin–Parkside shared his new findings on Gideon Mantell's role in the first discoveries of dinosaurs, which was especially magnanimous in that it meant giving me first chance to publish some fruits of his own research. A much fuller account of the Mantell discovery will be given in Dean's book, *Gideon Mantell: The Discoverer of Dinosaurs,* tentatively scheduled for publication in 1986. The following also provided invaluable help in interviews: Walter Alvarez, Frank Asaro, Robert T. Bakker, Marion Brandvold, A. W. Crompton, Leo J. Hickey, Nicholas Hotton III, David Jablonski, Farish Jenkins, Robert Long, Malcolm McKenna, Richard A. Muller, David M. Raup, Dale A. Russell, John E. Schowalter, J. John Sepkoski, Jr., Robert Sloan, Roman Smoluchowski, Sam Tarsitano, Leigh Van Valen, and Daniel Whitmire.

No one can write a book about dinosaurs without incurring a large debt to Edwin H. Colbert. His informative books gave me a running start down many avenues of investigation.

A special note of thanks is due to Stephen Jay Gould. I consulted him on some points of interpretation. But even more important to me were his engaging essays on evolution, extinction, and related subjects; his writings were a frequent source of inspiration and illumination.

For research I relied largely on the New York Public Library and the library at the American Museum of Natural History. Other research was conducted at the libraries of Duke University, Princeton University, the University of Wyoming, and Yale University's Peabody Museum of Natural History.

Those who were kind enough to read and comment on parts of the book were: Walter Alvarez, William Clemens, Dennis Dean, Richard Muller, John Ostrom, and John Sepkoski. Joan M. Kelly offered stimulating editorial suggestions along the way. Working with Ashbel Green again was a pleasure; it was reassuring to have as an editor someone with his high standards and long patience. Peter Hayes was a great help in the final stages of preparing the book for publication.

My wife, Nancy, managed to keep life in the present going while I had my head stuck in the deep past. For her and everyone else who lent support, I only hope that the results justify their generous assistance.

Bibliography

General

The literature on dinosaurs, vertebrate paleontology, historical geology, and evolution is voluminous. Following are some of the more recent popular and scholarly works that afford a general introduction to the subjects of this book:

Calder, Nigel. *Timescale.* New York, 1983. A history of the earth, with comprehensive chronology and glossary.

Charig, Alan. *A New Look at the Dinosaurs.* New York, 1983. Originally published in London in 1979. Perhaps the best short book reviewing current knowledge of dinosaurs, including excellent illustrations.

Colbert, Edwin H. *The Age of Reptiles.* New York, 1965.

———. *Dinosaurs: An Illustrated History.* Maplewood, N.J., 1983.

———. *Dinosaurs: Their Discovery and Their World.* New York, 1961.

———. *Men and Dinosaurs: The Search in Field and Laboratory.* New York, 1968. The best of Colbert's many works, especially concerning the stories of early fossil hunters. Reissued in 1984 by Dover Publications under the title *The Great Dinosaur Hunters and Their Discoveries.*

Desmond, Adrian J. *The Hot-Blooded Dinosaurs.* New York, 1976. Quite readable, though one-sided in favor of warm-bloodedness.

Eiseley, Loren. *Darwin's Century: Evolution and the Men Who Discovered It.* Garden City, N.Y., 1958.

Fortney, Richard. *Fossils: The Key to the Past.* London, 1982.

Gillispie, Charles C. *Genesis and Geology.* Cambridge, Mass., 1951. Comprehensive account of geological thinking at the time of the first dinosaur discoveries.

Glut, Donald F. *The New Dinosaur Dictionary.* Secaucus, N.J., 1982. A helpful guide through the thicket of dinosaurian nomenclature.

Halstead, L. B. *The Search for the Past.* Garden City, N.Y., 1982. Illustrated review of fossils and palentology.

———, and Halstead, Jenny. *Dinosaurs.* Poole, Eng., 1981.

Hotton, Nicholas, III. *Dinosaurs.* New York, 1963.

Lewin, Roger. *Thread of Life: The Smithsonian Looks at Evolution.* Washington, D.C., 1982. Colorful review of evolution and paleontology.

Mayr, Ernst. *The Growth of Biological Thought: Diversity, Evolution and Inheritance.* Cambridge, Mass., 1982.

Romer, A. S. *Vertebrate Paleontology.* 3rd ed. Chicago, 1966. The standard scholarly work in the field.

Silver, Leon T., and Schultz, Peter H., eds. *Geological Implications of Impacts of Large Asteroids and Comets on the Earth.* Geological Society of America, Special Paper No. 190. Boulder, Colo., 1982. Collected papers from the "Conference on Large Body Impacts and Terrestrial Evolution: Geological, Climatological, and Biological Implications," held Oct. 19–22, 1981, at Snowbird, Utah. Cosponsors were the Lunar and Planetary Institute, Houston; National Science Foundation; National Aeronautics and Space Administration; Office of Naval Research.

Simpson, George Gaylord. *Fossils and the History of Life.* San Francisco, 1983. Excellent illustrated introduction to paleontology. Issued as part of the *Scientific American* Library series.

———. *The Meaning of Evolution.* Rev. ed. New Haven, 1967. Indispensable.

Swinton, W. E. *The Dinosaurs.* New York, 1970.

Thomas, Roger D. K., and Olson, Everett C.,

eds. *A Cold Look at the Warm-Blooded Dinosaurs.* American Association for the Advancement of Science, Selected Symposium Series 28. Boulder, Colo., 1980. A valuable compendium of data on dinosaurs, as well as the fullest airing of one of the stormiest arguments in dinosaur paleontology.

Following are the research materials consulted in writing each chapter. In many cases, especially those concerning contemporary developments, interviews with scientists (see Acknowledgments) and visits to dig sites supplemented the published materials and were the source of background information, interpretative insights, and the "human element" so important to the narrative.

Time in Utah

Bakker, Robert T. "Dinosaur Heresy—Dinosaur Renaissance." In Roger D. K. Thomas and Everett C. Olson (eds.), *A Cold Look at the Warm-Blooded Dinosaurs.*

Darwin, Francis. *Life and Letters of Charles Darwin.* London, 1887, Vol. 2.

Eiseley, Loren. *The Invisible Pyramid.* New York, 1970.

Gould, Stephen Jay. *The Panda's Thumb.* New York, 1980. Chap. 26.

Simpson, George Gaylord. *Attending Marvels.* New York, 1934.

———. *The Meaning of Evolution.*

Wilford, John Noble. "A New Way of Looking at Dinosaurs." In *The New York Times Magazine,* Feb. 7, 1982. An article primarily about "Dinosaur Jim" Jensen.

1. *First Bones*

Adams, Frank D. *The Birth and Development of the Geological Sciences.* New York, 1954. Reprint of a 1938 book. Account of Lyell's visit to Paris.

Bourdier, F. "Georges Cuvier." In *Dictionary of Scientific Biography,* 3. New York, 1971.

Bowler, Peter J. *Evolution: The History of an Idea.* Berkeley, Calif., 1984. Chap. 5 on Cuvier and catastrophism.

Buckland, William. "Notice on the *Megalosaurus* or Great Fossil Lizard of Stonesfield." In *Transactions of the Geological Society of London,* 21, 1824.

Charig, Alan. *A New Look at the Dinosaurs.*

Colbert, Edwin H. *Dinosaurs: Their Discovery and Their World.*

———. *Men and Dinosaurs.*

Coleman, William. *Georges Cuvier: Zoologist.* Cambridge, Mass., 1964.

Cuvier, Georges. *Recherches sur les Ossemens Fossiles des Quadrupedes.* 4 vol. Paris, 1812.

Dean, Dennis R. Personal communication. Jan. 19, 1984, and Jan. 15, 1985. More details of Dean's research on the first bones will be included in Dennis R. Dean, *Gideon Mantell, Discoverer of Dinosaurs,* to be published in 1986.

Desmond, Adrian J. *The Hot-Blooded Dinosaurs.*

Geikie, Archibald. *The Founders of Geology.* London, 1897. On Cuvier and Buckland.

Gillispie, Charles C. *Genesis and Geology.*

Gould, Stephen Jay. "Making These Bones Live." In *New York Times,* Dec. 9, 1979.

Mantell, Gideon A. *The Fossils of the South Downs.* London, 1822.

———. "Notice on the *Iguanodon,* a Newly Discovered Fossil Reptile, from the Sandstone of Tilgate Forest, in Sussex." In *Philosophical Transactions of the Royal Society, London,* 115, 1825.

McGowan, Christopher. *The Successful Dragons: A Natural History of Extinct Reptiles.* Toronto, 1983.

Moore, Ruth. *The Earth We Live On.* New York, 1971. Chapter on Cuvier.

Nield, Edward W. "Was This, Then, Antediluvian Man?" In *New Scientist,* 100, Dec. 22–29, 1983. Assessment of Buckland's cave discoveries.

Outram, Dorinda. *Georges Cuvier: Vocation,*

Science and Authority in Post-Revolutionary France. Manchester, 1984.

Rupke, Nicholaas A. *The Great Chain of History: William Buckland and the English School of Geology.* London, 1983.

Spokes, Sidney. *Gideon Algernon Mantell: Surgeon and Geologist.* London, 1927.

Swinton, W. E. *The Dinosaurs.*

2. *Discovery of Time*

Adams, Frank D. *The Birth and Development of the Geological Sciences.*

Eiseley, Loren. *Darwin's Century.*

Geikie, Archibald. *The Founders of Geology.* Account of Hutton.

Gillispie, Charles C. *Genesis and Geology.*

Gould, Stephen Jay. "Hutton's Purposeful View." In *Natural History,* 91, May 1982. Also included as a chapter in Gould, *Hen's Teeth and Horse's Toes.* New York, 1983.

Greene, Mott T. *Geology in the Nineteenth Century: Changing Views of a Changing World.* Ithaca, N.Y., 1982.

Hutton, James. *Theory of the Earth with Proofs and Illustrations.* 2 vols. Edinburgh, 1795.

Knox, R. Buick. *James Ussher, Archbishop of Armagh.* Cardiff, 1967.

Lewin, Roger. *Thread of Life.*

Lyell, Charles. *Principles of Geology.* 3 vols. London, 1830–34.

McIntyre, D. B. "James Hutton and the Philosophy of Geology." In Claude C. Albritton, Jr. (ed.), *The Fabric of Geology.* Reading, Mass., 1963.

Moore, Ruth. *The Earth We Live On.* Chapter on Hutton.

Paley, William. *Natural Theology.* London, 1822.

Reese, Ronald Lane; Everett, Steven M.; Craun, Edwin D. "The Chronology of Archbishop James Ussher." In *Sky and Telescope,* 62, Nov. 1981.

Rudwick, Martin J. S. *The Meaning of Fossils.* London, 1972.

3. *Measuring Time*

Adams, Frank D. *The Birth and Development of the Geological Sciences.*

Albritton, Claude C., Jr. *The Abyss of Time.* San Francisco, 1980.

Eicher, Don L. *Geologic Time.* Englewood Cliffs, N.J., 1976.

Eiseley, Loren. *Darwin's Century.*

Faul, Henry. "A History of Geologic Time." In *American Scientist,* 66, March–April 1978.

Fenton, Carroll L., and Fenton, Mildred A. *The Fossil Book.* Garden City, N.Y., 1952. Chapter on William Smith.

Fortney, Richard. *Fossils: The Key to the Past.*

Fuller, John G. C. M. "The Industrial Basis of Stratigraphy: John Strachey, 1671–1743, and William Smith, 1769–1839." In *American Association of Petroleum Geologists Bulletin,* 53, 1969.

Geikie, Archibald. *The Founders of Geology.*

Greene, Mott T. *Geology in the Nineteenth Century.*

Halstead, L. B. *The Search for the Past.* Chap. 2 for discussion of the fossilization processes.

Harland, W. B., et al. *A Geological Time Scale.* Cambridge, Eng., 1982. Includes the most recent revisions in the dates for the geological time scale. These dates are used throughout the book. The most significant revision applies to the Triassic, found to begin and end much earlier than previously estimated.

Kulp, J. Laurence. "The Geological Time Scale." In *Science,* 133, April 14, 1961.

Needham, Joseph. *Science and Civilization in China.* Cambridge, Eng., 1959. Vol. 3. Quotation of Chu Hsi.

Toulmin, Stephen, and Goodfield, June. *The Discovery of Time.* Chicago, 1965.

Wetherill, George W. "Dating Very Old Objects." In *Natural History,* 91, Sept. 1982.

Wilford, John Noble. *The Mapmakers.* New York, 1981. William Smith as a geological cartographer.

4. *A Name for a Phenomenon*

Barber, Lynn. *The Heyday of Natural History, 1820–1870.* Garden City, N.Y., 1980. Chap. 12 on Owen.

Clarke, Arthur C. "In the Beginning Was Jupiter." In *The New York Times Book Review,* March 6, 1983.

Cohen, Daniel. *A Modern Look at Monsters.* New York, 1970.

Colbert, Edwin H. *Men and Dinosaurs.*

———, and Beneker, Katherine. "The Paleozoic Museum in Central Park, or the Museum That Never Was." In *Curator,* 2, 1959.

De Camp, L. Sprague, and De Camp, Catherine. *The Day of the Dinosaur.* New York, 1968.

Desmond, Adrian J. *Archetypes and Ancestors.* Chicago, 1984. Account of paleontology in Victorian London, with particular emphasis on Richard Owen.

———. "Central Park's Fragile Dinosaurs." In *Natural History,* 83, Oct. 1974.

———. *The Hot-Blooded Dinosaurs.*

Hawkins, Thomas. *The Book of Great Sea Dragons.* London, 1840.

Illustrated London News. Dec. 31, 1853, and Jan. 7, 1854. Accounts of dinner in the *Iguanodon* at the Crystal Palace.

Ingersoll, Ernest. *Dragons and Dragon Lore.* New York, 1928.

Kielan-Jaworowska, Zofia. *Hunting for Dinosaurs.* Cambridge, Mass., 1969.

Mayr, Ernst. *The Growth of Biological Thought.*

Ostrom, John H. "The Evidence for Endothermy in Dinosaurs." In Roger D. K. Thomas and Everett C. Olson (eds.), *A Cold Look at the Warm-Blooded Dinosaurs.* Includes the classification of the many families and orders of dinosaurs.

Owen, Richard. "Report on British Fossil Reptiles." In *Report of the Eleventh Meeting of the British Association for the Advancement of Science.* London, 1841.

Schowalter, John E. "When Dinosaurs Return: Children's Fascination with Dinosaurs." In *Children Today,* 8, May–June 1979.

Seeley, H. G. "On the Classification of the Fossil Animals Commonly Named Dinosauria." In *Proceedings of the Royal Society,* 43, 1887. Seeley's work established the basic classification system for the two branches of dinosaurs.

5. *Early Bird*

Barber, Lynn. *The Heyday of Natural History.* Quotation from *Family Herald.*

Barthel, F. Werner. *Solnhofen.* Thun, Switz., 1978. In German. An English translation is in preparation.

Bibby, Cyril. *Thomas Henry Huxley: Scientist, Humanist and Educator.* London, 1959.

Bowler, Peter J. *Evolution: The History of an Idea.*

Brooks, John Langdon. *Just Before the Origin: Alfred Russel Wallace's Theory of Evolution.* New York, 1984.

Clark, Ronald W. *The Huxleys.* New York, 1968.

Darwin, Charles. *On the Origin of Species by Means of Natural Selection, or the Preservation of Favored Races in the Struggle for Life.* London, 1859. Many subsequent editions are available in paperback.

DeBeer, Gavin. *Archaeopteryx lithographica.* London, 1954. Excellent description of the animal and how the London specimen was obtained, published by the British Museum (Natural History).

Desmond, Adrian J. *Archetypes and Ancestors.*

———. *Hot-Blooded Dinosaurs.*

DiGregorio, Mario A. *T. H. Huxley's Place in Natural Science.* New Haven, Conn., 1984.

Feduccia, Alan. *The Age of Birds.* Cambridge, Mass., 1980. Chap. 1 on *Archaeopteryx.*

Howgate, Michael. *"Archaeopteryx:* No New Finds after All." In *Nature,* 306, Dec. 15, 1983.

Huxley, Leonard. *Life and Letters of Thomas Henry Huxley.* London, 1900. Vol. 1. Quotations from Huxley's correspondence with Darwin.

Huxley, Thomas Henry. "Further Evidence of the Affinity between the Dinosaurian Reptiles and Birds." In *Quarterly Journal of the Geological Society of London,* 26, 1870.

———. "On the Animals Which Are Most Nearly Intermediate between Birds and Reptiles." In *Annals and Magazine of Natural History,* 4, Feb. 1868.

———. "Remarks upon *Archaeopteryx lithographica."* In *Proceedings of the Royal Society,* 16, 1868.

Leidy, Joseph. "Remarks Concerning Hadrosaurus." In *Proceedings of the Academy of Natural Sciences, Philadelphia,* Dec. 14, 1858.

Lucas, J. R. "Wilberforce and Huxley: A Legendary Encounter." In *Historical Journal,* 22, Spring 1979.

Ostrom, John H. *"Archaeopteryx."* In *Discovery,* 11, Fall, 1975.

———. *"Archaeopteryx:* Notice of a 'New' Specimen," In *Science,* 170, Oct. 30, 1970.

Von Meyer, Hermann. "On the *Archaeopteryx lithographica,* from the Lithographic Slate of Solenhofen." Tr. by W. S. Dallas. In *Annals and Magazine of Natural History,* 9, April 1862.

Wagner, Andreas. "On a New Fossil Reptile Supposed to be Furnished with Feathers." Tr. by W. S. Dallas. In *Annals and Magazine of Natural History,* 9, April 1862.

Wendt, Herbert. *Before the Deluge.* Tr. by Richard Winston and Clara Winston, Garden City, N.Y., 1968.

6. *Cope and Marsh: The Bone Wars*

Betts, Charles. "The Yale College Expedition of 1870." In *Harpers New Monthly Magazine,* 43, June–Nov. 1871.

Colbert, Edwin H. *Men and Dinosaurs.*

Cook, James H. *Fifty Years on the Old Frontier.* New Haven, Conn., 1923. New ed. Norman, Okla., 1957.

Cope, Edward D. "Vertebrata of the Tertiary Formations of the West." In *Report of the U.S. Geological Survey of the Territories,* 3. Washington, D.C., 1884.

Lanham, Url. *The Bone Hunters.* New York, 1973.

Marsh, O. C. "The Dinosaurs of North America." In *16th Annual Report of the U.S. Geological Survey,* Part I. Washington, D.C., 1896.

Osborn, H. F. *Cope: Master Naturalist.* Princeton, N.J., 1931.

———. *Impressions of Great Naturalists.* New York, 1924.

Ostrom, John H., and McIntosh, John S. *Marsh's Dinosaurs: The Collections from Como Bluff.* New Haven, Conn., 1966.

Penick, James. "Professor Cope vs. Professor Marsh." In *American Heritage,* 22, Aug. 1971.

Plate, Robert. *The Dinosaur Hunters: Othniel C. Marsh and Edward D. Cope,* New York, 1964.

Reingold, Nathan. *Science in Nineteenth Century America.* New York, 1964. Includes excerpts from correspondence between Cope and Marsh.

Schuchert, Charles, and LeVene, Clara Mae. *O. C. Marsh, Pioneer in Paleontology.* New Haven, Conn., 1940. The definitive biography of Marsh, with ample documentation of writings by and about him.

Shor, Elizabeth Noble. *The Fossil Feud Between E. D. Cope and O. C. Marsh.* Hicksville, N.Y., 1974.

———. *Fossils and Flies.* Norman, Okla., 1971. A biography of Samuel Williston.

Sternberg, Charles H. *The Life of a Fossil Hunter.* New York, 1909. Good on the flavor of fossil hunting in the American West.

7. *Collecting Far and Wide: North America*

Adams, Daniel B. "A Fossil Hunter's Best Friend Is an Ant Called 'Pogo.' " In *Smithsonian,* 15, July 1984.

Barton, D. R. "Father of the Dinosaurs." In *Natural History,* 48, Dec. 1941. About Barnum Brown.

Brown, Barnum. Archives at the American Museum of Natural History, New York. Includes most of his correspondence from the field to H. F. Osborn.

———. "Hunting the Big Game of Other Days." In *National Geographic,* 35, May 1919.

Brown, Lillian. *I Married a Dinosaur.* New York, 1950. A chatty, though unrevealing, memoir by Barnum Brown's second wife.

Colbert, Edwin H. *Men and Dinosaurs.* Chap. 7.

Hellman, Geoffrey. *Bankers, Bones and Beetles.* Garden City, N.Y., 1969. A history of the American Museum, including lengthy interview with Barnum Brown shortly before he died.

Holland, W. J. "Earl Douglass: A Sketch in Appreciation of His Life and Work." In *Annals of the Carnegie Museum,* 20, 1931.

Lanham, Url. *The Bone Hunters.* Good treatment of Hatcher's work.

Matthew, W. D. *Dinosaurs.* New York, 1915. Accounts of early dinosaur hunts by the American Museum of Natural History.

Preston, Douglas J. "Barnum Brown's Bones." In *Natural History,* 93, Oct. 1984.

———. "Sternberg and the Dinosaur Mummy." In *Natural History,* 91, Jan. 1982.

Schuchert, Charles. "John Bell Hatcher." In *American Geologist,* 35, 1905.

Shor, Elizabeth Noble. *Fossils and Flies.*

Simpson, George Gaylord. *Discoverers of the Lost World.* New Haven, 1984. Chapter on Hatcher in South America.

Stegner, Wallace. *Mormon Country.* New York, 1942. Moving chapter on Earl Douglass.

Sternberg, Charles H. *Hunting Dinosaurs on Red Deer River, Alberta, Canada.* Lawrence, Kans., 1917.

———. *The Life of a Fossil Hunter.*

8. *Collecting Far and Wide: Europe and Africa*

Broom, Robert. "On the Occurrence of an Opisthocoelian Dinosaur *(Algoasaurus bauri)* in the Cretaceous Beds of South Africa." In *Geological Magazine,* 5, 1904.

Charig, Alan. *A New Look at the Dinosaurs.*

Colbert, Edwin H. *Men and Dinosaurs.*

Dollo, Louis. "Première Note sur les Dinosauriens de Bernissart." In *Bulletin du Musée Royal d'Histoire Naturelle de Belgique,* 1, 1882.

Dupont, E. *Bernissart and the Iguanodons.* Brussels, 1898. A guide to the collections.

Parkinson, John. *The Dinosaurs in East Africa.* London, 1930.

9. *Gobi: The Stuff Is Here*

Andrews, Roy C. *Ends of the Earth.* New York, 1929. Includes autobiographical material.

———. *The New Conquest of Central Asia.* New York, 1932. The comprehensive account of the Andrews expeditions, including both a narrative of events and discussions of scientific results.

Hellman, Geoffrey. *Bankers, Bones and Beetles.*

McKenna, Malcolm C. "Studies of the Natural History of the Mongolian People's Republic and Adjacent Areas, Made by the American Museum of Natural History." In *Mongolian Society Newsletter,* 1, 1962.

10. *Revival and Revisionism*

Bakker, Robert T. "Dinosaur Renaissance." In *Scientific American,* 232, April 1975.

———. "The Superiority of Dinosaurs." In *Discovery,* 3, Spring 1968.

Colbert, Edwin H. *A Fossil-Hunter's Notebook.* New York, 1980.

Crompton, A. W., and Jenkins, Farish A., Jr. "Mammals from Reptiles: A Review of Mammalian Origins." In *Annual Review of Earth Planetary Science,* 1, 1973.

———. "Mesozoic Mammals." In V. J. Maglio and H. B. S. Cooke (eds.), *Evolution of African Mammals.* Cambridge, Mass., 1978.

———. "Origin of Mammals." In J. A. Lillegraven; Z. Kielan-Jaworowska; W. A. Clemens (eds.), *Mesozoic Mammals: The First Two-Thirds of Mammalian History.* Berkeley, Calif., 1979.

———, and Parker, Pamela. "Evolution of the Mammalian Masticatory Apparatus." In *American Scientist,* 66, March–April 1978.

Desmond, Adrian J. *The Hot-Blooded Dinosaurs.*

Kemp, T. S. *Mammal-like Reptiles and the Origin of Mammals.* London, 1982. Comprehensive and authoritative.

McLoughlin, John C. *Archosauria: A New Look at the Old Dinosaurs.* New York, 1979. An iconoclastic reassessment of ideas about dinosaurs.

———. *Synapsida: A New Look into the Origin of Mammals.* New York, 1980.

Ruben, John A. "Mammal-like Reptiles: Spreading the Word." In *Paleobiology,* 7, Fall 1981.

West, Susan. "Dinosaur Head Hunt." In *Science News,* 116, Nov. 3, 1979.

11. *Hot Times over Warm Blood*

Bakker, Robert T. "Anatomical and Ecological Evidence of Endothermy in Dinosaurs." In *Nature,* 232, July 14, 1972.

———. "Dinosaur Renaissance."

———. "Ecology of the Brontosaurs." In *Nature,* 229, Jan. 15, 1971.

———. "The Superiority of Dinosaurs."

Desmond, Adrian J. *The Hot-Blooded Dinosaurs.*

Marx, Jean L. "Warm-Blooded Dinosaurs: Evidence Pro and Con." In *Science,* 199, March 31, 1978.

McGowan, Christopher. *The Successful Dragons.* Good summary of the arguments for and against warm-blooded dinosaurs.

McLoughlin, John C. *Archosauria: A New Look at the Old Dinosaurs.*

Ostrom, John H. "A New Look at Dinosaurs." In *National Geographic,* 154, Aug. 1978.

———. "A New Theropod Dinosaur from the Lower Cretaceous of Montana." In *Postilla,* No. 128, Feb. 25, 1969. This is a publication of the Peabody Museum, Yale.

———. "Osteology of *Deinonychus antirrhopus,* an Unusual Theropod from the Lower Cretaceous of Montana." In *Bulletin,* No. 30, 1969. Peabody Museum, Yale.

———. "Terrestrial Vertebrates as Indicators of Mesozoic Climates." In *Proceedings of the North American Paleontological Convention,* Sept. 1969. The paper that formally launched the warm-blooded dinosaur debate.

———. "Terrible Claw." In *Discovery,* 5, Fall, 1969.

Silverberg, Robert. "Beastly Debates." In *Harpers,* 263, Oct. 1981.

Thomas, Roger D. K., and Olson, Everett C., eds. *A Cold Look at the Warm-Blooded Dinosaurs.* Most comprehensive discussion of the matter, based on a symposium at a meeting of the American Association for the Advancement of Science.

Weaver, Jan C. "The Improbable Endotherm: The Energetics of the Sauropod Dinosaur *Brachiosaurus.*" In *Paleobiology,* 9, Spring 1983.

12. *Living Descendants?*

Bakker, Robert T., and Galton, Peter M. "Dinosaur Monophyly and a New Class of Vertebrates." In *Nature,* 248, March 8, 1974.

Benton, Michael J. "No Consensus on *Archaeopteryx.*" In *Nature,* 305, Sept. 8, 1983.

Bock, Walter. "On Extended Wings." In *Sciences,* 23, March–April 1983.

Caple, Gerald; Balda, Russell P.; Willis, William R. "The Physics of Leaping Animals and the Evolution of Preflight." In *American Naturalist,* 121, April 1983.

Colbert, Edwin H. *Men and Dinosaurs.* Brief account of Franz von Nopcsa.

Desmond, Adrian J. *The Hot-Blooded Dinosaurs.*

Feduccia, Alan. *The Age of Birds.* Chaps. 2 and 3.

Hecht, Max K., and Tarsitano, Samuel. "The Paleobiology and Phylogenetic Position of *Archaeopteryx.*" In *Geobios. Mémoire,* 6, 1982. Lyon, France.

Heilmann, Gerhard. *The Origin of Birds.* London, 1926.

Jensen, James A. "Another Look at *Archaeopteryx* as the World's Oldest Bird." In *Encyclia,* 58, 1981. Journal of the Utah Academy of Sciences, Arts, and Letters.

Lewin, Roger. "How Did Vertebrates Take to the Air?" In *Science,* 221, July 1, 1983.

Nopcsa, Franz von. "Ideas on the Origin of Flight." In *Proceedings of the Zoological Society of London,* 1907.

———. "On the Origin of Flight in Birds." In *Proceedings of the Zoological Society of London,* 1923.

Ostrom, John H. "The Ancestry of Birds." In *Nature,* 242, March 9, 1973.

———. "*Archaeopteryx* and the Origin of Birds." In *Biological Journal of the Linnean Society,* 8, June 1976.

———. "*Archaeopteryx* and the Origin of Flight." In *Quarterly Review of Biology,* 49, March 1974.

———. "Bird Flight: How Did It Begin?" In *American Scientist,* 67, Jan.–Feb. 1979.

———. "The Origin of Birds." In *Annual Review of Earth and Planetary Sciences,* 3, 1975.

Padian, Kevin. "Macroevolution and the Origin of Major Adaptations: Vertebrate Flight as a Paradigm for the Analysis of Patterns." In *Proceedings of Third North American Paleontological Convention,* 2, Aug. 1982.

———. "Running, Leaping, and Lifting Off." In *Sciences,* 22, May–June 1982.

Tarsitano, Samuel, and Hecht, Max K. "A Reconsideration of the Reptilian Relationship of *Archaeopteryx.*" In *Zoological Journal of the Linnean Society,* 69, June 1980.

Thulborn, Richard A. "Dinosaur Polyphyly and the Classification of Archosaurs and Birds." In *Australian Journal of Zoology,* 23, 1975.

Walker, Alick D. "New Light on the Origin of Birds and Crocodiles." In *Nature,* 237, June 2, 1972.

Webster, Bayard. "Did Flight Begin on the Ground or in the Trees?" In *The New York Times,* Feb. 22, 1983.

Whetstone, K. N., and Martin, Larry D. "New Look at the Origin of Birds and Crocodiles." In *Nature,* 279, May 17, 1979.

Williston, S. W. "Are Birds Derived from Dinosaurs?" In *Kansas City Review of Science and Industry,* 3, 1879.

13. *Social Life of Dinosaurs*

Bakker, Robert T. "Ecology of the Brontosaurs."

Bird, Roland T. "We Capture a 'Live' Brontosaur." In *National Geographic,* 105, May 1954.

Charig, Alan. *A New Look at the Dinosaurs.*

Desmond, Adrian J. *The Hot-Blooded Dinosaurs.*

Farlow, James O. "Estimates of Dinosaur Speeds from a New Trackway Site in Texas." In *Nature,* 294, Dec. 24–31, 1981.

Gorman, James. "First of the Red-Hot Mamas." In *Discover,* 2, Oct. 1981.

Helyar, John. "Dinosaur Fever: Hunt for Fossils Is Hot, Tedious, Ill-Paid Job; Jack Horner Loves It." In *The Wall Street Journal,* Oct. 3, 1983.

Horner, John R. "Coming Home to Roost." In *Montana Outdoors,* 13, July–Aug. 1982.

———. "Cranial Osteology and Morphology of the Type Specimen of *Maiasaura Peeblesorum* (Ornithischia Hadrosauridae) with Discussion of Its Phylogenetic Position." In *Journal of Vertebrata Paleontology,* 3, March 1983.

———. "Evidence of Colonial Nesting and 'Site Fidelity' among Ornithischian Dinosaurs." In *Nature,* 297, June 24, 1982.

———. "The Nesting Behavior of Dinosaurs." In *Scientific American,* 250, April 1984.

Lull, Richard S., and Wright, Nelda E. *Hadrosaurian Dinosaurs of North America.* Geological Society of America Special Paper No. 40, New York, 1942.

Mossman, David J., and Sarjeant, William A. S. "The Footprints of Extinct Animals." In *Scientific American,* 248, Jan. 1983.

Rensberger, Boyce. "Dinosaurs' Nest Is Found in Montana." In *The New York Times*, Feb. 6, 1979.

Swinton, W. E. *The Dinosaurs*. Chap. 4 on the physiology of dinosaurs.

14. *The Great Dying*

Alexander, George. "Going, Going, Gone." In *Science 81*, 2, May 1981.

Cuppy, Will. *How to Become Extinct*. New York, 1941.

Fisher, Arthur. "The World's Great Dyings." In *Mosaic*, 12, March–April 1981. Publication of National Science Foundation. Good review of various extinction scenarios, including Raup's "Just So Stories."

Gartner, Stefan, and Keany, John. "The Terminal Cretaceous Event: A Geologic Problem with an Oceanographic Solution." In *Geology*, 6, Dec. 1978.

Gartner, Stefan, and McGuirk, James P. "Terminal Cretaceous Extinction Scenario for a Catastrophe." In *Science*, 206, Dec. 14, 1979.

Gould, Stephen Jay. "Free to Be Extinct." In *Natural History*, 91, Aug. 1982.

Hsü, Kenneth J. "K-T Event Debated; Conclusion: ?!" In *Geotimes*, 27, July 1982.

———, et al. "Mass Mortality and Its Environmental and Evolutionary Consequences." In *Science*, 216, April 16, 1982.

Jepson, Glenn L. "Riddles of the Terrible Lizards." In *American Scientist*, 52, June 1964. Published originally in *Princeton Alumni Weekly*, 64, 1963.

Newell, Norman D. "Revolutions in the History of Life." In Albritton, Claude C. (ed.), *Uniformity and Simplicity: A Symposium on the Principle of Uniformity of Nature*. Geological Society of America Special Paper No. 89. New York, 1967.

Raup, David M., and Sepkoski, J. John, Jr. "Mass Extinctions in the Marine Fossil Record." In *Science*, 215, March 19, 1982.

Russell, Dale A. "The Mass Extinctions of the Late Mesozoic." In *Scientific American*, 246, Jan. 1982.

Swinton, W. E. *The Dinosaurs*. Chap. 13.

15. *Out with A Bang?*

Allaby, Michael, and Lovelock, James. *The Great Extinction*. Garden City, N.Y., 1983. Procatastrophist account flawed by mistakes and little attention to contrary evidence.

Alvarez, Luis. "Experimental Evidence That an Asteroid Impact Led to the Extinction of Many Species 65 Million Years Ago." In *Proceedings of the National Academy of Sciences*, 80, Jan. 1983. Review of the evidence and the possible physical effects of the impact. Reflects the emotions aroused by the issue.

———; Alvarez, Walter; Asaro, Frank; Michel, Helen V. "Extraterrestrial Cause for the Cretaceous-Tertiary Extinction." In *Science*, 208, June 6, 1980. First widely published report of the asteroid hypothesis. The same authors had previously presented their findings in "Extraterrestrial Cause for the Cretaceous-Tertiary Extinction: Experiment and Theory." Lawrence Berkeley Laboratory Report LBL-9666.

Alvarez, Walter; Asaro, Frank; Michel, Helen V.; Alvarez, Luis. "Evidence for a Major Meteorite Impact on the Earth 34 Million Years Ago: Implications for Eocene Extinctions." In *Science*, 216, May 21, 1982.

Ganapathy, R. "A Major Meteorite Impact on the Earth 65 Million Years Ago: Evidence from the Cretaceous-Tertiary Boundary Clay." In *Science*, 209, Aug. 27, 1980.

Gould, Stephen Jay. "The Belt of an Asteroid." In *Natural History*, 89, June 1980.

Kerr, Richard A. "Asteroid Theory of Extinctions Strengthened." In *Science*, 210, Oct. 31, 1980.

———. "Impact Looks Real, the Catastrophe Smaller." In *Science*, 214, Nov. 30, 1981. Report on the Snowbird conference.

Lowrie, William, and Alvarez, Walter. "One Hundred Million Years of Geomagnetic Polarity History." In *Geology*, 9, Sept. 1981.

Muller, Richard A. "An Adventure in Science." In *The New York Times Magazine*, March 24, 1985.

Orth, Charles J.; Gilmore, J. S.; Knight, J. D.; Pillmore, C. L.; Tschudy, R. H. "An Iridium Abundance at the Palynological Cretaceous-Tertiary Boundary in Northern New Mexico." In *Science*, 214, Dec. 18, 1981.

Pollock, James B.; Toon, Owen B.; Ackerman, T. P.; McKay, C. P.; Turco, R. P. "Environmental Effects of an Impact-Generated Dust Cloud: Implications for the Cretaceous-Tertiary Extinctions." In *Science*, 219, Jan. 21, 1983.

Rampino, Michael R., and Reynolds, Robert C. "Clay Mineralogy of the Cretaceous-Tertiary Boundary Clay." In *Science*, 219, Feb. 4, 1983.

Raup, David M. "Large Body Impacts and Terrestrial Evolution Meeting, October 19–22, 1981." In *Paleobiology,* 8, Spring 1982.

Silver, Leon T., and Schultz, Peter H., eds. *Geological Implications of Impacts of Large Asteroids and Comets on the Earth.* Collected papers of the Snowbird conference.

Simon, Cheryl. "Clues in the Clay." In *Science News,* 120, Nov. 14, 1981.

Smit, J., and Klaver, G. "Sanidine Spherules at the Cretaceous-Tertiary Boundary Indicate a Large Impact Event." In *Nature,* 292, July 2, 1981.

16. *Out with a Whimper?*

Alvarez, Walter; Alvarez, Luis W.; Asaro, Frank; Michel, Helen V. "The End of the Cretaceous: Sharp Boundary or Gradual Transition?" In *Science,* 223, March 16, 1984. Rebuttal of the gradualists' arguments.

Alvarez, Walter; Kauffman, Erle G.; Surlyk, Finn; Alvarez, Luis W.; Asaro, Frank; Michel, Helen V. "Impact Theory of Mass Extinctions and the Invertebrate Fossil Record." In *Science,* 223, March 16, 1984. Further support for the impact hypothesis.

Archibald, J. David, and Clemens, William A. "Late Cretaceous Extinctions." In *American Scientist,* 70, July–Aug. 1982. Making the case for gradual extinction processes. Response by the Alvarez team in letter to *American Scientist,* 70, Nov.–Dec. 1982.

Bohor, B. F.; Foord, E. E.; Modreski, P. J.; Triplehorn, D. M. "Mineralogic Evidence for an Impact Event at the Cretaceous-Tertiary Boundary." In *Science,* 224, May 25, 1984.

Clemens, William A. "Patterns of Extinction and Survival of the Terrestrial Biota during the Cretaceous-Tertiary Transition." In Leon T. Silver and Peter H. Schultz (eds.), *Geological Implications of Impacts of Large Asteroids and Comets on the Earth.*

———; Archibald, J. David; Hickey, Leo J. "Out with a Whimper Not a Bang." In *Paleobiology,* 7, Summer 1981.

Gilmore, J. S.; Knight, J. D.; Orth, C. J.; Pillmore, C. L.; Tschudy, R. H. "Trace Element Patterns at a Non-Marine Cretaceous-Tertiary Boundary." In *Nature,* 307, Jan. 19, 1984.

Hickey, Leo J. "Land Plant Evidence Compatible with Gradual, Not Catastrophic, Change at the End of the Cretaceous." In *Nature,* 292, Aug. 6, 1981.

Kerr, Richard A. "Isotopes Add Support for Asteroid Impact." In *Science,* 222, Nov. 11, 1983.

Lewin, Roger. "Extinctions and the History of Life." In *Science,* 221, Sept. 2, 1983. Report on "Dynamics of Extinction" conference at Northern Arizona University.

Luck, J. M. and Turekian, K. K. "Osmium-187/Osmium-186 in Manganese Nodules and the Cretaceous-Tertiary Boundary." In *Science,* 222, Nov. 11, 1983.

McGowan, Christopher. *The Successful Dragons.* Chap. 10.

Officer, Charles B., and Drake, Charles L. "The Cretaceous-Tertiary Transition." In *Science,* 219, March 25, 1983.

———. "Terminal Cretaceous Environmental Events." In *Science,* 227, March 8, 1985.

Pillmore, C. L.; Tschudy, R. H.; Orth, C. J.; Gilmore, J. S.; Knight, J. D. "Geologic Framework of Nonmarine Cretaceous-Tertiary Boundary Sites, Raton Basin, New Mexico and Colorado." In *Science,* 223, March 16, 1984.

Schopf, Thomas J. M. "Extinction of the Dinosaurs: A 1982 Understanding." In Leon T. Silver and Peter H. Schultz (eds.), *Geological Implications of Impacts of Large Asteroids and Comets on the Earth.*

Sloan, Robert E. "The Ecology of Dinosaur Extinction." In *Athlon,* 1978. Royal Ontario Museum publication.

———, and Van Valen, Leigh. "Cretaceous Mammals from Montana." In *Science,* 148, April 9, 1965. Further research by Sloan, "Cretaceous and Paleocene Terrestrial Communities of Western North America," in *Proceedings of North American Paleontological Convention,* 1969.

Smit, Jan, and van der Kaars, S. "Terminal Cretaceous Extinctions in the Hell Creek Area, Montana: Compatible with Catastrophic Extinction." In *Science,* 223, March 16, 1984.

Surlyk, Finn, and Johansen, Marianne Bagge. "End-Cretaceous Brachiopod Extinctions in the Chalk of Denmark." In *Science,* 223, March 16, 1984.

Van Valen, Leigh. "Catastrophes, Expectations, and the Evidence." In *Paleobiology,* 10, Winter 1984. A review of the proceedings of the Snowbird conference and the most thorough point-by-point critique of the evidence for a sudden extinction, by a proponent of the gradualist interpretation.

Wolbach, Wendy S.; Lewis, Roy S.; Anders, Edward. "Cretaceous Extinctions: Evidence for

Wildfires and Search for Meteoritic Material." In *Science,* 230, Oct. 11, 1985.

Zoller, William H.; Parrington, Josef R.; Phelan Kotra, Janet M. "Iridium Enrichment in Airborne Particles from Kilauea Volcano: January 1983." In *Science,* 222, Dec. 9, 1983.

17. *Cycles of Extinction*

Albritton, Claude C., ed. *Uniformity and Simplicity: A Symposium on the Principle of Uniformity of Nature.*

Alvarez, Walter, and Muller, Richard A. "Evidence from Crater Ages for Periodic Impacts on the Earth." In *Nature,* 308, April 19, 1984.

Anderson, Charlene. "A Talk with Eugene Shoemaker." In *Planetary Report,* 5, Jan.–Feb. 1985. A geologist's evaluation of the extinction theories.

Bailey, Mark E. "Nemesis for Nemesis?" In *Nature,* 311, Oct. 18, 1984.

Berggren, W. A., and Van Couvering, John A., eds. *Catastrophes of Earth History: The New Uniformitarianism.* Princeton, N.J. 1984.

Clube, S. V. M., and Napier, W. M. "Terrestrial Catastrophism—Nemesis or Galaxy?" In *Nature,* 311, Oct. 18, 1984.

Davis, Marc; Hut, Piet; Muller, Richard A. "Extinction of Species by Periodic Comet Showers." In *Nature,* 308, April 19, 1984.

Fischer, A. G., and Arthur, M. A. In Cook, H. E., and Enos, P. (eds.), *Deep-Water Carbonate Environments.* Society of Economic Paleontologists and Mineralogists Special Paper 25, Tulsa, 1977.

Goodman, Ellen. "A Dinosaur Theory Tailor-made for Our Times." In Boston *Globe,* Jan. 3, 1984.

Gould, Stephen Jay. "The Cosmic Dance of Siva." In *Natural History,* 93, Aug. 1984.

———. "The Ediacaran Experiment." In *Natural History,* 93, Feb. 1984.

———. "Sex, Drugs, Disasters, and the Extinction of Dinosaurs." In *Discover,* 5, March 1984.

Hallam, A. "The Causes of Mass Extinctions." In *Nature,* 308, April 19, 1984.

Hills, J. G. "Dynamical Constraints on the Mass and Perihelion Distance of Nemesis and the Stability of Its Orbit." In *Nature,* 311, Oct. 18, 1984.

Hut, Piet. "How Stable Is an Astronomical Clock That Can Trigger Mass Extinctions on Earth?" In *Nature,* 311, Oct. 18, 1984.

Kerr, Richard. "Extinctions and the History of Life." In *Science,* 221, Sept. 2, 1983.

———. "Periodic Impacts and Extinctions Reported." In *Science,* 223, March 23, 1984.

Muller, Richard A. "An Adventure in Science."

Rampino, Michael R., and Stothers, Richard B. "Geological Rhythms and Cometary Impacts." In *Science,* 226, Dec. 21, 1984.

———. "Terrestrial Mass Extinctions, Cometary Impacts and the Sun's Motion Perpendicular to the Galactic Plane." In *Nature,* 308, April 19, 1984.

Raup, David M., and Sepkoski, J. John, Jr., "Periodicity of Extinctions in the Geologic Past." In *Proceedings of the National Academy of Sciences,* 81, Feb. 1984. First formal published report of the apparent 26-million-year periodicity of mass extinctions.

Schwartz, Richard D., and James, Philip B. "Periodic Mass Extinctions and the Sun's Oscillation about the Galactic Plane." In *Nature,* 308, April 19, 1984.

Simon, Cheryl. "Death Star." In *Science News,* 125, April 21, 1984.

Torbett, Michael V., and Smoluchowski, Roman. "Orbital Stability of the Unseen Solar Companion Linked to Periodic Extinction Events." In *Nature,* 311, Oct. 18, 1984.

Weissman, Paul R. "Cometary Showers and Unseen Solar Companions." In *Nature,* 312, Nov. 22, 1984.

Whitmire, Daniel P., and Jackson, Albert A., IV. "Are Periodic Mass Extinctions Driven by a Distant Solar Companion?" In *Nature,* 308, April 19, 1984.

———, and Matese, John J. "Periodic Comet Showers and Planet X." In *Nature,* 313, Jan. 3, 1985.

18. *The World Thereafter*

Alvarez, Luis W. "Experimental Evidence That an Asteroid Impact Led to the Extinction of Many Species 65 Million Years Ago." His presentation to the National Academy.

Charig, Alan. *A New Look at the Dinosaurs.*

Gould, Stephen Jay. "Continuity." In *Natural History,* 93, April 1984.

———. "Sex, Drugs, Disasters, and the Extinction of Dinosaurs."

Hopson, J. "Relative Brain Size in Dinosaurs." In Roger D. K. Thomas and Everett C. Olson (eds.), *A Cold Look at the Warm-Blooded Dinosaurs.*

Lewin, Roger. "No Dinosaurs This Time." In *Science,* 221, Sept. 16, 1983.

———. *Thread of Life.*

Overbye, Dennis. "Prophet of the Cold and Dark." In *Discover,* 6, Jan. 1985. Profile of Paul Crutzen and how he conceived of the "nuclear winter" scenario.

Russell, Dale A. "A New Specimen of *Stenonychosaurus* from the Oldman Formation (Cretaceous) of Alberta." In *Canadian Journal of Earth Sciences,* 6, 1969.

———. "Speculations on the Evolution of Intelligence in Multicellular Organisms." In James Billingham (ed.), *Life in the Universe.* National Aeronautics and Space Administration Special Publication. Washington, D.C., 1981.

———, and Seguin, Ron. "Reconstructions of the Small Cretaceous Theropod *Stenonychosaurus inequalis* and a Hypothetical Dinosauroid." National Museum of Natural Sciences Syllogeus No. 37. Ottawa, 1981.

Turco, Richard P.; Toon, Owen B.; Ackerman, Thomas P.; Pollack, James B.; Sagan, Carl. "The Climatic Effects of Nuclear War." In *Scientific American,* 251, Aug. 1984.

Index

A

D

E

G

H

I

J

K

L

M

N

O

P

T

U

V

W

Y

A Note About the Author

John Noble Wilford is a science correspondent for *The New York Times.* He won the 1983 American Association for the Advancement of Science/Westinghouse science-writing award and a 1984 Pulitzer Prize for his reporting of space and science. He was a Visiting Journalist at Duke University in 1984 and the McGraw Lecturer in Writing at Princeton University in 1985. He has worked for *The Wall Street Journal, Time* magazine, and, since 1965, the *Times.* He is the author of *We Reach the Moon* (1969) and *The Mapmakers* (1981); co-author of *Spaceliner* (1981) and *The New York Times Guide to the Return of Halley's Comet* (1985); and editor of *Scientists at Work* (1979).

A Note on the Type

The text of this book was set in a digitized version of Bembo, a well-known Monotype face. Named for Pietro Bembo, the celebrated Renaissance writer and humanist scholar who was made a cardinal and served as secretary to Pope Leo X, the original cutting of Bembo was made by Francesco Griffo of Bologna only a few years after Columbus discovered America.

Sturdy, well-balanced, and finely proportioned, Bembo is a face of rare beauty, extremely legible in all of its sizes.

Composed by The Haddon Craftsmen, Inc., Scranton, Pennsylvania. Color illustrations separated by Capper, Inc., Knoxville Tennessee, and printed by Coral Graphics, Inc., Plainview, New York. Printed and bound by The Murray Printing Company, Westford, Massachusetts. Designed by Anthea Lingeman.